P9-ASD-874

Giving Up on School

Student Dropouts and Teacher Burnouts

Margaret Diane LeCompte
Anthony Gary Dworkin

CORWIN PRESS, INC.
A Sage Publications Company
Newbury Park, California

For information address:

Corwin Press, Inc.
A Sage Publications Company
2455 Teller Road
Newbury Park, California 91320

SAGE Publications Ltd.
6 Bonhill Street
London EC2A 4PU
United Kingdom

SAGE Publications India Pvt. Ltd.
M-32 Market
Greater Kailash I
New Delhi 110 048 India

Printed in the United States of America

Library of Congress Cataloging-in-Publication Data

LeCompte, Margaret Diane.
Giving up on school : student dropouts and teacher burnouts/
Margaret Diane LeCompte, Anthony Gary Dworkin.
p. cm.
Includes bibliographical references and index.
ISBN 0-8039-3490-4. —ISBN 0-8039-3491-2 (pbk.)
1. Dropouts—United States. 2. Teachers—United States—Job stress. 3. Burnout (Psychology) 4. Alienation (Social psychology) I. Dworkin, Anthony Gary. II. Title.
LC143.L43 1991
371.2'913—dc20 91-28760
CIP

FIRST PRINTING, 1991

Corwin Press Production Editor: Judith L. Hunter

Contents

FIGURES

TABLES

Preface

Although the problems of student dropout and teacher burnout have been studied extensively, they have always been considered separate phenomena. In this book, we hold that both stem from the same source, the process of alienation that is prevalent in the school system, causing students and teachers alike to "give up on school." We extensively document student dropout and teacher burnout, demonstrate critical links between the two, and present a series of models that show how educational alienation is created and fostered by conditions in the school, the community, and society at large.

We also show that for each student or teacher who leaves the system there are many more trapped within it. These "tuned-out" students and teachers are equally alienated and pose a considerable challenge to anyone attempting to "solve" the problem by simply lowering dropout and turnover rates.

The conditions we describe in this book mandate an immediate and drastic reappraisal of our approach to education and employment because, as we shall demonstrate, few existing programs have been effective. Those that do seem to work have consistently been short-lived and underfunded; those that receive consistent and repeated attention are so innocuous and uncontroversial that they do little, if anything, to alter the conditions that lead to giving up.

In the first chapter we outline the size of the problem and some of the specific conditions that contribute to it. In Chapter 2, we examine what we call the context of cultural expectations—those macro-level or global changes that have led to alienation because they make obsolete the behaviors and beliefs that once constituted effective ways for people to confront their social, intellectual, and physical environments. In Chapters 3 through 6, we discuss characteristics of students who are "at risk" and who have dropped out and teachers who are entrapped, burned out, or planning to quit the profession, addressing many of the multitude of factors that led them to give up on schooling. We distinguish between students who "tune out" but continue to attend classes and students who actually drop out of school. We also examine the characteristics and social forces that lead teachers to burn out, plan to quit teaching, and actually leave education. Teachers who burn out are equivalent to students who tune out, as teachers who quit are equivalent to students who drop out. Many students see schools as irrelevant to their life goals and feel that nobody in the schools cares about them. Teachers who give up on schooling also believe that nobody cares. They feel that what they do is meaningless and that they are powerless to change conditions to make their work more meaningful.

In Chapter 7 we interpret and integrate the experiences of students and teachers with respect to current alienation theory. Chapter 8 presents a model to describe the process of giving up on school. It constitutes our own, eclectic theory, which we use to examine why teachers and students give up. Our model is heavily steeped in the traditions of conflict and critical theory. It emerges from a substantial body of scholarship in both anthropology and sociology, and draws upon work in strain theory and applications of drift theory. Our attempt is to demonstrate that teacher burnout and student dropout are forms of alienation. Further, we link the onset of that alienation from individual institutions to unreconciled strains in the larger technological, economic, political, and social contexts of schooling.

Chapter 9 examines what has been done in American education to reform it and how these reforms have failed. We show how policies designed to reduce student dropout and teacher burnout, improve student achievement, and enhance the morale of students and teachers are meliorist at best, and often exacerbate difficulties encountered in schools.

In the final chapter, we explicate the directions of future reform as informed by our theoretical models. This chapter offers a range of modest and immodest suggestions for change. It is not vested in "meliorism," whereby reforms attempt to "sweeten" or improve upon conditions without altering structures. Rather, we propose changes in both individual practices and educational and social systems.

ACKNOWLEDGMENTS

This volume began as a paper titled "Educational Programs: Indirect Linkages and Unfulfilled Expectations," which was presented in 1987 at a conference sponsored by the University of Houston's Center for Public Policy and dedicated to exploring nonwelfare ways to alleviate poverty. The conference organizer and editor of a volume titled *Beyond Welfare,* which came out of the conference, was Dr. Harrell R. Rodgers, Jr., dean of the College of Social Sciences at the University of Houston. We wish to thank Dean Rodgers and the staff of the Center for Public Policy for giving us the impetus to create this book.

Several other colleagues at the University of Houston read drafts of the manuscript and acted as sounding boards for our ideas. These include Dr. Janet S. Chafetz, who helped us pare down a much longer and less well-organized draft into something we hope is more readable; Dr. Helen Rose Ebaugh; and Dr. Jon Lorence, all of the Department of Sociology. Dr. Donna Deyhle of the University of Utah also provided helpful comments regarding our material on dropouts and school reform. A. G. Dworkin would like to thank the Hogg Foundation for Mental Health, which is housed at The University of

Texas, Austin, and, in particular, Adrian Rhae Fowler, for the funding that made possible the data collection and analysis on teacher burnout. Adrian has been Dworkin's project manager at the Foundation for nearly a decade. Her insights and especially her patience are greatly appreciated.

Several University of Houston graduate students participated in the initial analysis of the data on the effect of educational reform on teacher burnout. In particular, John York, Martha Vickers, Bruce Hunter, David Jones, Patricia Chandler, and Rhona Hurwitz were of particularly great help during the 1986-1987 seminar we held on educational reform. Several of these students conducted their doctoral or master's research on sections of the data set.

We would like to thank Mitch Allen of Sage Publications and the anonymous reviewers for their cogent observations and suggestions. In particular, Mitch gave us considerable assistance in the editing of the book, and his insights helped us meld what appeared at times to be two distinctive books—one on dropouts and one on burnout—into a single volume.

Finally, there is one special colleague we want to thank. Dr. Rosalind J. Dworkin has read, reread, commented upon, and provided us with encouragement over the two years that it took to produce this book. At times she added some degree of sociological imagination to our efforts; at other times she prodded us to finish when it appeared to all, including our editor, that the book would never be hatched. She often prevented us from "giving up on *Giving Up on School.*" We dedicate this book to her.

—MARGARET DIANE LECOMPTE
ANTHONY GARY DWORKIN

About the Authors

Margaret Diane LeCompte is Associate Professor of Sociology and Education at the University of Colorado—Boulder. She has served as Executive Director of Research and Evaluation for the Houston, Texas, Public Schools and has taught at the University of Houston and the University of Cincinnati. She received her M.A. and Ph.D. degrees from the University of Chicago and her B.A. from Northwestern University. She has published numerous articles from her studies of dropouts, school and community organization, classroom interaction and socialization, and the influence of cultural, class, and ethnic influences on education, as well as theoretical articles on qualitative and ethnographic methods of research and evaluation. Her books include *Ethnography and Qualitative Design in Educational Research* (1984), with Judith Preissle Goetz; *The Handbook of Qualitative Research in Education* (1992), with Wendy Millroy and Judith Preissle; and *The Way Schools Work: A Sociological Analysis of Education* (1990), with Kathleen Bennett. She is active in the American Educational Research Association and the American Educational Studies Association, and has been President of the Council on Anthropology and Education of the American Anthropological Association.

Anthony Gary Dworkin is Professor and Chair of the Department of Sociology at the University of Houston. He is also Director of Research for the University of Houston's Texas

Center for University School Partnerships. He holds a Ph.D. in sociology from Northwestern University (1970). In recent years, he has been the author of *When Teachers Give Up* (1985), *Female Revolt: Women's Movements in World and Historical Perspective* (1986, with Janet Chafetz), and *Teacher Burnout in the Public Schools* (1987), as well as a variety of articles on such issues as teacher morale; racial, ethnic, and gender stratification; and ethnic stereotypy. He is also working on a third edition of his text, *The Minority Report* (with Rosalind J. Dworkin). His areas of research include minority group relations and the sociology of education. He has been President of the Southwestern Sociological Association and has served on various committees of the American Sociological Association, including its Sociology of Education Section. Recently, he has served on task forces and advisory committees on public education reform and educational innovation for the Chamber of Commerce of the Greater Houston Partnership and the Educational Economic Policy Center of the State of Texas. He is currently editor of a book series titled The New Inequalities, published by the State University of New York Press.

ONE

Introduction

Since the publication of the National Commission on Excellence in Education's *A Nation at Risk* (1983), there have been some 300 panel, commission, and study reports issued on problems in education. The majority address one common theme: American public schools, as they currently are structured, the teaching that takes place in them, and their system of recruiting and training teachers are in disastrous condition. Our schools are out of step with current demographic and societal conditions in the United States, with changes in the world balance of economic power and the structure of scientific knowledge, and with the needs of the international labor market. The philosophy they reflect satisfies neither the Right nor the Left, and they not only fail to provide basic literacy to a significant portion of the student enrollment, but render even the most talented students stupefied with boredom.

Our analysis of American education—of both students and their teachers—begins with this dissatisfaction and attempts to indicate both its causes and its impacts upon educational institutions. We focus on the consequences of a failing education for teachers and students; that is, we emphasize teachers who burn out and quit and students who tune out and drop out as both symptom and symbol, rather than cause, of the crisis in contemporary schooling. If institutions cannot retain their practitioners and clients, they surely are failing to fulfill their stated and unstated functions in society. If they can neither retain practitioners and clients nor fulfill their stated functions, it is because they have grown increasingly out of touch with the social and cultural reality in which they are embedded and in which their participants live. That this mismatch between institutions and context is profound can be found in evidence of public dissatisfaction with many public institutions, including schools. During the 1970s and 1980s, polls showed that Americans grew increasingly critical of their public schools (Elam & Gallup, 1989).

The forces of concern in this volume are not limited to school-level issues. Rather, we include worldwide changes in the distribution of economic and political power, as well as changes in the demographic characteristics of U.S. society's population. These mandate drastic modification in the basic institutions of society. If these modifications do not occur, the consequent mismatch between institutions and the society in which they are embedded leads to alienation of the society's membership. We are, however, on the horns of an unfortunate dilemma: The cost of reducing incongruity between institutions, such as schools, and society may be insupportable without substantial sociostructural change, while at the same time the cost of *not* addressing it in the long run will be worse. The United States has not typically invested in long-term solutions to social problems in any field without tangible evidence of short-term improvements. The consequence has been meliorist "muddling through"—small improvements that do not solve problems, but forestall imminent collapse of the system.

In this book, we examine student dropout and teacher burnout in their global, social, economic, political, and cultural contexts. When we first started thinking about this book, we thought of teacher and student problems as conceptually different, and planned to treat student dropping and tuning out and teacher burnout and quitting as if they were separate and distinct phenomena. We now believe that these phenomena are generated by identical sociocultural and structural forces. Factors that lead teachers to quit teaching also cause students to drop out of school; the actual behaviors and attitudes exhibited by alienated students and burned-out teachers also are similar. As a consequence, we now treat dropping out and burning out as inextricably linked, and we develop a process model to explain how and why they occur.

We have centered our analysis of the crisis in schooling on sociological and social psychological conceptualizations of alienation. We use an eclectic approach to alienation theory and include its variant, strain theory, in our analysis. We integrate sociological and anthropological concepts by linking individual alienation to changes in the social and cultural context in which individuals live. Specifically, we contend that when structural factors no longer make possible the attainment of societally valued and individually desired personal goals, individuals come to lose faith in the institutions—such as schools—that structure their everyday lives. Although loss of faith on the part of individuals does not automatically create a shift to alternative means of goal satisfaction (as proposed by Merton, 1968), a considerable body of evidence suggests that under these conditions, institutions begin to unravel. Institutional participants, or actors, come to believe that the organizations in which they pursue their goals counter the attainment of those goals. They feel powerless, meaningless, personally isolated, culturally estranged, and self-estranged—all components of alienation (Seeman, 1959, 1967, 1975). These concepts clearly define the feelings expressed by students and teachers who say that they are giving up on school. Feelings of *powerlessness* exist when people perceive themselves as having no control over the events in their personal or work lives. *Meaninglessness* in this context refers to a sense that the world is absurd or incomprehensible. *Normlessness* is a feeling that the rules that govern the world either have disappeared or have become ineffective. *Personal isolation* sets the individual apart from other human beings, and *cultural estrangement* puts the individual in opposition to the values held by his or her community of reference. *Self-estrangement* exists when people must engage in activities that they deem to be intrinsically unrewarding. We believe that contemporary schools are structured in such a way as to foster this kind of alienation and that the consequence of alienation among even the most enthusiastic of school participants, whether teachers or students, is giving up on school. The genesis of alienating structure in schools and other social institutions can be found in the inability of institutions to adapt to a new socioeconomic order.

We have come realize that what we term *giving up on school* frequently has two stages. The first involves a long process of alienation, the causes of which act similarly on all inhabitants of school and lead them to become increasingly disaffected with their situation. It reaches a dramatic climax only when teachers or students leave. The second stage, actually leaving, is the last step in a long process of alienation. In this book we use the terms *tune-out* and *dropout* to refer to the processes and consequences for students and the terms *burnout* and *quitting behavior* to refer to analogous processes and consequences for teachers. Burned-out teachers and tuned-out students suffer from entrapment; that is, they are alienated, but cannot quit. External factors, or "side bets," may make the consequences of quitting too costly. Thus giving up does not always lead to quitting.

A variation on alienation theory that we also find helpful is strain theory. Strain theory maintains that when individuals perceive a gap between their aspirations and their expectations, they reassess either their goals or their means to achieve those goals. The decision to make such an adjustment is not automatic and mindless. Early strain theorists attempted to explain deviant behavior in terms of the replacement of structurally prescribed means (which did not seem to be effective) with alternatives in order to attain culturally prescribed (and hence individually desirable) goals (Merton, 1968). However, Cloward (1959) correctly notes that there may be structural barriers to alternative means, in addition to side bets, that inhibit choice. Thus, although both teachers and students may come to perceive school as meaningless and to believe that they are powerless to make their school situations more meaningful (see the conceptualization of burnout in Dworkin, 1987), the immediate and automatic consequence is not always that teachers quit teaching and students drop out of school. Many are simply trapped. Neither the students nor the teachers want to be in school, but they have few alternatives. Teachers without other salable skills are trapped in teaching jobs they hate because they need their salaries to survive. They spend entire careers teaching poorly, blaming—and sometimes abusing—their students as scapegoats. Meanwhile, students, under the surveillance of parents, school officials, and the legal system, and too young or unskilled to find work, continue to attend school but fail to learn because they fail to pay attention to teachers or to do their work.

People, whether teachers or students, leave school prematurely in two ways: *voluntarily*, either (a) because they have alternatives to participation in school or (b) because they find participation completely intolerable or impossible; or *involuntarily*, because they are actually excluded, through transfer, firing, suspension, or expulsion. Quitting behavior has received more publicity than burnout, entrapment, or tune-out, partly because rates of teacher burnout and student dropout have not decreased, despite considerable expenditure of funds, the results of a wealth of task forces and commissions assigned to study the issues, and innumerable programs designed to address the problems. In the following sections we discuss why quitting behavior has remained so visible and has seemed so intractable.

DROPPING OUT: STUDENTS

Despite considerable effort, expenditure of additional funds has not ameliorated dropout rates. New York City, for example, has spent more than $40 million annually in the last five years for state and locally financed dropout prevention programs, with no appreciable decrease in the dropout rate.

Second, the proportion of dropouts among certain populations is increasing. Conventional wisdom holds that only nonwhite students drop out. However, data show that students from all groups are increasingly at risk. For example, the dropout rate for white, blue-collar males is increasing in some urban districts. In at least some Texas school districts, the dropout rate for white students exceeds the overall dropout rate (Asin, 1990); in Houston, it exceeds the overall rate for black students (Houston Independent School District, 1989).

Third, the percentage of minority students, whose dropout rates consistently have exceeded those of whites, is increasing in the public schools (Hodgkinson, 1985). Since minority students constitute the major part of enrollments in most large urban districts in the United States, this means that the actual number of dropouts is increasing.

Fourth, educators fear that recent attention on academic "excellence"—as translated into increases in the academic requirements for graduation from high school—will mean higher rates of dropout by students who cannot meet the enhanced standards (Archer & Dresden, 1987; McDill, Natriello, & Pallas, 1985). Dropouts will be even more disadvantaged in the labor force as increasing use of new technologies and forms of workplace organization come to require higher levels of intellectual and social skills.

Dropping out also has a high cost to society. Much has been written about the costs of dropping out in terms of joblessness, crime, and lower wages to individuals. Only recently have these factors been considered in terms of their impact on society as a whole. Levin (1972; cited in Rumberger, 1987, pp. 114-115) identifies seven social consequences of the failure to complete high school: forgone national income, forgone tax revenues for the support of government services, increased demand for social services, increased crime, reduced political participation, reduced intergenerational mobility, and poorer levels of health. Citing Catterall (1987), the Carnegie Council on Adolescent Development (1989) estimates that each year's class of dropouts will, in their lifetime, cost the nation about $260 billion in lost earnings and forgone taxes. Furthermore, the economic consequences of dropping out are unequally distributed by race and ethnicity; the unemployment rates and forgone income of

Hispanic and black dropouts, for example, has been 25% to 100% higher than that of whites (Rumberger, 1987, p. 115).

Social service costs for dropouts, such as welfare, aid for food and shelter and emergency medical services, and access to the criminal justice system, also are high. Some 82% of inmates in U.S. jails and prisons are dropouts; the cost of maintaining a prisoner averages $20,000 per year. By contrast, the annual cost to taxpayers of sending an adolescent to college or a child to Head Start is approximately $3,500. States with high dropout rates also have high rates of incarceration; between 1980 and 1987, the greatest increase in expenditure for taxpayer-funded social services was for prison construction, which was far ahead of transportation, educational, health care, housing, and welfare. Whether it relates directly to dropping out or not, the United States now has the highest rate of incarceration in the world, with the exception of South Africa and the Soviet Union (Hodgkinson, 1989, p. 15).

Another cost to society of dropping out is the effect that alienation of students has on teacher retention and recruitment (Firestone & Rosenblum, 1988). Research indicates that people traditionally have selected the teaching profession because of their prior favorable experiences with the work that teachers do. However, teachers now work increasingly with alienated, uncooperative, and unsuccessful students. Few people, especially talented and academically able members of urban minority groups, would choose the kinds of working conditions and clients they now observe in the schools they attend (Haberman, 1989). Further, the cost of maintaining morale and the desire to teach of educators already in the classroom is overwhelming when most students would rather be anywhere else.

Finally, educational administrators and policymakers have come to view dropout rates as indicators of school and district quality. This makes the dropout problem a political one, as the ability to define, count, and reduce the number of dropouts becomes salient in the competition for funding and merit evaluations (Rumberger, 1987, pp. 101-103).

Notwithstanding that actual dropping out is a serious problem, we believe that far more important and critical to the future of schools and society is tuning out, or simply giving up on school. While the dropout problem has been well documented for decades, never before has the problem of giving up been so severe. When those who give up are added to the 25% of the youth cohort who drop out, the proportion of the school-aged population affected nears half to three-quarters. Giving up produces some graduates who eventually will make it in society because their family resources provide a cushion until they can find adequate training or some kind of job (Littwin, 1987). However, far more numerous are those who, while credentialed, do not have the skills—social and cognitive—that a high school diploma once represented. The result is a population that might as well have dropped out of school, because their capabilities are no better than those of actual dropouts. In fact, they may be worse off, because they are victimized by a system that promises a diploma will yield a job and then fails to produce it.

Underskilled tune-outs often have skill levels so low that they cannot be employed by most businesses and industries without extensive prior training. One New York City bank recently reported that only 15 out of every 500 applicants were qualified for entry-level jobs (Cook, 1989). As late as the period immediately following World War II, people who were semiliterate or dropouts had job options whether they finished school or not. Furthermore, possession of a diploma was taken as prima facie evidence of possession of skills. Now it does not. Changes—both real and perceived—in technology and the labor market have made the consequences of dropping out, as well as of leaving school poorly educated, more severe. Fifty years ago, dropouts were only slightly more likely than graduates to be unemployed. Twenty years ago, they were only 50% more likely. Now, however, dropouts are twice as likely as non-dropouts to be unemployed (see Table 1.1).

TURNOVER: TEACHERS WHO QUIT

Although data are mixed regarding the increase in teacher turnover rates, many urban school districts report that more

Table 1.1 Unemployment Rates and Unemployment Ratios of 18- to 21-Year-Old High School Dropouts and Graduates: 1960-1987

Year	*Graduate Unemployment Rate*	*Dropout Unemployment Rate*	*Dropout/Graduate Unemployment Ratio*	*Unemployment Rate for All Ages*
1960	11.6	17.2	1.48	5.5
1961	17.9	26.8	1.47	6.7
1962	10.6	25.4	2.40	5.6
1963	10.3	16.6	1.61	5.7
1964	10.8	16.6	1.54	5.4
1965	8.4	14.9	1.77	4.5
1966	9.2	18.0	1.96	3.8
1967	9.7	14.5	1.49	3.8
1968	7.8	14.9	1.91	3.6
1969	7.7	14.5	1.88	3.5
1970	11.6	21.5	1.85	4.9
1971	11.3	21.0	1.86	5.9
1972	10.9	19.2	1.76	5.6
1973	8.2	17.4	2.12	4.9
1974	11.0	22.0	2.00	5.6
1975	13.6	25.3	1.86	8.5
1976	12.5	27.4	2.19	7.7
1977	11.9	22.9	1.92	7.0
1978	9.4	20.5	2.18	6.0
1979	10.7	20.9	1.95	5.8
1980	12.5	25.2	2.02	7.0
1981	14.7	30.1	2.05	7.5
1982	17.9	36.0	2.01	9.5
1983	16.7	30.5	1.83	9.5
1984	13.4	27.7	2.07	7.4
1985	12.7	25.9	2.04	7.2
1986	11.5	24.3	2.11	7.0
1987	10.2	20.5	2.01	6.2

SOURCE: U.S. Bureau of the Census (1963, 1966, 1971, 1979, 1981, 1985, 1989).

of their experienced teachers, those who are far from retirement age, are leaving. Since the early 1980s, districts also have reported increasing shortfalls in key teaching specializations, including science, mathematics, bilingual education, and special education. Teaching historically has had a higher average turnover than most professions. In large part, this is a function of the gendered nature of the profession; since the

1850s, teaching has been dominated by women—for many years it was almost the only profession open to them. While many women did indeed plan to leave teaching when and if they married, early departure from teaching upon marriage was enforced until the 1930s; laws in most states forbade married women from teaching.

Now a new phenomenon has emerged: Career teachers—those in their 30s and 40s—are leaving the profession. This is in part a function of the greater career opportunities now available to women and of the unwillingness of women who are able to move to different jobs to suffer under the conditions in which many are forced to teach. A growing percentage of persons trained in teaching never even get through the classroom door as teachers; rather than face assignments in inner cities, in less desirable schools, or with the problem students often routed to neophytes, they elect to work outside of education. Haberman (1989) notes that 70% of all individuals who complete teaching degrees in college never apply for or accept teaching positions.

Individuals who elect to remain in teaching beyond the first five critical years now are drawn from two groups: people who cannot translate the skills they have as teachers into another kind of work, and those who sincerely enjoy working with children. Often the former are those who entered teacher training programs in college with the lowest SAT scores and who would have had difficulty with more demanding forms of professional or semiprofessional training (Schlechty & Vance, 1981). They may indeed be burned out, but they cannot leave, because they cannot easily find other employment.

THE GROWTH OF STRAIN AND ALIENATION

Like other institutions, schools are not purposefully constructed to facilitate alienation and incompetence; they have evolved to be that way in response to changes in the social, economic, political, vocational, and cultural life of modern society. In fact, they reflect the structure of modern society. However, modern society and its institutions, as we shall see, have changed faster than the capacity of their participants to cope. The result is strain—among the demands of society, its opportunity structure, the structure of schooling, and possible human responses. When the strain becomes too great, alienation, as defined by Seeman and others, results. In schools, the symptoms of this strain are the burning out and quitting of teachers and the tuning out and dropping out of students.

The strains affecting schools have been documented most vividly in urban and inner-city schools. However, while many of the specific examples we use in this book are drawn primarily from research in such schools during the 1980s, they are not and will not remain localized in the inner city. Increasingly, as changes in what we shall describe as distributive sectors, technological innovation, and global political economy become more widespread, all institutions in all sectors of the population and all geographic areas are subject to the same strains.

The problem is one that affects both teachers and students immediately, because disaffected students increase the tendency for teachers to find their jobs unrewarding and onerous. But the problem also has long-term implications for the whole structure of society, in that it casts doubt upon the validity of hegemonic myths connecting hard work and scholastic achievement with occupational attainment and economic success. To the extent that these links are shattered for more and more people, the influences that mobilize a labor force and legitimate its placements within the opportunity structure attenuate. The consequence for many has been an increasing gap between aspirations and expectations (see, e.g., Clignet & Foster, 1966; Foster, 1965; Littwin, 1987). For even more, it has meant that no jobs exist at all. Those who are employed often find that job conditions are not what they expected and, further, that the behavior they were trained to exhibit in their work does not produce the kinds of results they were led to expect. In social institutions this kind of gap

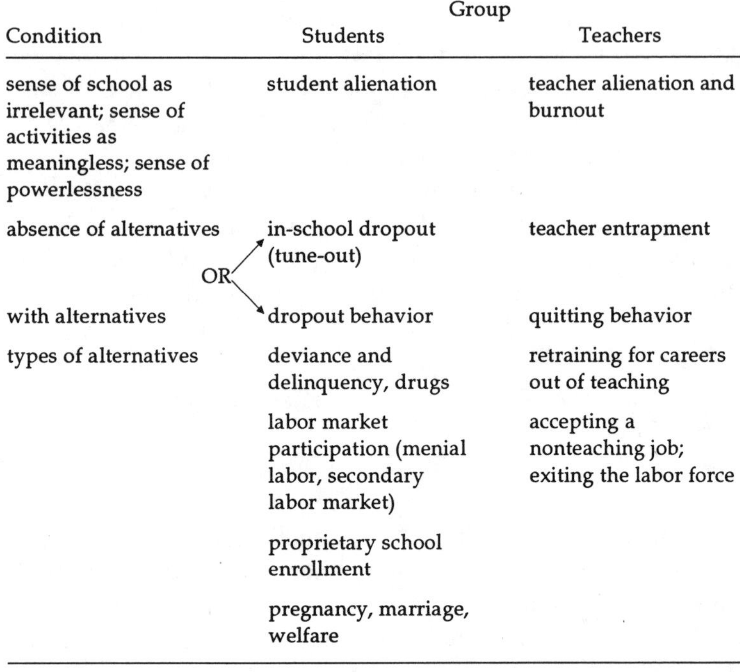

Condition	Group: Students	Group: Teachers
sense of school as irrelevant; sense of activities as meaningless; sense of powerlessness	student alienation	teacher alienation and burnout
absence of alternatives	in-school dropout (tune-out)	teacher entrapment
OR		
with alternatives	dropout behavior	quitting behavior
types of alternatives	deviance and delinquency, drugs	retraining for careers out of teaching
	labor market participation (menial labor, secondary labor market)	accepting a nonteaching job; exiting the labor force
	proprietary school enrollment	
	pregnancy, marriage, welfare	

Figure 1.1 Process Model for Giving Up on School by Students and Teachers

promotes alienation; at the societal level, it fosters loss of social cohesion. These conditions, and the processes they engender in public schools, are displayed in the context of alienation and strain theory in Figure 1.1.

A key issue, however, is why strain and alienation develop in the first place. What causes the dissonance between individual expectations, hopes, and aspirations and the societal and institutional ability to fulfill them? And, with respect to education, what forces act to impede schools from succeeding in what the public, school practitioners, and their clients believe their job to be? In the pages that follow, we explore the relationship between cultural and social change and the development of conditions of alienation.

THE DISTRIBUTIVE AND INSTITUTIONAL CONTEXTS OF SCHOOLS: THE MACRO LEVEL

Many forces have irrevocably changed the world in which schools exist. The geometric rate of technological change since the middle of the 19th century has led to rather major gaps between the cognitive maps—or patterns for behavior—that people use to guide their behavior and their interpretations of the environments in which they live. At the same time, schools have failed to change in significant ways in response. The term that we find useful to explain this phenomenon is *cultural lag*; the feeling of alienation it produces is culture shock. Cultural lag engenders at the societal level the same feelings of meaninglessness, powerlessness, loss of confidence, and dissatisfaction described earlier in alienated individuals, including students and teachers. People feel that neither the institutions that govern their lives nor their personal and social relationships are as efficacious and meaningful as they once were. This contributes to the sense of alienation that is key to our analysis of teacher burnout and entrapment and dropping out and tuning out among students.

Evelyn Jacob (1987), a cultural anthropologist, helps to explain social behavior by distinguishing between the patterns *of* behavior—which consist of real and explicit aspects of behavior, those things that are observable, measurable, and that people can talk about—and patterns *for* behavior, or ideal and implicit aspects of belief about behavior in given contexts. Patterns of behavior are relatively easy to observe. Patterns for behavior are not, because they must be either inferred from observed behavior or elicited verbally from the people who hold them. This may be difficult, insofar as people find it difficult to articulate the reasons for their actions, are so close to their actions that they may take them for granted, or do not wish to divulge their reasons to strangers.

Changes in the Cognitive Map

We are particularly interested in patterns for behavior because they determine what people ultimately will do. Patterns for behavior are based in large part upon past experience. They are created from what people learn from their historical experience as well as the accumulation of responses they have to the particular level of technology with which they live, the socioeconomic and ethnic mix of people surrounding them, and ways in which power and access to resources are distributed.

Patterns of response to environmental conditions become customary or normative; they constitute cognitive maps dictating for people "the way things are supposed to be." Ultimately, they come to constitute those rules or patterns *for* behavior described by Jacob. They form the basis for expectations about daily life as well as for what will happen in the future, including how to make life in the future successful. If, as frequently happens, these expectations are taken to represent the reality of a given culture or society *for all time,* these views encourage the preservation of existing social structural relations—a static perspective on what actually are dynamic social phenomena. This kind of thinking is common in education, which generally refers back to some assumed "golden age" of educational excellence that must be recaptured (LeCompte & Dworkin, 1988; see also E. W. Bennett, 1988; Bloom, 1987; Hirsch, 1988). Parents try to pass on to their children patterns for successful behavior, modeled either on their own behavior or on ways they feel they might have improved their lot. It is important to remember that these patterns are based upon current conditions, and they represent the best accommodation to current conditions that their practitioners have been able to make. They may not apply to conditions obtaining in the future, and they also may not be particularly successful patterns, at least from the point of view of outsiders.[1]

What Is Cultural Lag, and How Does It Cause Shock and Alienation?

Most of us are to some extent unaware of the fundamental postulates, assumptions, and biases of our own culture. They constitute the implicit patterns for behavior that govern how we act and our notions about reality. Culture *shock* develops when the world suddenly becomes unpredictable, as, for example, when individuals visit a foreign culture in which the postulates, assumptions, and biases are unknown to them. The normal cues that guide behavior are absent or, if present, require responses different from those customarily emitted. The manners, patterns of speech, and ways of behaving that seem normal at home produce unexpected, unusual, and even alarming responses in the foreign culture (LeCompte, 1978, p. 105). Even when fascinating, contact with an alien culture produces in individuals a constant state of anxiety, tension, and alienation, and often even paranoia and physical illness.

This sense of alienation, or culture shock, in individuals is paralleled at the societal level when rapid change occurs in the technology, demography, resource base, or political economy of an entire group of people. However, it is generated by time rather than distance; the difference is that between eras, not between cultures. It is a consequence of a lag between the extant patterns *of* cultural behavior developed for an earlier era and the yet-to-be developed patterns *for* behavior that need to be developed for the new conditions.

Cultural lag sets in when changes in the technological, demographic, sociocultural, economic, and political context of people's home culture outstrip the capacity of human beings quickly to develop appropriate new patterns of response. For example, beating a mule with a stick and feeding it sugar are possible ways to encourage a recalcitrant animal to carry its load faster, but beating a broken-down diesel truck will produce only dents, and sugar will destroy the motor and fuel system. Neither will make the truck work better. However, frustrated human beings retain the desire to beat their trucks. They transfer a stimulus that was appropriate in prior eras, when transport was not mechanized, to a contemporary mode of transportation for which it is totally ineffective. The result is a kind of culture shock; old patterns are not as effective in producing desired results as they were for the earlier environment in which they were developed. The differences between the old patterns and the new are so great that life becomes less predictable, more alienating, and more stressful.

Cultural lag is a normal consequence of changing conditions, and human beings usually are able to adapt to much of the change that occurs around them. However, long delays in adaptation, or ones that affect critical institutions in society, can alienate, depending upon the rate of change, the degree of disruption it causes, the number of aspects of life affected, the percentage of the population affected, and the degree to which changes affect the power and behavior of dominant societal groups. When reasonable accommodation to change cannot be made smoothly, the cultural context of life feels turned upside down, and human beings are left without satisfactory guidelines for their behavior. Furthermore, they cannot find satisfaction in or feel in control of any of their customary activities. It is this condition that we feel prevails in contemporary society, and particularly in public education. It is a cause of the failure of schools to retain teachers and students. We will discuss the components of alienation in subsequent chapters. Here we wish to address the cultural context that causes it to occur.

Nostalgia: What Is Lagging Behind?

To understand cultural lag, we must describe what is lagging behind. In large part, cultural lag is based on nostalgia for a presumably better, recently past way of life—often most strongly articulated by elites who feel that their privileged status and way of life is threatened. This nostalgia is structured around longing for old patterns, or rules, for behavior and values as well as expectations for public policies and institutional practice—including those in educational systems. It causes alienation because the conditions through which these longings can be requited no longer exist.

In our recent past, conventional wisdom held that the world was a rationally ordered one in which applied science could invent technological solutions for any problems faced by humankind. Nature was endlessly resilient, as well as a source of inspiration and comfort. While challenging, it also was controllable in all but rare and extreme conditions. In other words, people could be protected against the vagaries of nature by the inventions of science. While there was a constant tension between the romanticism of those wishing small, intimate democratically organized social structures and those advocating economies of large scale, bigness came to be accepted as better, and bureaucratic rationality was seen as a way to impose order and system on the necessary large systems that dominate modern life.

The world also was a Western European one. Certain enemies of Western European life and culture were clearly identified and contained, and while they provided constant tension and interest in political life, they posed no immediate challenge to the self-concepts and daily life of Americans. Furthermore, the nation-state provided a stable unit of social organization, with self-sufficient internal labor markets and more or less sovereign economic power. These in turn provided a center of political, civic, cultural, and patriotic focus.

While lip service was given to cultural and ethnic pluralism, and slow strides toward race, class, and gender equity were made, the domination of WASP males and their system of values was only mildly challenged. Traditional gender roles were valued, as were youth cultures that accommodated smoothly to the existing sociopolitical and economic status quo. Political, sexual, and religious morality was male dominated, hierarchical, conventional, and Christian. This is the portrait toward which nostalgia is directed; it established cultural patterns *for* predictable behavior.

What "Reality" Structures the Schools?

Conventional wisdom also shapes how schools operate. The American school day still is structured around the assumption that children live with more than one adult, one of whom is available during the day to meet with teachers and help out in the classroom and after school to provide custodial care. Schools still expect parents to act as auxiliary teachers, available at night to help with hours of homework. As a consequence, most intervention programs for at-risk students build in extensive "parent involvement" programs. Because teachers and school staff also expect that their custodial duties will end at the close of the school day, parent visitations usually are scheduled during working hours. When parents (who may themselves have jobs) do not show up for meetings, they are defined as uncaring; the low achievement of their children is blamed on irresponsible parents, not pedagogy.

Adherents of the conventional wisdom still portray teachers as dedicated, adequately trained, intellectually competent, and self-sacrificing public servants. This position justifies paying teachers poorly while expecting them to make superhuman efforts on behalf of children. Schools and labor markets are believed to be intimately linked; it is the task of schools and teachers to prepare students so that they will find jobs or college placement after graduation. It is assumed that jobs commensurate with ability exist for everyone with the ambition to work, so that a measure of school failure is the extent to which students drop out, remain unemployed, or fail to enroll in college.

The value of education is unquestioned, and its abilities to liberate the mind, channel the labor force, strengthen the nation's economy, and inculcate desirable social values are accepted as public functions that should be funded for all, at least at some minimal level. In truth, this portrait reflects the hegemonic domination of North Americans of European heritage or adoption. However, these beliefs and characteristics structure our thinking and policy-making about social reality, whether or not they are really considered true by every segment of society. The gap that exists between these beliefs and reality renders practice in schools absurd, alienating, and meaningless. What is needed is a new beginning that will bring practice and society closer together.

NOTE

1. For example, in their description of "folk theories for success," Ogbu and Matute-Bianchi (1986) suggest that members of castelike minorities in the United States may define success differently from members of the dominant culture and may engage in behavior that, while winning esteem from the minority peer group, prevents them from achieving success in school and long-term job security. Unlike Ogbu and Matute-Bianchi, Wilson (1987) believes that the issue is not one of caste, but of race, class, and geographical location. Wilson has defined as an "underclass" poor people who live in racially isolated inner-city neighborhoods that have lost most or all of their economic infrastructure and from which middle- and working-class residents have fled. The remaining members of the community are intractably poor because there are few, if any, licit job opportunities within the range of available modes of transportation. What enterprise there is often is owned by absentee members of other races. Under these conditions, poor people may develop notions of success that diverge from the mainstream because they are socially, racially, economically, and geographically isolated from it.

TWO

The Contemporary Context of Cultural Expectations

American social values are predicated upon the existence of a social structure undergirded by a manufacturing working class and the persistence of national economic independence. Dramatic changes in the political economy of contemporary life challenge this thinking. These changes include deindustrialization, or a shift from manufacturing to service economies in industrialized nations; loss of economic power among the traditional working classes and a concomitant increase in the proportion of the population in poverty; loss of the economic power of educational credentials; an increasingly large gap between the rich and the poor, at all levels of analysis; the development of alternative economies; shifts in dominance by regional and national economies to the hegemony of multinational and global corporations and economic arrangements; the rise of global alternative economies; loss of cultural, economic, and political dominance by white persons of European background; and dramatic developments in patterns of communication, technology, and the basis of scientific knowledge. These changes and their implications are discussed in this chapter.

INDUSTRIALIZATION AND DEINDUSTRIALIZATION

Today, once-powerful industrialized nations face three problems. First, nations in the Pacific Rim and Third World are industrializing and competing with the West. They have learned by copying and updating the experience of the West, and the products they make are increasingly competing with those from traditional industrialized countries. Newly industrialized powers are able to hold down costs by purchasing technologically advanced equipment; they also have surpluses of workers and lower pay scales for those workers (Bluestone & Harrison, 1982; Halberstam, 1986).

Second, the West has undergone decapitalization, or deindustrialization. In order to reduce their costs and remain competitive, North American and European industries have relocated many operations to regions where workers and materials are cheaper. The results have been loss of manufacturing jobs for entire sectors of the population and loss of attendant purchasing power for whole communities (Bluestone & Harrison, 1982).

A related problem has been the industrialization of the agricultural sector (Falk & Lyson, 1987).[1] In most countries, farmers are considered to represent the moral, if not the productive, backbone of the nation. However, the rate of urbanization in the farm sector, worldwide, is increasing to the point that independent family farms may soon be a rarity, except where they produce specialty crops requiring intensive hand labor.[2] The foreclosure of hundreds of thousands of family farms has had an unintended consequence—a major redistribution of land from independent, owner-operated farms to concentration in the hands of corporate agribusiness run by absentee owners. This has meant the demise of small rural communities, major shifts in land use and resource management, and considerable disruption in employment patterns in the countryside.

The third problem is that the rate of creation of high-wage jobs in the 1980s was only one-third the rate created at that level between 1963 and 1979, and not nearly enough to keep up with the increase in population and well-educated candidates for the jobs. Furthermore, of the other new jobs created, 44% were low-paying service sector jobs paying at or near poverty-level wages. In addition, many of the more desirable jobs now are shifting from full-time salaried jobs that include job security and employment benefits such as insurance, unemployment compensation, and retirement plans to temporary or contract work (Bluestone & Harrison, 1987; Chira, 1989). Among high school graduates not going on to college, employment rates dropped 72% from 1979 to 1985 (see Table 1.1 in Chapter 1).

LOSS OF ECONOMIC POWER IN THE WORKING CLASS AND THE GROWTH OF POVERTY

The War on Poverty and the Great Society included programs predicated on the premise that poverty could be eliminated or, at least, that the growth rate of income for the poor would exceed that of the rich if business cycles could be controlled, wealth could be induced to trickle down, and social policies favorable to the poor and minorities were implemented. However, these anticipated effects have not occurred. Since 1970, Americans have experienced increasing economic stagnation, a growing gap between the very rich and the very poor, and increasing poverty and economic inequality, especially for families with children (Danziger, 1988, p. 5).

A recent analysis of poverty among children in the United States indicates that even though average U.S. income levels reached an all-time high in 1988, the number of Americans living below the official poverty line remained the same for two straight years (Bane & Ellwood, 1989). Official guidelines are misleading, however, because they make no adjustments for local differences in the cost of living. Where living costs are high, families living above the official poverty line may actually have less disposable income than those below the line but who live in less expensive localities.

What this means is that ordinary working Americans can no longer aspire to a better life than their parents had. As the number of jobs in the service sector increases at the expense of high-paying interesting and lucrative jobs in the professional sector, fewer people will anticipate upward occupational mobility. Many will have to adjust their income and employment expectations downward. This has had a profound effect upon families and their expectations for the future. For example, young men who finish high school but do not attend college—the majority of the cohort—cannot expect to earn enough to support families for quite some time. However, their expectations for the future have not changed in accordance with the reality of their job situations. Weis's (1990) recent ethnography of white and black working-class students indicates that young men still have very traditional expectations—job, marriage, a few children, maybe a house, and settling down with a wife who will stay at home with the children. For most, those expectations are completely unrealistic. By contrast, young women expect to, and want to, work before settling down; they no longer see themselves as structuring their lives entirely around the presence of a husband. These altered expectations mean alienation, because the traditional ways people have expected to "grow up" are no longer possible. We now discuss some of the reasons this is so.

Poor Children, Poor Households

Increases in poverty among children in the 1980s can be accounted for by the worsening economic situation for two-parent families, rather than by increases in the number of children living in female-headed homes, as was the case in the past. Young families, those most likely to have young children, were hit hardest. In 1984, roughly half of all poor children lived in two-parent homes, and in California, for example, 52% of children living in poverty came from families in which at least one parent worked (PACE, 1989). In 1973, 12.7% of all married men with two children failed to earn enough to stay above the poverty line (Danziger, 1988). Much of this is a function of decline in the wages of male workers, but since the early 1970s average wage and salary incomes, adjusted for inflation, have been declining for nearly all groups in the population and in most industries. Some 44% of new jobs created pay poverty-level wages (Bluestone & Harrison, 1987). The situation is worst for minorities. Among males 20-24, real earnings for high school graduates dropped 30%; for black graduates, the drop was more than 50%. For dropouts in general, real earnings fell 42% from 1973 to 1984; among black dropouts, the plunge was 61%.

Families

The impact on families has been dramatic. In 1986, less than one-half (44%) of young men aged 20-24 earned enough to support a family of three above the poverty line. This represented a drop from 58% in 1973. For young black men, the situation was worse; in 1986, 24% earned enough to support a family of three, down from 54% in 1973 (W. T. Grant, 1988). Only one black dropout in nine earns enough to support a family of three above the poverty line (Children's Defense Fund, 1987). These factors help to explain the rise in the number of children who are born out of wedlock: While economic factors prevent young people from instituting viable marriages, these factors do not at the same time prevent them from producing children.

While a slight majority of all poor children live in two-parent families, predictions are that by the early 1990s, one out of every four children under 10 years old will be living in a family headed by a single woman (Rodgers, 1988, p. 42). Living in a "broken home" now has "become the normal childhood experience" (Hodgkinson, 1985, p. 3). Divorce rates and the increased incidence of unwed motherhood also affect the poverty status of children. The poverty rate for single-parent families has been about 50% since 1965; it is five times higher for female-headed families than for two-parent families. In

1985, 34% of all female-headed families were poor; the rate for those headed by a woman under age 25 exceeds 74%. For mothers who never married and are under age 25 and racial minority members, the rate exceeds 85%. Some 22% of all children lived in such families in 1985 (Rodgers, 1988). These children are at risk for dropping out both because they are poor and because they have less support from adults than do other children.

Social Policies

The United States is the only major Western industrialized country that has no statutory maternity benefits, no universal child-rearing benefits, and no universal health care benefits. U.S. welfare policies penalize two-parent families in which one or both parents work; these families are ineligible for cash income transfers in 27 states (Danziger, 1988; Rodgers, 1988; Smeeding & Torrey, 1988, p. 875). These policies also either preclude family members from working or penalize them by eliminating benefits such as health care and reducing their monetary benefits to the extent of their wages.

The Feminization of Poverty

As long as women are disadvantaged in the work force, welfare programs offer limited economic incentives or opportunities, and absent fathers fail to provide support, half of the children living in female-headed homes will be poor. Bane and Ellwood (1989, p. 1050) point out that the issue is not one of not working; one can work and still be poor in the United States. However, the average annual salary of a female-headed household is close to or below the poverty line. The impoverishment of women is partly a result of labor market choice, in that women typically choose or are forced to move into low-paying female-dominated and service sector jobs because of their lack of labor market experience and training relative to men. However, women also get smaller returns on their educational investments than men do (Rosenfeld, 1980); only half the sex gap in earnings can be explained by the types of jobs women hold compared with men (Bayes, 1988, pp. 93-94). Many women hold jobs that include no insurance or other benefits (Croke, 1989). Bayes (1988) indicates that the more children a women has, the less she earns (p. 97). Further, although women are entering the work force in increasing numbers, they are doing so at a time when the number of high-paying jobs for all workers is shrinking (p. 104).

No-fault divorce laws in 43 states also have contributed to the impoverishment of women. These laws eliminated alimony and often forced the sale of a family home—often the only valuable asset a couple has. The typical divorcee with children suffers a 73% drop in standard of living in the years after divorce, while the standard of living of ex-husbands jumps by 42% (Weitzman, 1985). Bureau of Labor Statistics data show that the number of women moonlighting has quintupled since 1970. At the same time, the number of men moonlighting has dropped. While some women moonlight to save money, gain extra experience, or pay off debts, the majority do so because it is the only way to keep themselves and their families above the poverty line or in the family home and a familiar neighborhood (Kilborn, 1990).

Teenaged Motherhood

Children who are born to children are much more likely to be poor, and as the incidence of teenaged motherhood increases, so do the numbers of impoverished children, especially if their mothers are unmarried. Teenaged mothers are likely to be dropouts, as are their children. It is not so much that teens intrinsically have unhealthy babies or abuse them, but that teenagers, especially single ones, are far more likely to be poor, undereducated, unemployed, and inexperienced parents. Teenagers who have babies also are more likely to come from homes that already are poor. And poor children are more prone to the alienation from school that causes them to drop out.

Ignorance about reproduction and contraception exacerbates the problem of teen pregnancy. Fewer than half of all sexually active teens know what part of the menstrual cycle constitutes the greatest risk of conception; often they have unprotected intercourse because they think they cannot become pregnant (Weatherley, 1988; Zelnik & Kantner, 1980). In 1982, the National Research Council studied sexual activity among 9.7 million girls ages 15-19. Of the sample, 40% initiated intercourse, and only 40% of those used effective contraceptives (Hayes, 1987). Political and religious conservatives foster such ignorance in their opposition to making information about family planning, sexuality, abortion services, and contraceptive devices readily available to minors, but even those contraceptives accessible to Americans are not well suited to an adolescent population because they are complicated to use, require discipline and motivation, are inconvenient and often messy, and have unintended side effects. Most important, those that are easiest to obtain are the most unreliable (Djerassi, 1989; Hilts, 1990).

The combination of high levels of sexual activity, ignorance, and inadequate prophylaxis has produced an epidemic of births. Unless there is intervention, a teenager who has a child tends to have a second child; each day, 40 teenagers in the United States give birth to their third children (Hodgkinson, 1985, p. 3). Since society has become more accepting of—or at least resigned to—the phenomenon of unwed mothers, more young mothers are keeping their babies. Before 1960, 95% of unmarried adolescent mothers gave their babies up for adoption. By 1982, 91% of white and 95% of black adolescent mothers elected to raise their babies themselves (Weatherley, 1988, p. 120). The president of the National Committee for Adoption feels that there is "almost a pressure to be a single mother if a woman becomes pregnant. People say, 'what kind of mother would give her baby away?' Their friends want to give them baby showers. Society is choosing parenting for the mother" (Sowers, 1989). As access to abortion and family planning services becomes more restricted and expensive, poor teenagers are increasingly likely to become parents and to be at risk for dropping out of school.

Housing

Lack of affordable housing is the primary cause of homelessness. Since 1970, housing prices have risen four times faster than incomes. Furthermore, the stock of existing older housing available to low-income families has diminished under pressures of gentrification, renovation, and condominium conversions. In 1987, 8 million members of the working poor were competing for 4 million low-income housing units (Hodgkinson, 1989). Local government policies and zoning laws act to keep poor and minority tenants and low-cost housing out, at the same time that federal housing assistance has been cut by more than two-thirds and the federal housing construction operation has been shut down completely (Jordan, 1987b). The poor pay an increasingly large proportion of their income for housing; for nearly half the families in poverty, 70% of income goes for housing. Under these conditions, loss of a paycheck brings forth the specter of homelessness (Hodgkinson, 1989), and one homeless person in four is a child ("Hungry Children," 1989).

Loss of housing can lead to doubling up and crowding of existing families, or even the breakup of families. One of the considerations in awarding custody of children is whether or not a parent can provide adequate shelter. Jordan (1987a) describes two such situations. One custodial father with a monthly income of $800 could not pay his $550 rent, and could not find another apartment in the Washington, D.C., area near his work for less; his ex-wife had sued for custody. Another woman moved back in with an abusive ex-husband because she could not find affordable housing for herself and her children. The chaos of being homeless makes children more prone to becoming dropouts; without even the security of a roof over one's head, life itself loses meaning. Under such conditions, school becomes the only safe refuge—but it is one that is increasingly scarce, since eligibility to attend depends upon being zoned to a school according to one's *home* address.

LOSS IN THE VALUE OF EDUCATIONAL CREDENTIALS

Americans no longer can trust that working hard to get an education will ensure success. At one time, a high school diploma served as assurance that one possessed the requisites for employment. However, the power that education wields to ensure occupational attainment has waned. Debate exists over whether what counts are skills or credentials. Arguing for skills, some theorists state that the education schools actually provide is so deficient that students must acquire higher levels of educational attainment simply in order to possess the same skills once provided by fewer years in school. Other theorists argue that schools act as finishing schools, to assure that, once on the job, employees will exhibit behaviors acceptable to their employers (Collins, 1971, 1974, 1979). Still others posit that as levels of educational attainment in the general population rise, people who wish to remain competitive in the job market must acquire ever more advanced credentials to distinguish themselves from other job seekers.

Whatever the reasons for educational "inflation," the consequences have been enormous. First, while most jobs really do not require more than elementary school skill levels in literacy and computation, the numbers of people educated beyond primary school continue to grow. Second, certification no longer guarantees a job commensurate with that level of education. Third, levels of skill demonstrated by individuals may in no way be commensurate with the levels of certification they have acquired; and fourth, levels of skill and certification acquired are distributed differentially by ascriptive characteristics such as race, gender, ethnicity, religion, and place of residence or origin. This means that certain segments of the population have become frozen on lower rungs of the occupational ladder (LeCompte & Dworkin, 1988, p. 149; Ogbu, 1978, 1983).

Inflation of credentials means that a college education is worth less at the same time that the cost of higher education to individuals and families is growing and the payoff to higher education is diminishing. Since 1977, college tuition costs have increased in constant dollars by as much as 25%. Students who take out loans to go to college often end up so deeply in debt that they cannot choose fields such as teaching and nursing, because they will not earn enough money to repay what they owe ("Student Debt Level," 1987).

If fewer people go to college, the drop in the number of college graduates probably will articulate better with the reality of the labor market. However, the resulting downward mobility will not sit well with people in a culture such as that in the United States, where higher education and the occupational prestige to which it leads have come to feel like entitlements.

THE RISE OF ALTERNATIVE ECONOMIES

Change in the distribution of income has several effects. First, it calls into question the validity of beliefs that it is possible, through hard work and moral behavior, to achieve economic success. Second, it leads those frozen out of the opportunity structure—those for whom these beliefs are fairy tales—to seek economic alternatives, whether licit or illicit. The frozen-out constitute an underclass (Wilson, 1987) defined as much by under- and unemployment as by race or ethnicity. There is a growing underclass in every nation, and it acts to destabilize existing social structures. It will remain static and passive only so long as there is no alternative pathway to status. Some standard alternatives, such as the military, are now becoming out of reach because of rising skill requirements that the children of the underclass do not possess. Where other alternatives do exist, they often disrupt cultural myths and aid the perception of alienation, since they violate standard norms and beliefs about success and well-being in the society, as well as laws regulating the stability of the social order.

Illegal Economies as Alternatives to Educational Success

Trade in illegal drugs, arms, highly organized theft, and prostitution has traditionally formed alternative and parallel economies, but until recently these economies have remained for the most part underground. Participation in these alternatives did not in any way constitute a viable avenue to success in the legitimate sphere. However, now these illegal economies are beginning to dominate those nations and cities where the underclass predominates and where no other hope exists.

The drug trade is the most obvious alternative economy. Notwithstanding all attempts by the U.S. government to stem the tide of illicit drugs, neither the demand fueling the traffic nor the highly sophisticated business operation that it supports have diminished. "In fact, the illicit drug business has been described—not entirely in jest—as the best means ever devised by the U.S. for exporting the capitalist ethic to potentially revolutionary Third World peasants" (Nadelmann, 1989, p. 946). In addition, interdiction of massive amounts of imported marijuana—the most successful of the control attempts, in large part because the bulky smuggled product is hard to conceal—has resulted in making the United States the world's leading producer of high-grade marijuana (p. 946).

Even the least elaborate drug rings display a remarkable level of business acumen, organizational skill, and technological sophistication (Bourgeois, 1989; Kolata, 1989). A dealer can get into the business with remarkably little capital; an ounce of cocaine bought for about $1,000 is enough to get started. The payoffs of drug trafficking are perceived to be enormous. Street wisdom holds that successful salespeople can make in excess of $500 a night—and the highest level of traffickers themselves are not addicts. While the risks of getting arrested, murdered, maimed, or addicted are substantial, the payoffs in terms of wealth, the ability to engage in conspicuous and status-raising display, and status are substantial, even irresistible. "Ambitious energetic inner-city youth are attracted to the underground economy precisely because they believe in the rags-to-riches American Dream. It is Horatio Alger with a needle" (Bourgeois, 1989). It is the same get-rich-quick scheme, the same "shimmering lure, built on myth and self-deception" (Kolata, 1989) that once was the catalyst for working hard in school. There are high risks, but also high gains for the successful.

Sociologists and anthropologists studying street drug culture suggest that participants in drug traffic really make far less money and have much shorter and unhappier lives than the news and entertainment media often portray. Even those who claw their way to the second level of the crack cocaine distribution pyramid may admit that they lead miserable lives, living in substandard housing or on the streets, in fear of arrest or death, and making little more than $20-$30 for a full day's work. For most, the drug trade may be no more than another minimum-wage job (Bourgeois, 1989; Kolata, 1989).

What may be overlooked in this analysis is that a minimum-wage job, even an illicit one, may be better than no job at all to someone in the underclass. For the young children who act as lookouts and delivery persons for dealers, it may be a very good job indeed. And even though it may be a minimum-wage job, with no benefits and high risks, it is unlike almost any other job available to young people in the underclass: It holds out the promise, however slim, of status and economic mobility. That is, the drug trade constitutes not only an alternative economy, but an alternative to the existing and inaccessible system of social status and power.

FROM REGIONAL AND NATIONAL TO GLOBAL ECONOMIES

As Americans, we can no longer view ourselves as first among world leaders. In the past, we quite clearly have seen ourselves as the vanguard of the world economic and political order, the makers of history. We have believed in an updated form of mercantilism, predicated upon the existence of upper-tier sovereign nation-states with intact self-sufficient internal labor markets and independent financial, entrepreneurial, and industrial sectors controlled, for the most part, by their own citizens—who were served by less developed client states that provided raw materials, exotic crafts, and markets for finished industrial products. The sovereignty of the United States now has been challenged by multilateral agreements that, although once limited to exchange of scarce resources and treaties aimed at control of warfare, now govern almost every aspect of Americans' lives as consumers. We find that almost everything we buy or use is produced, at least in part, in foreign places, by foreign workers, with foreign materials, or by enterprises that are owned or at least partly controlled by foreigners. The United States is accustomed to being the controller and owner, not the controlled and owned. To find ourselves in this predicament incites xenophobia and confusion over our new role and power in the world.

LOSS OF WHITE ETHNIC HEGEMONY

The culture that has dominated policy-making and institutional practice, and whose members have reaped the greatest proportion of societal rewards, has been that of the white middle and upper-middle class. This has led whites of whatever class to expect that they will be dominant politically and numerically in the majority in the institutions where they work and play and in the neighborhoods where they live. However, current U.S. population shifts mean that the feeling of numerical and social dominance that whites once enjoyed is becoming more illusory and harder to maintain. By the year 2000, one in three Americans will be nonwhite (Hodgkinson, 1985). The nonwhite immigrants—Asians, Hispanics, and non-Hispanic blacks—who increasingly come to the United

States as legal immigrants under new immigration legislation are skilled workers (Herbers, 1986) who constitute a great challenge to the economic, political, and cultural dominance of established white residents. For schools, this means that the teaching force, which still is predominantly white, will increasingly serve students whose cultures, classes, and races differ from their own, and students will attend school with classmates with whom they can no longer assume shared patterns of behavior and belief.

LOSS OF EUROCENTRIC HEGEMONY

The world underwent a massive round of decolonization during the two decades from 1950 to 1970. This changed the political map, but did not really affect who held power in the world. Neither did it alter the fact that a bipolar Cold War prevailed, creating a balance of terror whose dynamics kept the world, if not comfortable, at least relatively predictable and Eurocentric. Recent changes in patterns of political hegemony, however, have brought about a radical destabilization of the geopolitical map.

We already have noted the decline in the absolute and proportional numbers of white people in the Western world. Loss of numerical dominance is not necessarily associated with loss of hegemony. However, the latter part of the 20th century is witnessing the attenuation of white-dominated colonial empires of Europe, the United States, and the Soviet Union. Now, Asian nations—in particular, Japan, Korea, and Singapore—having noted carefully the strengths and weaknesses of American and European industrial organization (Halberstam, 1986), have begun to achieve dominance over many world markets and to translate that dominance into political muscle. The geopolitical importance of their location, as well as the centrality of their oil resources, makes the Arab nations of the Middle East increasingly powerful in the equation of world politics. The patterns of behavior and cognitive maps of North Americans and Europeans are no longer taken as the sole models upon which the progress and development of other cultures are predicated and assessed; neither is their ability to impose policy anywhere in the world taken for granted anymore.

THE IMPACT OF SCIENCE AND TECHNOLOGY

A Problem of Knowledge

During the last 25 years, the entire scientific world has changed. Test-tube babies no longer are an Orwellian fantasy, and the universe now seems to be organized around some dynamic form of chaos that has replaced the systemic order that once structured our thinking. We now know that DNA is not static matter, but that chromosomes seem to "talk" to each other and engage in dynamic activity. The Human Genome Initiative proposes to map each and every one of tens of thousands of mysterious genes in the human organism. The concept of continental drift now underpins our understanding of seismic activity. The uncertainty principle no longer is new. Theoretical mathematicians, physicists, and artificial intelligence experts now are challenging the whole theoretical structure of our universe. The popular press is full of books on these subjects, explaining as simply as possible everything from subatomic physics (Zukav, 1979) and theories of chaos (Gleick, 1987) to the genetic basis of evolution (Wills, 1989) and the origins of the universe (Hawking, 1988).

We believe that the changes in the last two or three decades are as earthshaking as the Copernican revolution in terms of the degree to which they challenge the view that ordinary humans have of themselves and their relationship to the universe. Unfortunately, developments in science have outstripped the ability of lay people to keep up with them. Further, these challenges are not just academic.

Issues such as depletion of the ozone layer, control of human fertility, disposal of nuclear waste, and use of recombinant DNA to create new organisms exemplify how scientific advances can surge ahead of public responses to them. These are the kinds of areas where cultural lag becomes most prominent. While it is tempting to view them as if they were outside our responsibility, we regard them as mere issues of morality, too complex or frightening to resolve, or capable of short-term solution, at our peril. In the succeeding chapters, we will develop a more complex model for depicting the strains, conflicts, and tensions that such forces cause, and indicate entry points where these strains might be alleviated. Here we wish only to indicate their relationship to cultural change and alienation.

Communications: A Problem of Scale

Contemporary humans are faced with a curious tension between intimacy and anonymity. Notwithstanding a persistent and often romantic effort to reform modern society by decentralization and the creation of smaller institutions and technologies, as the world has grown "smaller," the networks of its institutions have grown wider and more inclusive. Groups from different cultures are thrown together via telecommunications and transport networks that give an illusion of intimacy at the same time the institutions in which the groups live and work have become so large and unwieldy that intimacy is precluded. Children may know a great deal about people living in Tierra del Fuego from television documentaries, but virtually nothing about the people in the next block. Scale and complexity are only a part of the shift we describe. Also involved is the rapidity and depth with which modern means of communication have penetrated every aspect of all societies. In some cases, new modes of communication have made it possible to circumvent every effort at suppression; they have also increased the rate at which change is possible in societies. Only about three decades separate the laboriously hand-copied and carbon-paper-copied underground *samizdat* of dissidents in the Soviet Union and the use in 1988 by protesting Chinese students in Beijing of fax machines and computer networks to communicate with supporters and fellow dissidents in the outside world.

Allocation and Utilization of World Resources

A new version of the "Doomsday Book" heralding the "end of nature" (Schell, 1982) recently has called attention to the need for a radically different conceptualization of the relationship between humans and nature. Ever since the Enlightenment, Westerners have acted upon nature, assuming that, given sufficient time, study, insight, and technical expertise, nature could be controlled and put to the service of humankind. A corollary to this attitude has been the belief that any messes created in the process can be fixed by the same scientific processes. The background assumption was that nature was infinitely resilient, and that the demise of many biological species was irrelevant to the survival of the human race.

Now, however, nature is biting back. It has become clear that we may have tampered with the global ecological system—of which we only dimly realize we are a small part—too drastically. These realizations require that contemporary Western humans change their view of how they relate to the universe. They must recognize that they are not the universe's controlling masters. They cannot flee to an all-forgiving and resilient forest for solace, or envision world resources as infinitely exploitable. Complicating this realization are rising expectations for material comfort in every nation of the world. Role models for consumption from Europe and North America cannot be emulated by the whole world without even more radical exploitation of what is left of the world resource base—and unacceptable environmental degradation.

The rising demand for individual freedom and democracy also threatens the sense of collective responsibility, which may further endanger the global ecosystem. Examples include the nuclear arms race among Third World nations, who view attempts to control proliferation as an attack upon their sovereignty, or protests by less developed nations that controlling the use of refrigerants—in the name of protecting the ozone layer—will deny their people the cool and comfortable life enjoyed by more affluent nations. Because these issues require definitions of self and responses for which no guidelines exist, they constitute a primary source of cultural alienation. The human race drifts in an alarming new world ungoverned by rules dictating behavior.

The Rising Toll of "Acceptable" Levels of Violence

We believe that millions of people in the world are nearing saturation in their exposure to random—and, from the perspective of individuals, uncontrollable—violence. Violence is not limited to warfare, nor is it restricted to exotic foreign countries. The violence engendered by alternative economies of drugs, arms, and other illicit activities is deeply ensconced in American and European cities of all sizes. This is profoundly unsettling to people's perceptions of the quality of life. While it may be that the actual levels of global violence—in terms of numbers of people killed, maimed, hijacked, kidnapped, robbed, or otherwise injured—are no greater than in past eras, the forms the violence takes are becoming less institutionalized and less widely legitimated. Hence they have become much more difficult for everyday citizens to ignore or avoid. Because of the explosion of communications technology, violence has also become much more visible and intimate, no matter where it occurs; many people now find it hard to avoid seeing the citizens of distant countries as neighbors. The *perception* of insecurity, then, and the *feeling* that one is at risk—whether accurate or not—becomes all-pervasive, and increases the tensions and strains with which people spend their daily lives.

SUMMARY

So, here we are with a profoundly changed world, with our institutions seemingly incapable of responding because they cannot resurrect a world that no longer exists. The question is, What does all of this have to do with education? Let us return to the world of students and teachers for a moment.

From the students' perspective, school has simply ceased to be very relevant, both to the lives they currently live and to their futures. School is as irrelevant as current events and the political system, over which they believe they have absolutely no control. In a recent poll, 70% of American youth said that politics and government were too complicated for them to understand, and 57% admitted to very little interest in newspaper or television reports on developments in politics and government. Their concern is for self, not service and community; 72% said that career success was the most important goal in life, while 58% voted for "enjoying life and having a good time." This lack of concern is reflected by the fact that only 31% had volunteered for any kind of community service activity in the past year (Peter D. Hart Research Associates, n.d.; study cited in the *Houston Chronicle,* November 30, 1989, p. 1).

> I don't know anything about politics. I was going to vote, but then I thought about it and thought I didn't know anything about it. If you don't understand it and you vote, then you're going to mess things up. I don't watch news. I don't read. It's full of problems. It's one more headache. (18-year-old student and salesclerk, quoted by Reinhold, 1990)

> I look at my parents voting. The candidates they vote for make promises and promises and promises and nothing ever changes. (college student, quoted by Reinhold, 1990)

Some writers have described these attitudes as more than mere self-centered apathy or passive inaction. Rather, they feel it resembles the nihilism of punk culture—an aggressive and active rejection of the politicization of reality. Living in today's world does not "deny the need for action or the possibility of commitment, albeit as a localised, individual one" (Grossberg, 1989, p. 98). Young people "find it impossible to represent the world of their parents, to internalize their parents' affective relationship to the world, or to invest themselves in their parents' values" (p. 109) The existing "mattering maps" no longer correspond to the maps of meaning created by and relevant to young people. Thus overloaded, they withdraw into the authenticity of an inauthentic stance or pose, a punk nihilism.

> If we are without passion or affect, it is because we have decided that passion and affect are simply not worth the trouble. If we stand crouched in the shadows of a history in which we refuse to take part, it is because that's exactly where we have chosen to stand. . . . Characterlessness takes work. It is defiance and defense all at once. (Grossberg, 1989, p. 98)

And what of the teachers who face these young people in their classrooms? Let us conclude this chapter with a series of questions that such teachers face in day-to-day pedagogy:

- As a biology, chemistry, or physics teacher, how do you keep up with the rapid pace of change in your field, much less make it intelligible to students? Or cope with demands to give creationist notions of the origins of the species equal time with scientific evolution?
- As a social studies teacher, what stance do you take—during tensions among *perestroika, glasnost,* and the pressures of counterreform in Eastern Europe and the Soviet Union—when your state-mandated curriculum is predicated upon 1950s Cold War geopolitics?
- As an educator from any field or grade level, how do you cope with students who are hungry, homeless, abused and neglected, drug-addicted, frightened, and unable to study?
- Given the erosion of good opportunities in the labor market, how can you convince your students that if they work hard and get good grades, they will be able to attain a middle-class lifestyle?
- Do you blame their parents? Are you a single parent yourself? How much drug use and alcoholism and pregnancy is there in the schools your children attend?
- As a teacher, are you afraid of your students? Are you afraid to leave the school after dark?
- As a vocational teacher, what vocations do you teach?
- What inducements for achievement can you use when students believe that the alternative, or underground, economy garners

far more money with much less work in considerably less time than hard work in a straight job? Or that higher education—and its presumed payoff—are impossible dreams for most of your students? What if you know that even if they do graduate from high school or college, your students will not earn enough money to participate in the American Dream?

- Does a good life 50 years in the future seem possible for anyone in the face of impending environmental collapse?
- How do you react upon overhearing the following conversation between two 15-year-old male honor students?

  A: *What kind of woman do you want to marry?*
  B: *Awww . . . I don't think I'm going to get married . . .*
  A: *Why not, man?*
  B: *What's the use of thinking about getting married and all that when we're probably going to get blown up before we're even 25, anyway?*

Responding to these questions decenters everything teachers are taught to expect and do in classrooms. The consequence is alienation—a sense that they are powerless to do their job well, and that, as a result, their work is meaningless. In the chapters that follow, we will explore in detail the implications of this alienation for students and teachers.

NOTES

1. In 1987, the federal government held between 4.5 and 7 million acres of foreclosed farmland. In four states (North Dakota, Kansas, Nebraska, and Iowa) this land has been offered for sale at bargain prices—10% to 40% down and as little as 4.9% financing—but even at these rates, poor farmers and young people cannot obtain financing to buy land ("Growing Inventory," 1987).

2. The U.S. Department of Agriculture reports that from June 1985 to June 1986, 65,000 farms were lost—a rate of one every eight minutes. If each farm supported some three people, this means that an estimated 195,000 rural Americans had to seek new lives. Often those who were displaced were pillars of their communities—hardworking role models, innovative farmers who went bankrupt under the pressure of loans the government itself encouraged them to undertake to finance the very programs for which they were admired (Malcolm, 1987).

THREE

Turned Off, Tuned Out, Dropped Out

In this chapter and the next, we define who student dropouts and tune-outs are, how big a problem they constitute, and what leads to tune-out, alienation, and dropping out. While we draw on a wealth of quantitative and qualitative data on student experiences in school, including extensive research on dropouts in a major urban school district conducted by one of the authors, we have been struck by the fact that there simply is not as much in-depth information about students who drop out as there is about teachers who become burned out and leave the profession. Actual data from students are relatively limited; most of what we know about how students feel is based upon correlational studies or upon inferences made from descriptions of students by adults (LeCompte & Preissle, 1992). Dropouts, because they leave school, are not around to be studied, and they tend not to leave addresses through which they can be traced. Notwithstanding these limitations, we try to delineate how students come to be defined and counted as dropouts, and suggest that the issues that affect these most alienated students severely also affect most other children in school.

WHAT IS A DROPOUT?

A dropout is a pupil of any age who leaves school, for any reason other than death, before graduation or completion of a program of studies and without transferring to another elementary or secondary school (Houston Independent School District, 1989; LeCompte, 1985b; Putnam & Tankard, 1964). This definition permits us to examine the impact of in-school factors on the ability of schools to hold students long enough to complete their courses of study. It does not include people who might, after a time, choose to return to school and finish, or who find alternative paths to certification, such as the GED or early admission to college. Since studies of dropouts do not all use the same definition, our choice of one definition creates real anomalies in determining how many students actually drop out.

The Problem of Enumeration

A major problem is that it is difficult to determine how many students really drop out. Estimates vary depending upon how dropouts are defined, the span of time used for computations, whether attrition is calculated from a cohort or an annual class, and how well records are maintained and reported by school districts (Hammack, 1986; LeCompte & Goebel, 1987; Morrow, 1986; Rumberger, 1987). Rumberger (1987) points out that there are two primary statistics used to estimate the number of students who drop out. U.S. Bureau of the Census figures are designed to determine the number and proportion of persons from a given demographic cohort who are dropouts. States also aggregate dropout data based upon attrition from school. These data consist of the proportion of a given entering ninth-grade class that graduates four years later (see Table 3.1). Census data rates are lower, ranging in 1984 from 6.8% for 16- and 17-years-olds to 15.2% for 18- and 19-year-olds (Rumberger, 1987, p. 104). States vary considerably in their rates of attrition; the average for 1984 was 29.1% of a cohort, with a high of 43.3% for Louisiana and a low of 10.7% for Minnesota.

An even more variable statistic comes from specific school districts. At a conference on dropouts in 1985, participants provided conferees with statistics from their own districts for dropout rates ranging from 2% to 15% annually. They privately admitted that actual rates might exceed 30% to 50%, especially for minorities (Mann, 1987). In general, scholars report that approximately 25% of all 18-year-olds fail to graduate from high school (McDill et al., 1985). In urban areas and for minority students the figures are much higher (Holley & Doss, 1983; Orum, 1984; Whelage, 1983).

How to overestimate dropouts. The U.S. Bureau of the Census does not count as dropouts people over the age of 18 who obtain high school equivalency certification after dropping out of formal educational programs. However, most state agencies include as dropouts all persons who have not graduated and who are not currently enrolled in school, even if they have completed the GED or other high school equivalency examination. Some districts count as dropouts students who transfer to other schools. Many districts even count as dropouts gifted students who gain early admission to college and skip their senior years, even though the colleges grant them high school credit for their course work (Asin, 1989). Since many people do reenter school after a period of having dropped out, and since many states do not permit individuals to take the GED until they have been out of school for two years or have passed the age of 18, state figures may be too high.

How to underestimate dropouts. On the other hand, and probably more serious, are underestimates of the size of the dropout population. In the past, traditional school accounting procedures calculated dropout rates on the basis of the nine-month school year; dropouts were students who left during the months from September to June. Students who failed to return the following September, the "summer dropouts," were omitted from the tallies. Even when schools moved to year-round accounting procedures, many students were missed. "Involuntary dropouts," or students who have been suspended or expelled from school, and students who become "lost" when they transfer to another school district (and hence are not in attendance) but fail to have their records transferred to the receiving district may be counted as dropouts. These may account for as many as 25% of the students counted as dropouts (LeCompte & Goebel, 1987). Students who repeatedly drop in and out of school may be counted several times. Political considerations also affect how dropouts are counted. When districts are pressured to reduce dropout rates, especially when the sanctions include reductions in state or federal funding, whole categories of students once counted as dropouts suddenly are excluded from the tally of dropouts. These include long-gone "ghosts" who are maintained on school records to increase the enrollment base for funding, truants whom school districts "forgot" to discharge when they were absent more than the legal maximum, students who allegedly transferred but for whom no documents were requested, and students who completed their schooling nontraditionally, such as by getting a GED in a district-run adult education program (Deyhle, 1989; Hahn & Danzberger, 1987, p. 10).

The labels assigned to students also cause school districts to underestimate the population. School districts create administrative categories to classify students for whom they can no longer account. These categories often obscure both the actual count and the reasons students drop out. Some districts have a specific category called "dropped out of school," into which only those students who self-identify as dropouts are placed. Unfortunately, most students who leave school before graduating do not announce their intentions. Their act of dropping out is disguised in such categories as "needed at home," "married," and "cannot adjust" (Hahn & Danzberger, 1987, p. 10). Many simply compile increasingly poor records of performance and attendance until they fail to show up at all. They then fall into such ambiguous catchall classifications as "lost—not coming to school," "nonattendance," and "whereabouts unknown," which can account for more than

50% of the students who might be dropouts (LeCompte & Goebel, 1987).

However they might be measured, some trends do seem clear. One is that the overall dropout rate in the United States, which declined steadily from 40% in 1960 to about 25% in 1965, has not changed substantially in 25 years. In fact, 1988 figures from the Department of Education indicate that the rate now may be as high as 29%. Another identifiable trend is that dropout rates for inner-city minorities are rising. More important, however, are the problem areas that aggregated statistics mask. In the following pages, we attempt to develop an accurate picture of students who are at risk and drop out.

WHO ARE THE DROPOUTS?

A number of studies have used quantitative data on the personal, family, and social class characteristics of students from sources such as the Project TALENT, Youth in Transition, and High School and Beyond data bases to construct a profile of dropouts (see, for example, Bachman, Green, & Wirtanen, 1971; Coleman & Hoffer, 1987; Coleman, Hoffer, & Kilgore, 1982; Peng, 1983; Rumberger, 1983). Among their findings are the following. First, dropout rates are substantially higher in urban areas, in public schools, and among minority youth. Second, dropouts generally are low-income students. In fact, social class is the most reliable predictor of a student's dropping out of school (Rumberger, 1983). Dropouts also are students who are low achievers, poor readers, discipline problems, and frequent truants. They also are likely to come from broken homes. These studies have created a conventional, if mistaken, wisdom that often views dropping out simply as a problem characteristic of poor and minority students. This fosters intervention policies predicated only on the existence of what we call the "traditional profile" of dropouts (Ekstrom, Goertz, Pollack, & Rock, 1986; LeCompte & Goebel, 1987); using it, teachers consistently report that they can identify those at risk for dropping out by second or third

Table 3.1 Dropout Rates by Age, Sex, Race, and Ethnicity, Selected Years, 1968-1984 (in percentages)

Cohort	*1968*	*1978*	*1980*	*1982*	*1984*
3- to 34-year-olds	18.3	12.9	12.7	12.7	12.6
white males	17.1	12.2	12.2	12.4	12.5
white females	17.3	12.4	11.9	11.9	11.7
black males	25.8	17.2	16.5	16.7	15.7
black females	25.6	16.2	16.2	14.9	15.0
Hispanic males	—	28.1	28.3	26.9	27.0
Hispanic females	—	29.0	27.3	27.3	26.7
18- to 19-year-olds					
white males	15.7	16.7	15.7	16.7	15.2
white females	14.3	16.3	16.1	16.6	15.8
black males	23.8	25.8	22.7	26.4	19.7
black females	24.7	22.8	19.8	18.1	14.5
Hispanic males	—	36.6	43.1	34.9	26.2
Hispanic females	—	39.6	34.6	31.1	26.0
16- to 17-year-olds					
white males	7.8	8.8	8.8	7.3	6.8
white females	6.9	9.6	9.3	7.3	7.3
black males	10.1	5.2	7.2	6.4	5.5
black females	14.2	9.4	6.6	5.5	4.9
Hispanic males	—	15.6	18.1	12.2	13.6
Hispanic females	—	12.2	15.0	15.9	12.7

SOURCE: Rumberger (1987, p. 20). Data from U.S. Bureau of the Census *School Enrollment* (Current Population Reports, Series P-20), various years.
NOTE: Dropout rates represent the percentages of cohorts who are dropouts. Dropouts are defined as persons of a given cohort who are not enrolled in school in October of the year in question and have not received a high school diploma or an equivalent high school certificate.

grade. It has been bolstered by research findings that typically examined the records of students who had been enrolled in grades 9-12 and failed to consider that dropouts might be younger.

In some respects, the traditional profile is helpful in identifying collective trends and future problems. The high dropout rate currently exhibited by minorities, for example, is of critical importance, because by the year 2000, one of every three Americans will be nonwhite (Hodgkinson, 1985). The map presented in Figure 3.1 shows the extent to which the nonwhite population has become predominant in many states. In

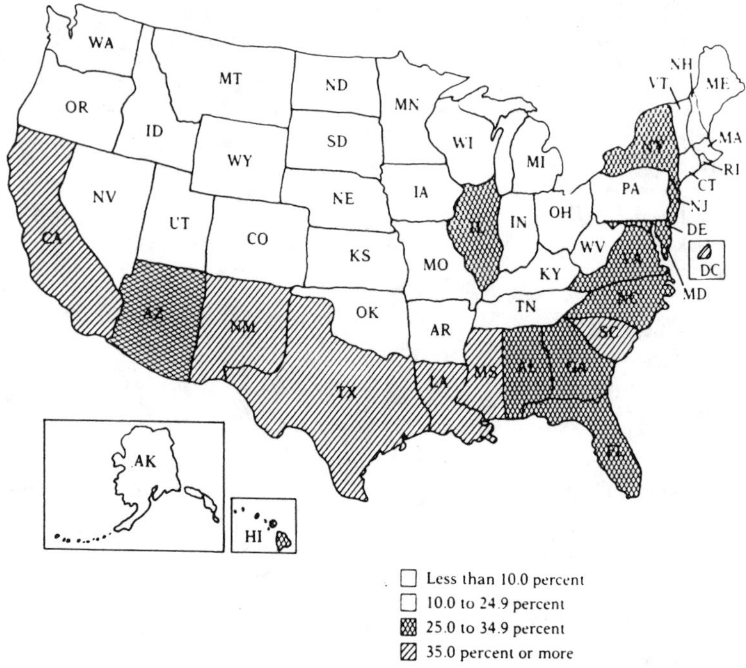

Figure 3.1 Minority Enrollment as Percentage of Public Elementary/Secondary School Enrollment, by State
SOURCE: National Center for Educational Statistics (1984).
NOTE: Percentage minority enrollment in public elementary secondary schools was generally greatest in southern and southwestern states and California. The percentage black enrollment was highest in southern states, and percentage Hispanic enrollment was highest in New Mexico, Texas, California, and Arizona.

the near future, the proportion of nonwhite young people will be even higher, because the bulk of immigrants to the United States are both young and nonwhite, and because the nonwhite population, in general, experiences higher birthrates than whites. This means that public school enrollments, even outside of urban areas, will become increasingly dominated by nonwhite children—who constitute those most at risk for dropping out. Adhering to the traditional profile can, however, obscure other even more dramatic trends and problems.

The Nontraditional Dropout

We have been confronted consistently by data that signal that other, more nontraditional, students now are dropping out, including able students from the middle class. We call the replacement of at least a portion of this low-income, low-achieving traditional cohort with one with very different characteristics the "gentrification" of the at-risk population (LeCompte, 1986; LeCompte & Goebel, 1987). Our own cohort analysis of dropouts in Houston confirmed that schools are losing many students who do not fit the traditional profile. Of those identified by the district as dropouts for 1983-1984, the year studied, 25% scored above the seventy-fifth percentile in standardized tests; 10% scored above the ninetieth percentile, and one male with scores in the ninety-ninth percentile dropped out in the last semester of twelfth grade.

The able dropout. Two examples illustrate what we mean by the nontraditional dropout. One was a white, middle-class senior high school girl who had scored in the ninety-seventh percentile on standardized tests, and who was enrolled in the program for gifted and talented students for most of her academic career. In her senior year, she became pregnant. She was transferred to a special school for pregnant teens, where she was not permitted to continue her work in the gifted program. The only curriculum provided at the school was an entirely remedial program, aimed at students whose achievement was far below grade level. Bored beyond toleration, she dropped out. Hess and Green (1988) summarize the similar experiences of young women in Chicago, where pregnant girls receive not only inappropriate academic handling, but little, if any, emotional or prenatal counseling and medical care.

Another example is that of Jay, a white, middle-class, third-year B student enrolled in the High School for Performing and Visual Arts. After flunking second-year algebra, he was placed back in a regular school because, under the "no pass, no play" rule mandated by the Texas legislature, attendance in the magnet school for the performing arts was defined as an "extracurricular activity." Despite the fact that he had passed first-year algebra, he was not allowed to satisfy the remaining year of math required for graduation with a less rigorous course—a substitution that many of his classmates at the High School for Performing and Visual Arts had already made. Jay dropped out of school rather than return to a traditional program. After obtaining a GED, he apprenticed himself to a painter. Subsequently, he enrolled in college, then transferred to another college with a strong art program in advertising, where he has maintained a B+ average.

Clearly these students were able and motivated. They were not at risk to begin with; rather, they were *put* at risk by rigidities in the school system that pushed them out. And they are not alone. Deyhle (1989), for example, reports that 55% of the Navajo dropouts she studied—her population included the entire student cohort from 1980 through 1988—left school in the twelfth grade. A recent study by Texas A&M University of six Texas school districts indicates not only that the majority of the dropouts were white, but that they had not been identified as at risk—or performing below grade level—under state guidelines (Asin, 1990). Districts in the Texas study had constituencies that were, with the exception of San Antonio, white and suburban, or predominantly white college communities. Similar findings were published in an analysis of dropout characteristics published by the Houston Independent School District (1989).

At least as far as academic performance, persistence in school, and ethnicity are concerned, these students do not fit the traditional profile. Their tested ability indicated that they were intellectually able, and the fact that they did not leave school until just before graduating indicates that they were motivated sufficiently to stick it out almost to the end. Most certainly they would not have been identified by teachers to be at risk in the third grade. Cases like these demonstrate that dropping out is increasingly a phenomenon that affects not just remedial students, but able ones as well.

The underaged dropout. Another nontraditional group of dropouts is made up of students younger than ninth grade.

Although records on this population are not kept systematically, there is scattered evidence that dropout rates for this group may be increasing (Hahn & Danzberger, 1987, p. 45). For example, in a 1985 study conducted in Houston, 21% of the students who dropped out did so in grades 6-8. This study also noted a big drop in the size of the cohort from elementary to middle school—although whether the drop was a consequence of dropping out or something else could not be ascertained directly, because no centralized data were collected from the elementary schools.

In 1987-1988, Houston reported dropout rates of 10.6% for seventh graders and almost 15% for eighth graders (Houston Independent School District, 1989). Many school districts, including Houston, now are aggregating data for middle school and junior high students, and trends of attrition for this population may become clearer in the future. However large the population may be, it poses a particular problem for intervention and remediation. The Houston data indicate that these children were far below grade level. They also were too young to work or to qualify for most of the job-oriented programs aimed at dropouts. Begging the question of a "self-fulfilling prophesy," or the fact that statistics are not even kept on the number of preteens and very young children who drop out of school, we feel that the fact that increasing numbers of children are leaving school for a world where they are too young to work, marry, or drive a car legally is of critical importance.

Teachers have long stated that by the second or third grade they can predict which children will drop out of school. In many cases, this is because actions of the schools themselves can actually begin the downward spiral toward student dropout. For example, in many districts, retention is routinely prescribed for students performing below grade level. However, the efficacy of retention has been widely debated (Labaree, 1984), especially given evidence indicating that retention itself may put children at risk and, indeed, may be the single most important predictor of dropping out (Cipollone, 1990; Fine & Zane, 1989). Retention of one grade increases the risk of dropping out by 50%, while retention of two grades increases the risk by 100% (Elmore, 1990). Being identified as "average" can put children at risk in school systems where great emphasis is placed on identification for specialized programming, because the term "average is just a catch-all category for kids who fall into no other category" (Barron, 1989). In a way, average students constitute a new minority that gets the least interesting and the least enriched educational programs of all (LeCompte, 1985a).

The Tune-Outs

Even more important than the number of dropouts, and more difficult to portray statistically, is the number of students who give up on school. Tune-outs differ from dropouts out because they actually are physically present in school. However, they are entrapped by truancy policies, parental expectations, personal aspirations, and child labor laws, and their consequent level of alienation prevents them from being deeply affected by what goes on in school. In Chapter 4 we will discuss in some depth what seems to cause students to tune out. One problem with these students is that the causes of their alienation seldom have been studied systematically (Newmann, 1981, p. 548); however, proxies for alienation may be found in reports on increasing rates of vandalism, absenteeism, apathy and hostility toward school, in-school cutting, and declining achievement (Carnegie Council on Adolescent Development, 1989; Coleman & Hoffer, 1987; Coleman et al., 1982; Hess, Wells, Prindle, Liffman, & Kaplan, 1987; Marotto, 1986; McLaren, 1980; McLeod, 1987; Powell, Farrar, & Cohen, 1985).

We believe that some estimate of the numbers of tune-outs might be found in the resoundingly poor performance that students in the United States exhibit in their studies. Haberman (1987) reports that during the 1980s, more than 300 national commissions and blue-ribbon panels were convened to assess the state of education. Their reports uniformly begin with a litany of horror stories regarding the poor performance of American students. They report, for example, that students do not know the most basic facts about history and geography (National Endowment for the Humanities, 1989), lag far behind their counterparts in other countries in science and math (LaPointe, Mead, & Phillips, 1989), and are deficient in the basic skills of reading and writing. These reports almost uniformly lack a theoretical grounding in social or educational theory. Further, their suggestions for reform ignore past research on educational reform initiatives, most of which have been proven ineffective. A 250-page report of the National Science Foundation titled *Educating Americans for the 21st Century*, for example, devotes only one paragraph to discussion of previous curriculum innovations, the ultimate impact and effectiveness of which were "far less than had been hoped." The report then proceeds to call for yet another wave of curricular programs similar to those that had failed (Puckett, 1989, p. 280).

While some blame can be laid at the feet of poor teaching and ill-advised curricula, we believe that there are much larger social and structural issues that lead students to underachieve. It simply does not make sense that more than half the students in many school districts drop out because they are too lacking in mental ability to graduate. Similarly, it makes no sense that report after report shows that even those students in the United States who do stay in school demonstrate profound gaps in their knowledge base.

WHAT PUTS STUDENTS AT RISK?

Long before they actually drop out of school, students who drop out are subject to a great many pressures, both endogenous and exogenous to the school, that put them at risk. The term *at risk*, however, does not have a fixed meaning. In its original derivation, from epidemiology, it refers to the possession of some identifiable demographic characteristic (e.g., place of birth, sex, age) or biological trait (e.g., inherited

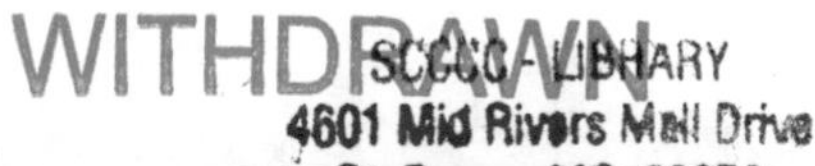

genetic traits, color of hair and skin), or engagement in some behavior (e.g., abuse of alcohol or overeating) that is statistically associated with the onset of some ailment. In some circumstances, being at risk may have a juridical meaning, such as when states mandate tutorials, retention, or other intervention for students performing at a specified level below grade expectations on standardized tests. The recent work of Richardson, Casanova, Placier, and Guilfoyle (1989), however, indicates that in educational settings defining who is at risk is far more fluid. Unlike the rather straightforward legal and epidemiological definitions above, the concept used by educators is situation specific and constructed. Furthermore, it varies according to the characteristics of the children and the beliefs and expectations of individual teachers; children defined as at risk by one teacher will not be so defined by another.

Richardson et al. (1989, p. 135) divide at-risk children into four categories:

(1) *readily identifiable:* possessing physical, cognitive, or emotional conditions that lead to academic problems in the regular classroom, such as brain damage or blindness
(2) *severe:* having family or background circumstances that make it extremely difficult for the school to provide adequate instructional programming, such as being sexually abused or the child of a migrant worker
(3) *context dependent:* having sensitivity to classroom and school settings and seen as at risk by some educators, but not others
(4) *masked:* having the ability to adapt well to classrooms socially, and so often not diagnosed as having learning problems and hence not provided with needed services

Since these definitions can include almost all children in school, it could be argued that all children are potentially at risk. This does not mean that the term *at risk* is meaningless; while it is, we believe, no longer useful as a diagnostic tool, it does serve as a quite meaningful argument for prophylactic action for all children. An analogy can be made with measles; the fact that all children are at risk is the strongest argument for universal vaccination.

Our convictions about the magnitude and scope of the problem are reinforced by the fact that, as indicated earlier, dropping out no longer is a phenomenon limited to the poor, urban, minority underachiever. Tuning out and dropping out are, in fact, facilitated by factors that contribute to the alienation students feel from school and to their sense that major discrepancies exist between what the school promises and what it can deliver.

ARE ALL STUDENTS AT RISK?

We have been struck by how gifted, as well as normal or ordinary young people (Ferrell & Compton, 1986; Littwin, 1987; Powell et al., 1985), describe school with the same unhappy litany of complaints as do dropouts. What is bad for dropouts is not experienced uniquely by them, but also by an increasingly large number of other students. It is clear that schools have fallen out of touch with the lives of contemporary young people and the opportunity structure they face, and that school programs and educational policy are based upon obsolete conceptions of student characteristics, life experiences, family structure, labor market experience, and customary ways of learning. Schools are, in fact, operating on the basis of cultural myths, not real assessments of what students think and are like and how schools and society are linked. Thus what students are supposed to do and can do in school do not match. What they expect to happen in and after school is different from what does happen. This conclusion has led us to feel that all students can be defined as being at risk. They are alienated and powerless in a meaningless world, especially as it is reflected in public education. In Chapter 4 we discuss some of the factors that put children at risk and that ultimately make it difficult or impossible for them to remain in school.

FOUR

Creating Failure: Why Students Drop Out

In this chapter we discuss the many factors that lead students to drop out. Researchers have identified four categories of factors associated with identification of at-risk students. Roughly, these are as follows:

(1) *Pupil-related factors:* These pertain to the experiences and characteristics that students bring to school with them. They include economic, familial, and sociocultural factors that often push students out of school; activities and incentives that pull students out of school and away from schoolwork because they offer rewards perceived to be greater than those offered by further education; peer pressure; and poor academic performance. These are the factors most commonly emphasized by researchers, educators, and policymakers. They also are factors over which schools feel they have little control.

(2) *School-related factors:* These are related to the microsystem of schools or to characteristics of the particular school, educational staff, and district that serves the student. They include inadequate teaching; unresponsive staff and school structure; systematic stratification of knowledge and information, including information relating to careers and employment; and other school factors that make continued attendance difficult or unbearable for students.

(3) *Constructed factors:* These are products of the interactions among other factors listed above. They result from the ways

the attitudes and perceptions that teachers and students have about schools and each other negatively or positively affect their interaction over curricular and other school-related tasks, consequently affecting the willingness or ability of children to perform adequately.

(4) *Macrosystem factors:* These are related to the social, political, and economic contexts in which school systems are embedded. They include how forces external to schools—including the labor market, demography, and changes in the structure of society and the family—affect life in the classroom for teachers and students. These factors may be the genesis of what are perceived to be student characteristics, such as family income level or ability of parents to participate in school-related activities.

PUPIL-RELATED RISK FACTORS

We now move to a discussion of what have been termed pupil-related factors. Some of the most obvious pupil characteristics, such as age and gender, usually are not considered to be problematic for students.

Age

The recruitment policies of schools, which are predicated upon age grading rather than developmental levels, often result in the enrollment of children who lack the cognitive maturity for academic work and are unable to adjust to the social demands of classroom life. We realize that the definition of *readiness* in this sense often is socially and culturally constrained. Poor children in a wealthy district may be deemed unready in comparison to others simply because they come to kindergarten unable to read or without the experience of years of preschool and day care. By contrast, the desire to make children more than ready leads to middle-class practices such as "kindergarten red-shirting" (Eisenhart & Graue, 1990; Smith & Shepherd, 1989, p. 228), or holding children out of school a year so that they will be more advanced socially, physically, and intellectually than their classmates, and thus will have a chance at exceeding the performance of those children. Notwithstanding the difficulty of defining readiness, the fact that age, rather than intellectual or cognitive issues, determines entrance can put immature children at risk.

Gender

Fine and Zane (1989) point out that simply being female puts girls at risk. The most obvious gender-related dropout factor is that girls who become pregnant and have children find it difficult to stay in school. However, there are other issues as well. Girls generally outperform their male peers in elementary school, but their performance begins to slip as they enter middle school, about at the onset of puberty. One explanation that has been offered for this phenomenon is that it is at puberty that girls begin to realize that success in male roles clearly articulates with success in school, whereas success in female roles does not (see, for example, Coleman, 1961; Eder & Parker, 1987).

Fine and Zane (1989, p. 34) argue that schools put adolescent girls in a contradictory position, wherein they are caught between the culturally mandated standards for appropriate female behavior and aspirations and school-mandated rewards and standards for achievement. The latter, what goes on *in* school, constitutes a public sphere that must be kept separate from the private sphere, or what goes on *outside* of school. School staff often consider the problems of low-income families to be a nuisance, extraneous to school affairs. They also do not believe that matters of the private sphere should be discussed in class. To be successful in school, girls, particularly minority and low-income girls, must ignore the complex needs of family, friends, and jobs when they interfere with school, maintain an appearance of sexual innocence in the face of a society steeped in open and flagrant sexual advertisement and assault, and deny that the moral and intellectual structure of the universe is complex, contradictory, ambiguous, and multifaceted (p. 37). However, as we have pointed out elsewhere, the complex, ambiguous, and multifaceted array of activities outside school often is more important to achievement than what goes on inside (Bennett & LeCompte, 1990).

A further explanation is that girls, especially white girls, get ignored. Because they do not cause trouble, they neither engage teachers' interest nor constitute challenges to be taught. Tizard, Blatchford, Burke, Farquhar, and Plewis (1989) found that while white girls had the fewest behavior problems of all students (male or female, black or white), and hence received less negative feedback, they also rated their own achievement lowest, enjoyed school least, and were the least self-confident. These researchers suggest that the feedback that white girls do get is about their work, not their misconduct, and it usually is given in terms of their lack of ability to achieve, rather than, as is the case for boys, their simple lack of effort. Girls come to feel as if they are incompetent to achieve, rather than that they could do better if they just would try harder (pp. 149, 182-183).

Fine and Zane (1989) point out that the consequence of poor performance is more devastating for girls than for boys. Girls who do not graduate are far more likely than boys to be unemployed. Girls who are retained are far more likely to express bad feelings about the experience and to drop out before age 18 than are boys. They also are much less likely to obtain high school equivalency certificates. Nevertheless, school staff do not view dropping out to be as disastrous for girls as for boys, especially if they get married. Perhaps the lack of concern reflects cultural norms; school staff evince the belief that female dropouts who pursue traditionally feminine roles—such as marrying and having children—will be "taken care of" because they will have males to take care of them.

> Mr. Perry to Michelle Fine, about Elisa, in the attendance office: Don't worry. She's dropping out, but it's a good case. She's fifteen, pregnant, but getting married. She'll go for a G.E.D. (Fine & Zane, 1989, p. 37)

The girls, however, know that male support is neither certain nor an unmixed blessing:

> Jennifer: You have to support yourself some way. Even if you do get married and you're happy now . . . you could have an unhappy marriage and get divorced. You can't say I'm gonna have a happy marriage . . . (Weis, 1988, p. 199)

> Ilana: Like I say to my girlfriend, "what's wrong?" and she said, "I'm married." (Fine & Zane, 1989, p. 37)

Fine and Zane also suggest that girls are more vulnerable than boys to societal contradictions regarding gender and competence. The young women they studied said that welfare makes them feel as if they are "no good"; at the same time they realize they need it to survive. They want to stay in school, and feel that they should not be promoted if they cannot perform at grade level, but find it difficult to study when they have children themselves or siblings who need to be cared for. They also find it difficult to articulate with a reward structure that promises good jobs in return for academic performance when they are aware of the kinds of jobs most commonly available to women. All of these issues can combine to make it more difficult for girls to participate as enthusiastically as boys in the reward structure of school, especially when academic achievement and consequent career success appears to obviate being "feminine," is threatening to relationships with men, and conflicts with demands of the family. Finally, if girls do drop out, less concern often is evinced for them if they pursue traditionally feminine roles.

Poverty

Researchers have long identified the relationship between the degree of poverty experienced by children and their tendency to drop out of school. One of the most pressing problems putting children at risk is, as noted in Chapter 2, the growing number of children who are poor. Children now constitute the largest group of poor people in the United States. Since 1965, at least 20% of the nation's children have lived in homes with incomes below the federally set poverty line. Half the nation's poor are children under the age of 18 (Barringer, 1989). Almost 10% of the children in the United States exist at 25% or more below the official poverty line. These are not all urban minority children: 30% of poor children in 1987 lived in rural areas, and 28% lived in suburbs; 44% were non-Hispanic whites. Thus one cannot understand the overall poverty of children without looking beyond the inner-city ethnic ghettos.

How does poverty put children at risk in school? The impact of poverty on children has been devastating. When framed in terms of mean income and proximity to the poverty line, poverty remains an abstraction. For this reason, we try to portray here what being poor does to the school performance of children. Poverty is more damaging than simple lack of exposure to cultural amenities and educational toys. It means wearing shabby or inappropriate clothing that calls attention to one's status and damages self-esteem. Poverty also means inadequate housing, with concomitant noise, crowding, and lack of privacy. It means shared beds and bathrooms—or none at all. At best, somewhere to study may consist of a shared seat on a convertible couch in a crowded living room next to a noisy kitchen (Hodgkinson, 1989).

Richardson et al. (1989) document the devastating double bind this situation creates for low-income students. Many teachers assume that homework is a natural extension of the school day. Failure to complete assignments after school means that children are failing to accomplish tasks that teachers assume are necessary and appropriate for all students. Educational reformers agree, and bolster their beliefs with research that shows a correlation between hours of homework done and student achievement—studies that do not take into account the socioeconomic conditions of students. As a consequence, many legislative reform packages in education call for additional hours of homework. However, many poor children find it virtually impossible to do work at home. As Richardson and her colleagues (1989) put it, "If important work is to be done at home, the at-risk child will fall farther and farther behind" (p. 129).

Poverty also means insecurity, hunger and poor nutrition, poor hygiene, and sometimes homelessness. According to a recent study by the U.S. Conference of Mayors, homelessness and hunger rose most among children in 1989. In the 27 major cities surveyed, 36% of the homeless are families with children, up from 27% in 1985 and 34% in 1988. Three-fourths of the cities could not meet demands for food and shelter and had to turn families away; requests for emergency housing were up 25% from 1988, and requests for emergency food for families were up 19%. Poor children also now face the added burden of cutbacks in school meal programs and income-support programs such as food stamps.

Homelessness simply makes consistent schooling experiences impossible. It exacerbates all the well-known problems of inadequate housing, and adds to them the burden of long commutes to school or frequent transfers as students move from one makeshift housing situation to another. Poverty also often means lack of adequate transportation and even telephone availability. In most cases, this is because U.S. cities lack convenient, safe, affordable, and adequate public transportation. "Housing is too far from jobs, which is too far from school, which is too far from day care" (Hodgkinson, 1989). The result is that poor families find it difficult to maintain good communication with teachers—a factor that almost without exception leads teachers to define them as "parents who don't care" (Deyhle, 1992; Richardson et al., 1989). In 1980, 85% of Americans used private transportation to get to work. Only 6.4% used public transportation (Hodgkinson, 1989). For the poor, getting to work can be an excruciating combination of buses and subways; when multiple transfers are required, one miss can mean loss of part of the workday and problems with employers—a chain reaction that can cause loss of the job, the house, and the stability children need. Under these conditions, getting to school for parent conferences becomes impossible.

Poverty means that children have little medical, optical, or dental care. Less than half as many children are immunized against disease in the United States as are immunized in France and Spain. Some 25% of all pregnant women get no prenatal care (Hodgkinson, 1989). The United States is one of the only industrialized countries in the world that has no universal health care program for families with children (Smeeding & Torrey, 1988). Not going to the doctor means missing more school, and lack of other kinds of services means that conditions that might impede learning, such as poor vision, go undetected or are rendered too expensive to remediate.

Finally, poverty forces children to work, often in violation of child labor laws, under conditions that exploit their minor status or in illegal enterprises. William J. Gainer of the U.S. General Accounting Office has stated that since 1983 the number of violations of child labor laws has increased by 150% (quoted in Shearer, 1990). Many of the reported 4 million young workers in America are employed in sweatshops, grocery stores, and fast-food emporiums, places most likely to exploit minors and violate the laws protecting them. Sanctions against employers are insignificant; in the 59 cases in 1987-1988 involving the death of a youthful employee, the average fine levied against an employer was $740.

Disincentives and Alternatives to School

The daily routine of school itself can put students at risk. Often the school day is boring, humiliating, and unappealing to students. Students find that there is little connection between doing well in school and any real reward out of school. Absent any obvious extrinsic value for life inside school, what goes on outside constitutes a far more attractive alternative to getting an education. In the pages that follow, we analyze some of these disincentives.

Grades don't pay off. Working hard to get good grades does not pay off for students who do not immediately go to college. And since the majority do not go to college, one of the major incentives offered by schools—good grades for a good job—has become meaningless. While employers themselves might benefit from hiring good students because they often prove to be more productive workers, they do not offer job candidates any incentive by paying higher wages for those who come with good academic records. Employers generally do not use transcripts in the hiring process, in part because it takes too long to get them from the schools. Because high schools are oriented to the longer time lines of colleges and universities, they are ill equipped to get records of non-college-bound students to potential employers in a timely fashion—for hiring decisions that must be made in a few days or weeks. A recent survey of more than 2,600 middle-sized and small employers indicates that only 3.15% use aptitude test scores and only 13.7% use high school transcripts in their hiring decisions (Bishop, 1989).

Furthermore, it can take more than 10 years for young people to notice any difference in their wages that might be attributed to good grades—and then the difference is only a 1-2% increase in salary for each grade-equivalent level (Bishop, 1989). Many students already know that simply getting an education really will not result in satisfactory employment.

> Frankie: They dropped out of school, and they got better fucking jobs than we do. I got my fuckin' diploma, and I ain't got jack shit. Look how many fucking college graduates ain't got jobs. . . . They got educations. What the fuck they doin' with it? They ain't doin' shit. So fucking school ain't paying off for no one. (McLeod, 1987, p. 104)

Jobs. Half of all high school juniors are working, and 76% work more than 20 hours a week ("Learning Conditions," 1989). In a representative sample of high school seniors, 70% reported that they had part-time jobs while attending school; 40% worked between 11 and 25 hours a week (White, 1986).

Two-fifths of employed sophomores and three-fifths of employed seniors work more than 15 hours a week (Lewin-Smith, 1981). While the jobs they hold usually are not full-time, they often consume the afternoon and evening hours, depriving students of time for homework or sleep. They also act to retard later employment opportunities; holding a job while in high school often is associated with lower employment rates for non-college-bound students (Lewin-Smith, 1981; cited in G. Grant, 1989, p. 206).

Most teenaged workers come from families making more than $16,000 a year (Greenberger & Steinberg, 1986). Their jobs give students a good deal of disposable income; 37% report they earn between $50 and $125 per week. According to Scott Thomson of the National Association of Secondary Principals, the typical 15-year-old, a junior in high school, has at least $60 per week to spend from various jobs and allowances ("Learning Conditions," 1989). Students not planning to go to college have few economic incentives to get good grades, and all students have many incentives to hold jobs in order to finance an adolescent life-style, purchasing the consumer goods their parents cannot or will not buy for them (Greenberger & Steinberg, 1986; "Learning Conditions," 1989; McNeil, 1984). They are encouraged in active consumerism by the focus of television marketing strategies on teenagers, which has shifted downward from 18-year-olds to 15-year-olds, reflecting the increasing amounts of money children have at their disposal.

Schools, however, are still structured as if students have at least several hours each day to devote to homework, which is assumed as a normal extension of the school day. Teachers are faced with students who fall asleep in class, do not do their homework, have little time to read books, and otherwise do not let school interfere with their work lives. In many cases students need to work because of low family income or other responsibilities, and the indignation that school authorities demonstrate about the conflict of jobs with learning puts students in a double bind. One young woman put it well: "[I] just can't do it all. I've got a baby and I have to work. School will just have to wait for now" (Fine & Zane, 1989, p. 33).

Illicit jobs and drug trafficking. Many children work illegally in legal jobs—such as at fast-food emporiums and in the garment trade—because they are too young to receive work permits. Still others find work in illicit employment, working as sellers, couriers, and lookouts in the drug trade, pimping, and engaging in prostitution. The number of children engaged in these activities is unknown; the more flamboyant cases are those who get caught and receive media publicity. But their existence is a consequence of the lack of legal—and lucrative—employment available to young people in many regions, and of the perceived higher payoff from illicit than from licit jobs.

Peer group pressure to resist school. Peer group pressure to avoid success in school has long been documented. Some of the earliest studies of adolescence describe how top students are viewed as deviant and how popularity is enhanced by getting reasonable grades without the appearance of having to work too hard (Coleman, 1961); working-class students actively reject the rewards of success in school because they realize that it has little value for what they know to be their ultimate career destination (Furlong, 1980; Stinchcombe, 1964; Willis, 1977). Students may feel that they must eschew getting good grades or merely get by with, at the very best, a "gentleman's C" in order to be accepted by peers. They also may practice school avoidance, or participate in a "culture of cutting" (described by Hess et al., 1987; Marotto, 1986; McLeod, 1987), wherein students actually spend more time hanging around outside classrooms than they do inside them being instructed.

More important, students who succeed in school may be scapegoated. Fordham and Ogbu (1986) describe how black students who do well are accused of "acting white"; Willis's (1977) "lads" described achieving students as "ear'oles"—people who cozied up to teachers and curried favor. For these students, friendship—belonging to and being accepted by the group—is more important than achievement. They stick together even when peer group loyalty hampers striving for upward mobility.

Poor academic performance, retention, and poor attendance. Poor academic performance, being retained in a grade level, and truancy are characteristics ascribed to students that are highly correlated with dropping out. While many dropouts do possess these characteristics, we do not believe that they are inherent in most children. Something happens to make students perform poorly, become truant, or, as we shall discuss later, be defined as "in need of retention." The reasons often have little to do with their intellectual abilities (M. L. Smith, 1989); they can include being immature, having poor language skills, being learning disabled or hyperactive, possessing poor social skills, and having limited English-language proficiency. We believe that retention is a consequence of contextual factors in school, as well as poor teaching, nonteaching, and dilution of the curriculum. While they may predict dropping out, these factors—poor academic performance, retention in a grade, and truancy—are not the first causes. Many studies have indicated that home- and pupil-rated variables are less important than school and teacher variables in explaining the differences in children's progress in school.

In a study of economically disadvantaged students, Tizard et al. (1989) found no relationship between single-parent family status and children's reading, writing, and math skills at the end of nursery school. Children from single- and two-parent homes had comparable levels of skills (p. 113). Underachievement of children of single mothers has been shown to relate to poverty, not to single-parent status as such (Essen & Wedge, 1982). The children of working mothers do not, on average, underachieve (Hoffman, 1974). In fact, none of the commonly used measures of social disadvantage—income, family marital status, mother's education, parental satisfaction with school, and attitudes of parents toward helping their children at home—predict strongly the progress of individual children in basic skills (Tizard et al., 1989, p. 118). What does seem to matter is how individual children encounter the school setting and how that experience is interpreted by them and translated into a response to schooling. We now move to a discussion of school-related factors in the at-risk equation.

SCHOOL-RELATED RISK FACTORS

Why do children give up on school? One of the most important factors is the way they feel about being there. Table 4.1, which details the most common reasons given for dropping out, indicates that for all groups, the primary reason is that they "disliked school." But what does "disliking school" mean? Repeated studies of students' attitudes toward school and their description of their school experiences indicate that they are bored and find their experiences meaningless (Deyhle, 1989; Fine, 1987; Fine & Zane, 1989; Hess et al., 1987; Holley & Doss, 1983; McLeod, 1987; Powell et al., 1985; Valverde, 1987; Williams, 1987). They feel that their teachers are prejudiced against them and care very little either about individual students or their own teaching. Students interviewed for the studies cited here did not often say that they hated school—although, as in the case studies recounted earlier, they often felt caught in institutional rigidities and powerless to extricate themselves. They seldom said that they hated *learning*. But by deconstructing what students say about schools, it becomes clear that schools face serious problems in holding the interest and enthusiasm of their clients. Much of the problem derives from the treatment students receive from teachers and the unintended consequences of school organization and practice. In this section, we first discuss why students who are at risk are bored and find school meaningless; we shall then address the subject of "normal" children.

School Is Boring

When at-risk students say that school is boring, they mean that regardless of their status—be they low achievers or gifted—they are treated as if they uniformly have IQs of 4. Often, the more organized a school is to help at-risk students, the more students are labeled as such, and labeling often creates "at-riskness" (Richardson et al., 1989, p. 160). First, it creates a mind-set among teachers that a student can be expected

Table 4.1 Primary Reasons High School Dropouts Left School, by Sex, Race, and Ethnicity: 1979

	Males			*Females*			
Reason	*White*	*Black*	*Hispanic*	*White*	*Black*	*Hispanic*	*Total*
School-related							
poor performance	9	9	4	5	5	4	7
disliked school	36	29	26	27	18	15	29
expelled or suspended	9	18	6	2	5	1	7
school too dangerous	1	0	0	2	1	1	1
Economic							
desired to work	15	12	16	5	4	7	10
financial difficulties	3	7	9	3	3	9	4
home responsibilities	4	4	13	6	8	8	6
Personal							
pregnancy	0	0	0	14	41	15	17
marriage	3	0	3	17	4	15	9
Other	20	21	23	19	11	25	19
Total	100	100	100	100	100	100	100

SOURCE: Rumberger (1983, p. 201).
NOTE: Data are for persons 14 to 21 years of age.

to have trouble. Second, and perhaps more important, the label sets into motion a whole constellation of practices that are designed to help but that often make things worse. Most special intervention at the elementary level is provided in "pullout" programs that remove children from the normal flow of instruction and complicate and interrupt their daily schedules. Attempting to "fix" schools with high numbers of at-risk students often creates pressures toward standardization and increased fragmentation of the curriculum into ever smaller and more "doable" objectives. Standardization often causes students and teachers to focus on the form, rather than the substance, of instruction. At-risk students are particularly prone to missing the point of instruction, copying blindly, reciting from memory, skipping lines, and never comprehending what they are doing. Such students may spend all of their time trying to write neatly or spell correctly and forget all about telling a story. They may read only paragraphs, never write term papers, and seldom think an investigation problem through from start to finish, whether in science, social studies, or language arts (Apple, 1986; Bennett & LeCompte, 1990; McNeil, 1986; Richardson et al., 1989). Richardson et al. (1989) cite the example of Carmin, a Hispanic third grader who produced sophisticated, grownup conversations in Spanish and seemed in no way intellectually deficient. In language arts class, she was learning word lists with common phonological characteristics. Students went through these lists, pronouncing the words by syllables, and then writing them down.

> When asked what she was learning in reading . . . Carmin responded that she was learning "che" and "cha," that is, Spanish syllables. She did not seem to understand the process of reading: that syllables combine to form words, and these combine to form sentences. When she was asked to read . . . Carmin "read" letters and sometimes sounds, seldom words, and never sentences. And when asked to read a whole sentence she combined words that did not match the sense of what she had already read. (p. 111)

Thus instruction itself impeded the literacy of this child, who showed no sign of linguistic difficulty in her native language.

Departmentalization and moving from teacher to teacher prevents at-risk students from bonding with individual teachers—a factor critical in maintaining their interest and commitment to school—and causes them to lose much instructional time while in transit from class to class (K. P. Bennett, 1986; McNeil, 1988a, 1988b, 1988c; Richardson et al., 1989). In fact, elementary students who are not considered to have special needs really have the simplest school schedules and have to make the fewest adaptations to school. Since they are not pulled out for special instruction, they have more time to complete their tasks, receive the full complement of subject-matter instruction, and develop more consistent relationships with homeroom teachers. In contrast, high school remedial students face constant failure and isolation. They are relegated to vocational and basic tracks where even they term themselves "retards" (Page, 1989). They are caught in an endless cycle of remedial, repetitive, contextless, skills-based instruction, often at an interest level more appropriate for primary school. Often their instruction is isolated from other students in a computer-assisted instruction lab. Frequently they cannot exit from remedial instruction until they pass the competency tests that drive the curriculum. Since many cannot, and some will not, pass the tests, they spend semester after semester repeating the same reading or math "lab." Recent emphasis by educational reformers on "excellence" means, in effect, raising the passing scores on competency tests. The effect will be to encourage more students to drop out rather than continue futile efforts to pass tests for which they are unprepared (Archer & Dresden, 1987; Kreitzer, Madaus, & Haney, 1989).

Even students who are not conventionally considered to be at risk and who are not in remedial programs find school boring and irrelevant (Powell et al., 1985). Whelage (1989) suggests that there are several reasons students do not become engaged with the knowledge presented in schools. First, primary emphasis is placed upon the college bound. All other objectives are secondary, for both students and teachers. Since academic learning is not structured to be extrinsically rewarding except for the few who compete for college entrance, there is no payoff for working at academic achievement for the remaining majority of students (Bishop, 1989; Whelage, 1989, p. 10). Second, the learning process is too restricted, rewarding only that narrow range of intellectual competence developed and displayed in school. This makes school uninviting for students with skills that go unrewarded, including physical, technical, and artistic talent (Whelage, 1989, p. 10). Third, the learning tasks that structure the curriculum have become so divided and subdivided into minute tasks and activities that students have no sense of cognitive goals or overall topics, much less the grand sweep of knowledge in any particular field.

The delivery of instruction also is not designed to inspire enthusiasm. John Goodlad's (1983) landmark analysis of 1,000 elementary and secondary classrooms found that recitation, in which the teacher lectures or the students work as a total class on written assignments, is the predominant form of instruction. In an analysis of the observational data from Goodlad's study, Sorotnik (1983) found that less than 3% of instructional interactions are devoted to corrective feedback, less than 5% involve direct questions, and less than 1% elicit complex cognitive or affective responses. Even in elementary classrooms, going to school is a passive activity; children are expected to sit quietly. Tizard et al. (1989, p. 91) found that primary school teachers deliver instructional facts, ideas, and concepts—whether by explaining, informing, lecturing, demonstrating, suggesting, or questioning—to children 69% of the time. If management time for activities such as getting organized for instruction is added, teacher delivery constitutes 80% of the school day. Comments on social and personal contacts, life outside the classroom, and children's health and appearance make up less than 1% of classroom interaction. Children learn to initiate less and less, and simply to attend to teacher talk.

The way children have to do work also can involve a frustrating series of interruptions and discontinuities in tasks and thought. Less than half the primary children in Tizard et al.'s (1989) study found their lessons interesting. Reading was frustrating because it was hard to get help with unfamiliar words:

> Every time I don't know a word and I feel sad. 'Cos you sometimes need a teacher to tell you what you don't know and she is talking to someone else and she says wait a minute. (p. 145)

Writing was similarly frustrating, because of the focus on correct form and spelling:

> It's boring 'cos you have to keep walking round the classroom to get a word.

> Sometimes you think you're going to be so clever but you need a hard word and you have to rub it out and it looks horrible. (p. 146)

Adding to the problem is that teachers seem to be quite able to recognize when a task proves too difficult for a child, but appear to be "totally blind" when the demands of a task are too easy. From the teacher's point of view, if the children are busy, the work given is probably at an appropriate level (Bennett, Desforges, Cockburn, & Wilkinson, 1984). But busywork does not challenge, and too much of the school curriculum, whether in elementary school or in high school, is devoted to work sheets and scholastic drudgery.

School Is Meaningless

Meaninglessness in this context refers to the connection, or lack of connection, between schools and an orientation toward the future. What students really want to know is, What does all this mean for what I want to do with my life? One aspect of meaninglessness relates to jobs. Students are fully aware that credentials, schooling, and occupational and economic opportunity are weakly linked. Even good grades do not count for much when translated into impact on careers and wages (Bishop, 1989; Littwin, 1987; McLeod, 1987).

Another aspect of meaninglessness has to do with discontinuities between the culture of the student and that of the school. Students describe this in terms of teacher prejudice. They cite in support of their complaints sins of both omission and commission. The former include the dearth of authentic, nontrivial materials linked to students' heritage—class, culture, ethnicity, or gender—and the latter involves overt bigotry and ignorant blunders interpreted as prejudice. Going to school constitutes a constant assault by teachers and school staff on students' ethnic heritage and their place as functioning adults in their own community.

Minority students still find members of their ethnic groups underrepresented or portrayed stereotypically in texts. Adult members of minority groups have painful memories of coping with racism. Emmi Whitehorse, a noted Navajo artist, has said that during American history class she had to pretend that the vicious and disreputable Indians described in battles between the U.S. troops and indigenous peoples were different Indians from her own family. Disassociation was the only way to come up with "correct" answers on tests and tell the teachers what they wanted to hear (personal communication, 1989). Elementary school texts, which once portrayed boys and girls in stereotypical gender roles and avoided portraying minorities at all, have dodged the issue of sexism and racism by avoiding humans altogether; heroes of children's stories have become neutral figures such as animals, anthropomorphized machines, and ghosts. A contemporary social studies textbook used in the Santa Fe, New Mexico, public schools devotes one paragraph to the Pueblo Indian culture. The entire paragraph is written in the past tense, as if the Pueblo no longer exist.

Teachers attempt to impose Anglo modes of success on ethnic minorities, and reward most those students who are least like traditional members of their communities. Sometimes this is done with the best of intentions; teachers will state that minority students have to learn how to get along in the white world, because, after all, that is the world in which they will have to live. In so doing, however, they draw an obvious and invidious comparison between white and minority cultures.

Despite the fact that there is little hard evidence that a strong ethnic identity interferes with academic achievement, success in school alone is valued, and any kind of success in a student's own culture is ignored. Deyhle (in press), for example, indicates that Navajo children who still have strong ties with traditional grandparents fare far better in school than those whose families are more assimilated and fragmented. Studies of immigrants also support the relationships among ethnic identity, self-esteem, and academic achievement (Gibson, 1988). Deyhle also found that all of the young women in the Navajo community she studied underwent a *kinaalda,* a ceremony celebrating a girl's first menstrual period, during which her family and the community pray for her success as an adult—and particularly in school. School officials knew nothing of this practice, denied that the Navajo had any intact culture at all, and flatly stated that Navajo parents had no interest in schooling. This kind of ignorance works tremendous hardship on students who value their heritage, and it may act to encourage dropping out, insofar as students feel that the choice between home and Anglo culture is too painful.

Teachers Don't Care

Like their teachers, who state that students don't care about their work, students believe that teachers don't care about children. There are two aspects to this belief. First, teachers who are unwilling to help students with their lessons—in class or outside of class time—are defined by students as uncaring. Although teachers may in fact not have time for such activity because they are overloaded with paperwork mandated by new educational reforms, the lack of attention is interpreted by students as disinterest. The alienated, overworked teacher, then, helps to create the alienated, uncooperative student (Firestone & Rosenblum, 1988).

Another problem is that "getting help," asking questions, and demonstrating that one knows the correct answers in schools are governed by certain norms dictating how to communicate competently and appropriately. For example, students must show they need help by raising their hands or singling themselves out by some other means as not-knowing. This is most difficult for those who feel most incompetent, who are most in need of help, and for those whose cultures forbid as a breach of etiquette singling oneself out for attention (Brice-Heath, 1982; Philips, 1972; Vogt, Jordan, & Tharp, 1987; Wax & Thomas, 1961).

Students also complain that teachers do not care about their personal problems. Sometimes this is because teachers lack cultural understanding, which leads them to do things that students interpret as uncaring (Deyhle, 1989, 1992; Erickson, 1984). In addition, because students view teachers as personifying the institution, they feel that neither the teachers nor the institution itself cares when teachers cannot or will not extricate them when they get caught in a bureaucratic crack. Lack of concern is further demonstrated by institutions that lack the flexibility to accommodate to the terrible personal and family problems many students have. These problems often force students to drop out because school demands and home demands are too difficult to reconcile. Valverde (1986) describes the plight of one tenth grader whose grandmother, with whom he had been living, was comatose in a hospital across town. Distraught at his guardian's condition, and lacking adequate transportation, the student had missed many days of school to be at her bedside. Since his grandmother was unable to provide absence excuses for him, he was failed in all his courses because of school rules that mandated failing grades for students with more than 10 unexcused absences. Not permitted to make up the work, and rather than fail, he dropped out.

> Slick: Certain teachers you can talk to up there. But most of the teachers . . . They don't know how it's like to hafta come to school late. "Why'd you come to school late?" "I had to make sure my brother was in school. . . . I had to make sure that there was breakfast."
>
> Shorty: Responsibilities. See, that's what I mean. . . . He ain't got no father, right? . . . just like me. He's the oldest kid. And he has big responsibilities at home because his brothers are growing up and his sister—he's got to keep an eye on them. Now you gotta do all that, and you got teachers giving you a fucking hard time. (McLeod, 1987, p. 109)

Schools Are an Administrative Nightmare

The ultimate lack of caring is exhibited by school administrators who permit the continuation of bureaucratic foul-ups and incompetence that make learning impossible. Recent student walkouts in a number of cities were triggered by conditions so chaotic that students were without textbooks, desks, and class schedules seven weeks into the school year. A male senior found that his algebra class was scheduled in the girls' restroom, and 900 students were scheduled into lunchroom shifts that could accommodate only 600. Computer classes lacked computers, piano classes lacked pianos. Toilets in the restrooms would not flush (Horswell & Markley, 1989). Teachers who tried to protest the same conditions were ignored or were transferred if they attempted to channel student protest into less aggressive action (Markley, 1989). While such conditions are extreme, similar situations—lack of textbooks, inability to register for needed classes, science programs without labs and materials—exist in virtually every urban school district. Even those students who can cope with teachers who do not care cannot tolerate situations in which even the minimum conditions for learning are absent.

School structures and practices create low achievement. Some of the most common institutional practices of schooling actually retard the development of children and act to handicap minorities and the poor further. Some traditional instructional practices require spending a great deal of time on material children find easy, and little on those areas in which they have most difficulty. For example, preparatory reading workbooks typically emphasize text and word decoding skills. Yet children have the most difficulty with comprehension, not decoding. Spending so much time in early primary school on decoding can be wasteful, particularly for children whose families do not supplement comprehension activities by devoting significant amounts of time to reading stories aloud to their children (Feitelson, 1988).

Ability grouping. The all-pervasive practice of ability grouping for instruction (tracking), especially the practice of having lower groups proceed at a slower pace, not only does not appear to solve learning problems of low aptitude students, it actually seems to exacerbate them (Barr, 1974; Oakes, 1985). Students in the slower groups receive fewer minutes of instruction, more often are instructed by aides or paraprofessionals, cover less material, are given fewer complex cognitive tasks, and experience a more technical-managerial teaching style from teachers than do other students

(K. P. Bennett, 1986; Borko & Eisenhart, 1986). Grouping increases the variance in achievement, even among children who begin school with equal abilities and interest levels. Barr's (1974) classic study of grouping involved a suburban middle- to upper-middle-class white neighborhood elementary school. She found that by second grade the gap between children in slow groups and children in other groups had grown so wide that teachers began to have difficulty adjusting instruction appropriately. Further, considerably less learning was demonstrated by slow-learning students in the grouped school than by slow students in a socioeconomically similar nongrouped school nearby. Page (1989) has demonstrated how curriculum differentiation in an affluent white parochial high school acts to widen further the gaps in achievement between students in different tracks. In fact, Lee and Bryk (1988) argue that the vaunted "Catholic school effect" (minority students doing better in Catholic than in public schools) can be attributed not to selection effects or the schools' sense of community (Coleman & Hoffer, 1987; Coleman et al., 1982), but to the fact that Catholic schools have fewer resources than public schools and therefore cannot offer as wide a range of curricular choices. As a consequence, all students must enroll in a rather restricted group of "hard" subjects—far more than they might were they allowed the choices provided by the "cafeteria-style" public school curriculum.

Retention. Retention is one of the most common interventions prescribed for students whose achievement is lagging behind expectations. Nearly all teachers, parents, and principals favor retaining children when grade-level expectations are not met (Byrnes, 1989; M. L. Smith, 1989). However, a meta-analysis of all known studies of retention effects has shown that retention is an ineffective means for increasing student achievement (Holmes, 1989). Consistent across districts of very different socioeconomic levels, retained students experience a greater risk for dropping out that cannot be explained by their poor achievement. Wherever high school graduates and dropouts are compared, it is always the case that a substantially larger proportion of the dropouts have repeated a grade (Shepherd & Smith, 1989a, 1989b). Retention has demonstrated positive effects only with middle-class, suburban, largely white children with IQ ranges above 100 and who score at or near national norms on standardized tests. Thus in those few cases where retention has "worked," children systematically were more able and advantaged than the traditional population of retainees, which is constituted of slow learners with below-average IQs and achievement. On average, retained children are worse off in the following year than their promoted counterparts, with respect to both personal adjustment and academic achievement (Holmes, 1989, p. 27). The threat of retention also does not serve as an effective motivator, nor does it make economic sense for school districts. It greatly increases the cost of education for retained individuals—because they remain longer in school—without benefiting the vast majority of them (Byrnes, 1989).

One reason retention is one of the strongest predictors of dropping out may be that it stigmatizes children who are older than other children in their classes as failures. Another is that retention almost always means simply repeating the previous year's material. It is considered a treatment by itself, such that it almost never is associated with additional remediation. Even when retention takes place in kindergarten, its negative effects persist. In states that have increased their retention rates, dropout rates have increased accordingly (Shepherd & Smith, 1989b). Whatever the reason, retention, like ability grouping, is a time-hallowed school practice that is both ineffective and harmful to children.

Lack of information. Schools often do not provide students with the information they need to gain access to appropriate programs, succeed in their lessons, and articulate with desired career aspirations. Sometimes withholding of information is a deliberate, if covert, policy, triggered by the belief that students who have no chance to excel in careers should not be encouraged to try. The consequence is that they are not given information about the courses they need to pursue particular careers; the kinds of tests, deadlines, and hurdles they will need to cope with; and how to apply for jobs and for admission to college (Cicourel & Kitsuse, 1963; Fine, 1987; Sarason, 1971; Shultz & Erickson, 1982). Fine (1987) calls this practice the "silencing" of students' needs and aspirations; Clark (1960) refers to the "cooling-out" function of schools—the process of lowering student aspirations that teachers perceive to be inappropriate for the student's social class, ability, ethnicity, personality, or gender. He calls the teachers and counselors who execute the cooling-out function "agents of consolation." Instead of simply failing students, a "soft" response is tailored for unpromising students. They are sidetracked rather than dismissed; the counselors' objective is to make them disengage from inappropriate aspirations and accept less attractive alternatives (p. 515).

Another factor that impedes the adequate flow of information to students is counselor and teacher overload. Counselors typically handle as many as 300 to 400 students annually. They can do no more than practice counseling "triage," which helps only the most desperate and most persistent (Hess et al., 1987; Powell et al., 1985; Shultz & Erickson, 1982).

The panic for educational reform. Throughout this chapter, we have alluded to ways in which educational reforms often act to exacerbate the very problems they were intended to solve. We will discuss specific reforms in detail in Chapter 9. At this point, we merely wish to state that from the students' point of view, the most harmful—and the most likely to increase failure and dropout rates—probably have been competency-based exit testing (Kreitzer et al., 1989; McDill et al., 1985), the fragmentation and decontextualization of objective-based curricula (McNeil, 1986; Richardson et al., 1989), and the disruptions caused by pullout programs (K. P. Bennett, 1986; Richardson et al., 1989).

CONSTRUCTING FAILURE: CREATING AT-RISK FACTORS

Recent research on school failure has focused less on the characteristics of individual students and teachers and more on the reality that teachers and students construct in the course of their interaction about schoolwork. This research is informed by the work of symbolic interactionists and phenomenologists who posit the strong effect that people's beliefs and expectations about role-appropriate behavior have on their social interaction. Early research on the construction of school-related identities described what was termed the "Pygmalion effect" (see, for example, Rosenthal & Jacobson, 1968). It posited that teachers were more supportive of children whom they believed were capable of good work. These children were given higher grades regardless of their actual measured ability. Thus performance was not a function of the inherent capabilities and motivation of a child, but was dependent upon the beliefs and expectations teachers held about the specific characteristics of individual children in any given school or classroom. Since the publication of *Pygmalion in the Classroom* (Rosenthal & Jacobson, 1968) considerable research has documented the differential treatment of children on the basis of state, school district, and teacher beliefs and expectations about the academic and career potentials of different categories of children. These expectations are structured by presenting characteristics of the children—dress, hygiene, language use, the structure of their families, ethnicity, and social class (Brophy, 1983; McDermott, 1987; Rist, 1970).

Recent work by Richardson et al. (1989) expands the concept of social construction to include teacher expectations about proper conduct and how well children adjust socially to the specific mix of children in any given classroom. The teachers studied by Richardson and her colleagues identified problems from home—family problems, parents who do not care, high mobility, divorce, the lack of educative experiences at home—as those most likely to put a child at risk, rather than characteristics of their own teaching, the school, or the child (p. 19). However, they often were unable to agree upon which children were at risk. Furthermore, being at risk was a fluid condition, not one predicated upon academic performance. While teachers seemed always to have a stable number of children whom they considered to be at risk, the specific students so identified changed. If students with more severe problems than those currently in the classroom enrolled, the problems of students once considered at risk often seemed minor by comparison, and resulted in their being "dis-labeled." While teachers had different criteria for being at risk, "improvement in academics usually was not the sole [or primary] reason for de-labelling a child from the at risk group" (Richardson et al., 1989, p. 36). Conversely, children who were judged to be a pleasure to have in class and who were well behaved were described as having high academic potential (Crano & Mellon, 1978). A child who is "a pleasure to teach," who is described as "a trier," as having "a lively mind, and as "eager and curious" is not generally described in terms of ability, but generally is thought to have higher attainment (Tizard et al., 1989). Thus children at risk in one classroom might not be at risk in another. Constructed factors seem particularly crucial to student achievement in two areas: retention and relationships of school personnel with parents.

The Role of Retention

Elsewhere in this chapter we have described how retention puts children at risk for dropping out. How a child is identified for retention is of interest here. Being retained is a great deal like being at risk. The decision to retain very often is not based upon objective measures of a child's ability—or incompetence. Rather, it is constructed out of such disparate factors as parents' and teachers' beliefs about pupil readiness and achievement. Some teachers just believe more strongly than others in the efficacy of retention. They are the "nativists" (M. L. Smith, 1989), who believe that children develop readiness for school in a process that cannot be rushed or pushed. Children who are not "ready," then, should be retained until their development is enhanced. However, readiness itself is a negotiated condition. Certain artifacts of a given school—including a policy to retain many children, a "promotional gates" program that ties promotion to cut scores on criterion-referenced tests, the desire of parents to make sure a child is emotionally and physically mature enough to be a star athlete or social success in high school, and the practice of retaining children whose English-language proficiency is deemed deficient—affect whether or not children will be retained, and children who might be retained in one school could easily be eligible for promotion in another (Eisenhart & Graue, 1990; M. L. Smith, 1989; Smith & Shepherd, 1989).

Relationships With Parents

Few teachers say that the problems children have are related to school factors. Behavior problems in school usually are attributed to factors at home, particularly inadequate home relationships—lack of attention, lack of affection, or overstrictness. In fact, teachers generally can find something wrong with the family of a child they consider to be at risk (Richardson et al., 1989, p. 121). Children of minority parents and single parents are far more likely than other children to be described as having behavior problems (Tizard et al., 1989).

Further, children who are perceived to have problem parents are perceived to be problem students. Parents typically are viewed by schools primarily as sources of information on the home and health history of children, not as equal partners in decision making with teachers and principals (Richardson et al., 1989, p. 92). When minority parents intervene in school affairs, their children may be scapegoated and attempts may be made to defuse or dilute their efforts, particularly if they try to contradict the actions of a teacher (Stern, 1987).

The progress of children is significantly related to the level of contact parents have with the school and to their knowledge of school timetables, programs, and teaching methods. In addition, parents of all social classes and ethnicity usually are both enthusiastic about their children's attendance in school and as actively supportive as they can be of their schoolwork. Evidence of this interest notwithstanding, teachers generally do not believe that parents will provide adequate support for their children's learning at home. Further, many teachers—whether consciously or not—act in ways that sabotage efforts by parents to help their children. Most teachers send home assignments without any accompanying information on how to complete the work or how parents could help (Tizard et al., 1989, p. 78). Teachers are much more likely to tell parents that their children are doing well than that they are doing poorly, and are likely to avoid giving indications to parents that their children are having difficulties with schoolwork, even when it is apparent that they are. Tizard et al. (1989) indicate that the majority of parents—especially black parents—in their study of primary school children were not told whether their children's performance in math and reading was at, above, or below average. Parents of below-average children, in particular, were not so informed (p. 91). Because many parents have unrealistically optimistic perceptions of their children's progress, they do not seek help for them. By failing to ask for help, they demonstrate to teachers their "lack of interest."

EXTERNAL FACTORS: MACRO-LEVEL RISK FACTORS

Up until now, we have been discussing risk factors that are particular to the contexts of individual children and the experiences they have in school. However, these experiences do not occur in isolation. The conditions of life of individual children are profoundly affected and shaped by the social, economic, and political conditions obtaining in their neighborhoods and communities. In Chapter 2 we discussed the genesis of some of these factors, especially the growth of poverty. In the section above on pupil-related risk factors we discussed how being poor alienates students from school and makes achieving success exceedingly problematic. Poor children participate in a shakier network of social and health services than do more affluent students. They often lack adequate food, clothing, transportation, and housing, and their parents often are overworked and ignored by school personnel. Their needs go unmet, and the consequence is that schools are seen as uncaring and meaningless. Whether students are poor or not, the changes in the labor market described in Chapter 2 herald the death of the American Dream—the promise that if a student works hard and gets good grades, his or her reward will be an interesting, lucrative job. The demise of this myth also has badly damaged the promise of a better life that schools once held out as a reward to good students. In this section we wish to elaborate on other external issues that affect the alienation of all students, and their consequences for schooling.

Drugs, Violence, Abuse, and Disease

Four factors that are external to schools—drugs, violence, abuse, and disease—have the capacity to render life itself meaningless and difficult. They have significant bearing on persistence in school, because staying in school is predicated in a belief that the future is possible. These factors lead students to question the validity of that belief.

What students know about drugs is that they are pervasive—in corridors, on playgrounds, in restrooms, in the schools they attend, and in their homes (Martin, 1988). Drug traffic in schools is by no means limited to the inner city; it also afflicts rural areas—especially those with a declining economic base—and suburbs alike. The pervasiveness of drugs in their lives makes children skeptical about drug abuse information campaigns and their ability to resolve the problem. "The FBI, the White House drug guy, a judge—all the rest of you experts don't have a clue what to do. How could we possible know what to do?" (Martin, 1988). They also are skeptical of the sincerity of officials. In response to President Bush's televised broadcast to schoolchildren about drugs, a middle school student said, "We've heard it all before. We hear it all the time. How can we take seriously what he says when he nominated an alcoholic to the Cabinet?" (referring to Bush's nomination of Senator John Tower for secretary of defense; Weintraub, 1989).

Drugs make it more difficult for children both to perceive the connection between educational achievement and future success and to act upon that perception if it occurs. Drug abuse both increases the risk of school failure and creates whole categories of emotionally, socially, and physically impaired children who cannot cope with the social and cognitive demands of school. Further, while rates of use for most illegal drugs have declined among high school seniors, current rates are unknown among middle school students and dropouts, and there has been no decrease in the rate of use of alcohol, cigarettes, and crack cocaine. One recent study indicates that 92% of the high school class of 1987 had begun drinking before graduating, and, of these, 56% began to drink alcohol in the sixth to ninth grades (Johnston, O'Malley, & Bachman, 1989). The problem is worse for black teenagers and preteens, who are four times more vulnerable to drug abuse and twice as likely to use crack or inhalants as their white counterparts (Foltz, 1989).

An added problem is that of addicted babies. It is estimated that 1 in 10 newborns is exposed to illegal drugs during the mother's pregnancy. As many as 375,000 infants may be affected annually in the United States (Ogintz, 1989). Cocaine is the drug of choice, and even one episode of significant coke use can interfere with neurological development. Babies born to crack-addicted mothers are hyperactive and exhibit poor ability to concentrate. They also fail to show much emotional response, whether it be pleasure, anger, or distress, apparently because the neurological pathways affecting reward and pleasure, which appear to be particularly vulnerable to cocaine, are damaged. Children with fetal alcohol syndrome, known to affect as many as 25% of the children among certain American Indian groups, are both physically and mentally disabled; they also are hyperactive and unable to understand cause-and-effect relationships (Blakeslee, 1989; Kolata, 1989).

Federal and local governments estimate it will cost $15 billion to prepare drug-damaged children to enter kindergarten and another $6 billion a year get them through high school (Labaton, 1989). These figures do not include the costs of these children's disruption of normal classroom activities.

Violence. Drug use encourages the spread of violence and disease. Teenagers are victims of crime more frequently than any other age group, and a quarter of the crimes against them take place in or near schools (Carnegie Council on Adolescent Development, 1989, p. 65). More and more schools are riddled with gang activity; in many cities, fear of gangs in and around schools has become a primary reason for dropping out (Hahn & Danzberger, 1987, p. 15). More than half of the deaths among 10- to 14-year-olds are caused by violence—homicide, suicide, motor vehicle accidents, and other accidents (Carnegie Council on Adolescent Development, 1989, p. 27).

> Craig: Well, to be truthful, the main reason I picked Fundamental [a remedial school] was cuz the main high school was real tense. Y'know, there was fights up there—a white kid got stabbed to death, and when I was in the eighth grade it was still pretty bad. (McLeod, 1987, p. 90)

Much of the violence in and around schools today is related to drug trafficking. While students may be safe inside the building, outside and on the way home they may be in a war zone (Lee, 1989b). Most elementary school children know someone who has died or been killed as a result of drug use (Weintraub, 1989). Some violence is wreaked in retaliation for deals gone bad, money owed, confidences betrayed, or recruitment schemes gone awry. Students who do not use drugs are ridiculed, harassed, and even threatened by their using peers for being straight. Often the cost is ostracism and loneliness. And what happens if they "say no"? As one teacher in the Roxbury area of Boston said, "What are these kids going to do if they don't do drugs? These kids are still living in the projects where the dealers and drugs and guns are. Where can they go if they decide to say no?" (Weintraub, 1989).

Child abuse. The incidence of child abuse—by parents, friends, family members, caretakers, and even educators—has reached virtually epidemic proportions. The actual or feared consequences of abuse interfere with the ability of students to do well in school.

> Patricia: I just can't concentrate in school, thinkin' about my mother gettin' beat up last night. He scares me too, but I just don't understand why she stays. (Fine & Zane, 1989, p. 33)

> Corinna: I am really pissed. All the boys [friends of her live-in boyfriend] got real drunk last night and made like enough noise to keep me from getting any of my English sonnets and French memorized for class. . . . He'll ask if I'm busy when I'm obviously studying. And then I'll say, "I don't want to talk to you." And then [she waves her hand toward her jaw] smack! There goes his hand right into my face. (Roman, 1989, p. 15)

Sexually transmitted diseases. Sexually transmitted diseases add to the uncertainty and instability of life, while making concentrating on the payoff to schooling less appealing. Their spread is aggravated by the use of drugs, by participation in prostitution, and by other sexual activity. To the consternation of health officials, AIDS is on the rise among adolescents; in areas such as Miami and New York, as many as 1% of the 15- and 16-year-olds are HIV positive. For 21-year-olds the rate is two to three times as high. Since 1987, 1 in 100 babies born to 19-year-olds in New York State has had AIDS antibodies. Some 3% of all applicants for the Job Corps and the military are HIV positive. Teenagers are particularly at risk because they are highly sexually active, do not use condoms, and deny that they can get AIDS. However, AIDS patients who are now in their 20s or early 30s probably were infected as teenagers ("Experts Alarmed," 1989; Puga & DeSoto, 1989). While the AIDS threat may seem remote to life in school and still affects a relatively small proportion of teenagers, other sexually transmitted diseases, such as syphilis and gonorrhea, are achieving epidemic proportions among teenagers and add to the uncertainty of growing up safely.

In Chapter 3, we suggested that all children are, at least potentially, at risk for dropping out. In this chapter, we have detailed the factors that we believe justify such a belief. The factors described here—school and pupil characteristics, constructions of reality, and external conditions—all render life for young people less stable, certain, and hopeful. It is upon just such certainty and hopefulness that close articulation with schoolwork is built. Lacking it, students fall into the kind of alienation that we believe is the genesis of dropping out. In the next two chapters we discuss how similar conditions affect the teaching force, with similar consequences.

FIVE

The Who and Why of Teacher Burnout

This chapter parallels the previous one, but its focus is on teachers rather than on students. Our concern is with those aspects of work alienation that cause teachers to burn out, to quit teaching, or, even worse, to become entrapped in a hated career for their working lifetimes. Much of the information presented in this chapter represents the cumulative product of ongoing research by one of the authors, beginning with data collected more than a decade ago. However, we go beyond a recitation of prior research, presenting new data on the impact of educational reform on levels of teacher burnout, attitudes toward quitting, and entrapment.

WHAT IS TEACHER BURNOUT?

The construct of burnout has held considerable currency in many academic fields, including sociology, education, industrial psychology, and business administration. Unfortunately, as it sometimes has been defined, burnout is a very nebulous construct. Part of the problem is that it has often been conceptualized as a "trait definition." Trait definitions are those that enumerate the characteristics (or traits) that typify individuals possessing the construct. Often the construct, its causes, and its effects on other constructs get intertwined (see Dworkin, 1987). For burnout, characteristics of the trait definition range from depression to bruxism, or excessive grinding of teeth (Cedoline, 1982).

Psychological and Sociological Views

Freudenberger (1974), a psychologist, is generally credited with coining the construct of burnout to describe the sense of "wearing out" that characterizes many human service professionals. His focus and that of most psychologists is upon the individual as the unit of analysis. Social structure and social systems, which are crucial to sociology, are less salient to psychology, which is more concerned with how people, given their personalities, learn to cope with their "realities," including mental images from their past. Consequently, psychologists are more likely to look for causes of dysfunction within the person and his or her relations with others. Burnout is seen by psychologists as a problem in coping with stress that necessitates new modes of thinking for the burned-out individual, rather than structural and organizational changes in schools. For the most part, psychologists, including Maslach (1978a, 1978b), Maslach and Jackson (1982) and Cherniss (1980), view burnout as a loss of idealism and enthusiasm for work (or a role) characterized by exhaustion, depersonalization, depression and low morale, and withdrawal. Faced with a growing discrepancy between reality and ideal expectations, Maslach's respondents externalized the blame for their failures, placing it on their patients or clients (including their students). They further came to redefine their efforts as futile and divorced from their ambitions, goals, and "nature." In short, they came to view their work as meaningless. Cherniss (1980) describes burnout as "a process in which the professional's attitudes and behavior change in negative ways in response to job strain" (p. 5).

The link between stress and burnout is unproblematic. Most investigators describe burnout as a product of stress, one that is found especially among new professionals who work for bureaucracies (e.g., Cherniss, 1980; Cherniss, Egnatios, & Wacker, 1976: Maslach, 1978a, 1978b; Paine, 1982; Schwab & Iwanicki, 1982). Without the ability to negotiate agreements on role performances and to determine what the role expectations are within social service bureaucracies, such professionals soon acquire a strong sense of powerlessness. In Maslach's (1982) view, burnout is a stress response characterized by a sense of exhaustion (that one can no longer make an effort to perform as one did in the past), depersonalization (that one develops negative and cynical attitudes toward the patient or client), and lack of personal fulfillment (including a negative evaluation of one's own contributions). These elements lead to a strong sense of meaninglessness. Thus meaninglessness and powerlessness become essential elements in burnout.

The strong sense of inefficacy among many burned-out professionals has also been documented by Shinn (1982). Numerous investigators have also reported that burnout is accompanied by withdrawal as well as feelings of rejection by clients (some of whom are blamed by the burned-out professional for refusing to get better, or to learn, or to improve, in order to spite the professional). Schwab and Iwanicki (1982) have factor analyzed the Maslach Burnout Scale (Maslach & Jackson, 1979, 1981); they observe that the items that have the highest factor loadings are those that convey a sense of meaninglessness and powerlessness on the part of the respondents. Cherniss (1980) reports that burnout appears to be an alienation from work that sometimes serves to protect the worker from further disillusionment. Thus burnout may actually be a coping mechanism that makes hopeless tasks more palatable by minimizing the perceived consequences of inadequate task performance. For example, one burned-out teacher once reported that her pupils in an inner-city school "are unteachable and will probably stay on welfare anyway. So not doing a bang-up job teaching is no big deal." Like the ritualist in Merton's (1964a, 1964b) paradigm of alienation, the professional who is burned out no longer embraces the goals and ideals that attracted him or her to the profession, but now mechanically "goes through the motions," mindlessly pursuing the means to those goals.

Burnout also involves a sense of normlessness. Schwab and Iwanicki (1982), Cherniss et al. (1976), Maslach (1978a, 1978b), and Paine (1982) all speak of the individual's sense of conflict between rival expectations on the job and ambiguities regarding the appropriate rules of behavior. Some, such as Schwab and Iwanicki (1982), report that an important element of burnout is the sense of role conflict and role ambiguity. In a study of child-care workers, Mattingly (1977) noted that burned-out professionals reported a sense of a conflict between the need to give help and the inability to help enough. In the absence of appropriate norms for actions, such workers experience both role conflicts and role overloads. Further, Sparks and Hammond (1981) report that central to the construct of burnout among teachers is a sense that the norms are unenforceable. A majority of the urban public school teachers in a series of surveys conducted in Houston between 1977 and 1987 agreed or strongly agreed with the statement "School rules are so rigid and absurd that good teachers have to break them or ignore them" (Dworkin, 1987, 1990b; Dworkin, Haney, Dworkin, & Telschow, 1990; Dworkin, Haney, & Telschow, 1988; Dworkin, Sanders, Black, McNamara, & Webster, 1978). Sparks and Hammond (1981) further argue that burned-out teachers also have feelings of powerlessness and inefficacy, isolation, and meaninglessness. In the previous chapter we observed that student dropouts report the same feelings about schools and teachers. *When students and teachers feel the same way about the schooling experience, it makes sense to look for systemic causes of such alienation.*

It is clear that underlying many definitions of burnout, at least those that are not simply trait definitions, is a construct strikingly similar to the definition of perceived alienation, a more sociological construct because it suggests that systemic strains and contradictions underlie the experiences of individuals who are burned out. That is, meaninglessness, powerlessness, normlessness, isolation, and estrangement all have social referents. Each element of alienation posits the existence of a gap between what people are socialized to expect and what they experience because of the ways in which society and supraindividual structures operate, whether they be bureaucracies or institutions (we shall address this matter more fully in Chapter 7). Prior to the fascination with trait definitions in recent years, some researchers working on burnout thought of it in terms of the sociological construct of alienation. Berkeley Planning Associates (1977) measured burnout as job-related alienation.

In light of the strong similarity between alienation and burnout, the following conceptual definition of burnout has been offered by Dworkin (1987):

> Burnout is an extreme form of role-specific alienation characterized by a sense that one's work is meaningless and that one is powerless to effect changes that could make the work more meaningful. Further, this sense of meaninglessness and powerlessness is heightened by a belief that the norms associated with the role and the setting are absent, conflicting, or inoperative, and that one is alone and isolated among one's colleagues and clients. (p. 28)

Burnout is not the same as the desire to quit, nor is it the same as actual quitting behavior. Many who burn out never leave their jobs; many who want to quit do not do so. The belief that one can have an alternative role is often a necessary precursor of actual quitting behavior. Likewise, burnout can, in itself, be a coping mechanism that makes work less stressful, as it allows one to care less about the quality of one's work. Thus some who burn out would prefer to remain on the job. Cherniss (1980), Jackson, Schwab, and Schuler (1986), and Dworkin (1987) found only weak associations between burnout and quitting and between the desire to quit and actual quitting behavior. Therefore, we shall not include intentions toward quitting and actual role exits in our definition of burnout. To do so would ignore prior research and dismiss a priori another problem found in many urban public schools: *teacher entrapment,* or the condition in which a substantial number of teachers possess all of the attitudinal components of burnout, or role-specific alienation, but remain in disliked jobs for entire careers. People who have invested much in their careers and who must rely upon their work for their livelihoods or to purchase a sense of meaning through leisure and activities away from work cannot be expected to abandon that work without desirable alternatives. Experienced employees do not run *from* careers; they mainly run *to* new careers. We rarely abandon roles without embracing new ones, since role exits are simultaneously role entrances. There is a direct parallel between the entrapment of burned-out teachers and the entrapment of students who "tune out" rather than drop out (see Chapter 3). In the absence of options, they remain in school.

HOW MANY TEACHERS BURN OUT?

It is very difficult to estimate the percentage of the teaching population that is burned out. The figure is likely to vary by size of school district, ethnic mix of students and faculty, region of the country, and the current state of educational reform in the district. Litt and Turk (1985) report that 79% of public school teachers feel that their job is a major source of stress (compared with 38% of nonteaching semiprofessionals matched by age, sex, and marital status). Since burnout is often an end product of stress, one might imagine that the burnout rate is fairly high among public school teachers. However, this requires some extrapolation, especially since not all who are stressed burn out (Farber, 1982). While student dropout and teacher turnover statistics[1] are fraught with complications due to counting procedures, and, as we have noted, in-school dropout rates (the functional equivalent of burnout and entrapment) are nearly impossible to estimate, the estimation of burnout rates for teachers across districts is a morass. Dropping out and quitting are relatively easier to count because the rates depend upon particular action on the part of students or teachers—individuals leave an organization that keeps some sort of records on such leavings. Because we conceptualize burnout as something distinct from job dissatisfaction, surveys of teachers' attitudes toward their jobs, especially the national surveys conducted by the Gallup organization and reported each fall by *Phi Delta Kappan*, cannot be used as surrogates.

A search of studies of teacher burnout suggests that national estimates, or even estimates within a teaching population of a school district, are rare, qualitative in nature, or involve nongeneralizable case study analyses (Riggar, 1985). However, using a survey of studies, Cedoline (1982) estimates that the burnout rate among teachers is somewhere between 10% and 80%. Obviously, such a range is too great to be useful. In fact, burnout may actually be a continuous variable rather than a discrete one (burned out, not burned out), with the range reported in studies affected by the cutting points applied by the investigators.

Most studies of burnout have used small, nonprobability samples or case studies; for instance, Cherniss (1980) based his work on burnout on 28 respondents. Many other investigators, including Schwab and Iwanicki (1982) and Maslach and Jackson (1981), have either relied upon small, nonrandom samples or pooled data across numerous human service occupations to expand their sample sizes. While these investigations are useful in assembling an initial portrait of burned-out teachers, and even in assessing some of the corollaries of burnout, they do not permit us to determine the prevalence of burnout in the population or to aid in the construction of causal models of burnout or of the role of burnout in creating other outcomes for teachers or students.

We believe that Dworkin's (1985, 1987, 1990a, 1990b) work represents a plausible estimate for burnout rates among urban public school teachers because the samples are large and population parameters are known and matched with sample characteristics, thereby permitting generalizations to be made. The first study investigated the linkages among teacher burnout, teacher turnover, and student achievement in the Houston Independent School District between 1977 and 1982 (Dworkin, 1987). The study merged several large data sets: questionnaire data collected from a random sample of nearly 3,500 urban teachers, follow-up exit interview data on all of the teachers in the original sample who quit teaching within five years of the initial enumeration, two-year comparisons of standardized achievement test and attendance behavior of the elementary students taught by a subgroup (elementary teachers only) of the first sample of teachers, and a random sample of union members from the same teaching population enumerated in 1981-1982 to assess social buffering mechanisms on burnout.

The second study assessed the impact of educational reform legislation in Texas on the morale of urban and suburban teachers in the Houston metropolitan area (Dworkin, 1990b). It surveyed 1,060 teachers randomly selected from the Houston Independent School District and five adjacent suburban districts. Using the same measures of burnout, stress, support, plans to quit teaching, and other social psychological measures as were used in the previous data sets reported by Dworkin and his associates, the study permitted us to determine how educational reform affected teacher attitudes and behaviors by comparing the newer results with baseline data from the prior studies.

The survey data collected by Dworkin (1985, 1987) yields a stable estimate of the magnitude of burnout. Utilizing his burnout scale, Dworkin estimated that approximately one-third of all teachers in a large urban district were burned out. However, even that figure is subject to conjecture. Burnout was measured as a response to a factor-analytically developed 10-item scale that pooled the 10 responses of each individual into a single factor score. Although the details of factor analysis need not be explored here, a factor score is in Z-score form, with a mean of zero and a standard deviation of one. Selecting a cutting point that will distinguish high and low burnout is arbitrary. One could dichotomize the scale scores at the median or even the mean, thereby concluding that one-half of the teachers were burned out, or one could define burnout as a score that is beyond one standard deviation above the mean, thereby defining about 16% of the teaching population as burned out.

Dworkin noted that the items describing powerlessness and meaninglessness were most highly loaded on the burnout factor; he thus concluded that individuals whose scores were at or above the median of the sample and who agreed or strongly agreed with the powerlessness and meaninglessness items could provide a relatively conservative estimate of the magnitude of burnout in the urban teaching population. This procedure provided an estimate that 22.8% of the teachers were burned out. A slightly more liberal definition might also consider as burnouts those who failed to disagree with the powerlessness and meaninglessness items (that is, strongly agreed, agreed, or were neutral on the items). Using the neutral response as well elevated the burnout rate to 37.3% of the teachers.

These data were collected prior to the publication of *A Nation at Risk* in 1983 and the enactment of educational reform legislation in Texas and elsewhere. Between 1986 and 1987, Dworkin and his associates and students readministered the burnout measures to a sample of urban teachers, as well as to a sample of suburban teachers in the Houston area to see if the reforms implemented had any effect upon burnout. The data were collected during the period when the school districts were first implementing in-class teaching evaluations and teacher competency testing. These and the mandated increase in paperwork and record keeping by teachers that accompanied the call for greater accountability were associated with greatly heightened burnout rates. Among the urban teachers burnout rates escalated to 40.9%, using the conservative figure, and 64.1% using the neutral responses as well. Pooling the urban and suburban data yielded burnout rates of 30.9% and 63.6%, respectively. Thus, depending upon whether or not teachers are experiencing new stresses due to education reform, burnout rates hover between one-third and two-thirds of a district's teaching staff.

WHO BURNS OUT? TEACHER CHARACTERISTICS

A survey of National Education Association and Educational Research Information Clearinghouse pamphlets on teacher burnout is instructive, even if misleading. Teachers who burn out are thought to be drawn from all areas of the teaching population, but tend particularly to be those whose students are uncommitted to education, or who teach in very large or very small schools, who teach in school districts where resources and supplies are limited, who work under principals who are either laissez-faire or autocratic, who have colleagues who are less than enthusiastic about their work, who find that their role is complex and characterized by role ambiguities and role conflicts, and who live in communities where teachers' salaries have not kept pace with the cost of living. The inclusiveness of this list is such that one is reminded of Eric Hoffer's itemization of the characteristics of people who are susceptible to becoming true believers. That list is so inclusive that one can conclude that the entire population is vulnerable. However, because the concept of burnout is widely used to describe any malady associated with human activities that persist over some duration, it our belief that not every teacher is equally at risk of burnout.

Who Is Most at Risk?

Although the level of teacher burnout is substantial, it is an overstatement to contend that all teachers are burned out. Some categories of teachers are more likely to burn out than others. Cedoline (1982, pp. 40-57) notes seven major factors that contribute greatly to burnout among teachers. While not specifically a portrait of teachers likely to burn out, one might assume that individual teachers exposed to some combination of these factors are more likely to burn out than those not so exposed. Cedoline notes that individuals who have little control over their destinies are more likely to burn out. While efforts by legislatures, school boards, and community groups that diminish teachers' professional autonomy through increased bureaucratization and demands for educational reform and accountability affect all teachers (Apple, 1986; McNeil, 1988a, 1988b, 1988c), teachers in highly politicized urban districts and new teachers who have not yet learned to cope and adapt are candidates for higher levels of burnout.

Individuals who receive little feedback or communication on how well they are performing are candidates for burnout. Clearly, teachers in schools with unsupportive principals who consider faculty members to be expendable employees are more vulnerable to burnout than those not assigned to such principals (Dworkin, 1985, 1987; Dworkin et al., 1990). Individuals who are either overworked or have a significant underload will burn out. Teachers in bureaucratized systems or in systems undergoing demands for greater public accountability tend to burn out because they are overburdened by paperwork and the compounding of responsibilities (Farber, 1982; Richardson et al., 1989). Also, teachers who are never challenged because their work is tedious and boring are likely to burn out. Teachers who experience contact overload from oversized classes and too many class periods are candidates for burnout. Likewise, teachers who must satisfy a multiplicity of conflicting and competing demands placed upon them by students, other teachers, administrators, and parents are likely to burn out. Such role overloads may involve having to engage in behaviors that are mutually exclusive, such as providing individualized instruction while making sure that a common curriculum mandated by the state or district is taught (McNeil, 1986; Schwab & Iwanicki, 1982). Jackson (1968) has reported that urban high school teachers interact with as many as 1,000 different people a day. This is more prevalent among teachers in large districts and on large campuses, who consequently are more susceptible to burning out.

Cedoline (1982) further suggests that individual personality factors are relevant. Teachers who are not adequately prepared to work in bureaucracies or who are not familiar with the demands of the teacher role are likely to burn out. Unfortunately, these conditions hold for most new graduates of colleges of education. In short, candidates for burnout are those who, partly because of training, are too idealistic and too likely to expect miracles in education. Even new teachers who are not starry-eyed are at risk; administrators may see such teachers as uncommitted to teaching, which can lead to diminished administrative support and more negative teacher evaluations. These alone can increase the likelihood of burnout.

In their early work on stress, Kahn, Wolfe, Quinn, Snoek, and Rosenthal (1964) suggested that there are distinctive personality factors that heighten the loss of job idealism. Neurotics and introverts tend to experience more stress in teaching. Flexible and democratic thinkers (who often cannot say "no" to organizational demands and who have difficulty working under rigid autocratic administrators) also tend to experience greater stress and burnout when faced with rigid school systems.

A brief anecdote may be instructive in understanding why flexible, open-minded, democratic thinkers may have difficulty with dogmatic administrators. A group of very bright education students who were in the Teacher Corps program were assigned to a predominantly minority Houston high school. The preservice teachers were very enthusiastic about the opportunity to help disadvantaged children, and several began putting up posters about colleges and college opportunities around their classrooms. Unfortunately, some of the posters partially covered over the small glass windows the principal had installed in the doors of all the classrooms. In response to this "obvious" challenge to his authority, the principal reprimanded the teachers, had all of the posters removed, and asked that the Teacher Corps trainees be replaced with more respectful teachers. Nearly all of the trainees involved in the incident elected to enter some other line of work than public school teaching.

Finally, status-oriented people, as opposed to security-oriented people, are likely to experience burnout. Cedoline (1982) notes that the status-oriented individual "is striving, highly involved in work, independent, and seeking advancement." The security-oriented individual "is more dependent, worries about job stability, wants to be liked by others, and attributes power to others" (p. 54). Status-oriented people are more likely to be frustrated by obsolete practices and conventions that block both their advancement and their ability to get things done.

Summarizing studies of gender differences in burnout, Cedoline (1982) concludes that women are more likely than men to consider their jobs unrewarding and thus are more likely to burn out. However, most of these studies were based upon small data sets or left uncontrolled other factors such as school size, racial composition, whether urban or suburban, and principal behavior. Dworkin (1987) has reported that once organizational and social psychological factors were included in the regression equation, gender failed to account for any significant amount of variance in burnout.

The burnout data collected by Dworkin (1985, 1987) underscore many of Cedoline's observations. Specifically, teachers who are most susceptible to burnout are (a) younger, less experienced, and untenured; (b) white, although Hispanics also burn out more than do black teachers; (c) likely to believe that their destinies lie not in their own hands, but rather in the hands of chance, fate, or luck; (d) racially isolated in terms of the composition of the student bodies of their schools; (e) assigned to schools where there is little interracial cooperation among faculty and where they believe they are subjected to racial discrimination on campus; (f) prone to dislike the racial composition of the student bodies at the schools to which they are assigned; (g) able to rely upon sufficiently large alternative sources of income (usually derived from a spouse) that they could live without the income from their teaching salaries; (h) likely to disagree with their principals on appropriate management style; and (i) assigned to campuses where principals consider them to be expendable employees and not valued colleagues. These general correlates with burnout can be aggregated under five rubrics: teacher demographics, teacher personality variables, campus demographics, campus social climate, and administrator behaviors. These are discussed in turn below.

Teacher Demographics

Teachers are not all equally susceptible to burning out. A variety of teacher characteristics are correlated with higher burnout rates, including inexperience, race, social class, and personality. In general, these demographic characteristics typify individuals who are relatively powerless in their social settings and hence are likely to perceive themselves as victimized by social forces in their schools. Their sense of powerlessness also prevents them from effecting changes in school routines should they conclude that their activities are unappreciated by colleagues, administrators, and students.

Inexperience. Burnout tends to be a malady of the inexperienced. There is a large body of research in the sociology of work and occupations that demonstrates that idealism and enthusiasm are necessary to attract a professional to a career (Stevens, Beyer, & Trice, 1978). Such idealism tends to be replaced by other factors—including career investments and collegiality—as an individual matures in a profession; with increased experience, naive enthusiasm is abandoned. Perhaps this is not unlike the usual stages that occur in mate selection, courtship, and marriage. Starry-eyed ebullience and enthusiasm are eventually replaced by more "mature" accommodations and interdependence.

Most individuals enter teaching because of a desire to make a difference in children's lives. The gap or contradiction between what preservice teachers are socialized to expect from their training in schools of education and what they experience in urban districts is a central element in the creation of burnout and alienation. It is also one reason burnout is generally more frequent among young, freshly idealistic teachers than among old hands, many of whom have abandoned idealism, learned to cope, or learned to work the system.

Preservice teachers come to expect that they will instruct and shape young minds, plan and develop curricula, evaluate students, and manage classrooms and maintain discipline. Some may even recognize that they are expected to serve as role models for children; to act as surrogate parents, especially when the children's own parents abrogate such responsibilities; to work with students of diverse ability levels, backgrounds, disadvantages, and problems; and to combat racism, sexism, child abuse, drug abuse, and learning disabilities. However, they often assume that they will be granted the professional autonomy to exert control over the roles they are assigned to perform. Some investigators, such as Sarason, Davidson, and Blatt (1962), Sarason (1977, 1978-1979), and Duke (1984), see colleges of education as failing to prepare preservice teachers for the "real world of teaching," in which autonomy is significantly restricted. Others, such as Bartholomew (1976) and Ginsburg (1988), blame the modularization and compartmentalization of knowledge in colleges of education, which separate learning from practice, for "deskilling" teachers so that they are unable to generalize what they have been taught from setting to setting.

Colleges of education rely upon student enthusiasm in recruiting education majors, and they are unlikely to attempt to extinguish such enthusiasm through course work. If they did, the colleges would have too few majors to justify faculty slots. Additionally, as Duke (1984) notes, most who teach in colleges of education have had little hands-on experience in public school classrooms, and are thus not likely to be able to recount too many horror stories about teaching, especially in urban schools.

Race. Racial isolation is significant in urban schools. Many urban school districts are under federal faculty desegregation mandates such as the "Singleton ratio," which came out of the *Singleton v. Jackson Municipal Separate School Districts* court case (*Singleton v. Jackson Municipal Separate School Districts et al.*, 419 F.2d 1211, January 14, 1970). This court ruling, which has been applied to approximately 300 school districts, assigns teachers to campuses on the basis of racial composition of the faculty districtwide, thereby ensuring proportional numbers of minority and majority faculty at each school. While there are similar mandates to desegregate student bodies, most large urban districts no longer have enough white students to provide meaningful desegregation of campuses, barring metropolitan desegregation plans. Thus faculty desegregation is more successful than student desegregation (Center for National Policy Review and National Institute of Education, 1977a, 1977b). As a consequence, most white teachers are assigned to predominantly minority schools.

When black teachers are assigned to white schools, they tend to be assigned to campuses in which there is a slight plurality of students who are white, but where there are sizable percentages of black students. When white teachers are assigned to black schools, they find themselves on campuses where a minuscule percentage of the students are white. Minority communities perceive, sometimes correctly, that minority group teachers care more about minority group children than do majority group teachers, and they are often suspicious of the motives of majority group teachers. Principals in minority schools have been known to make their preferences for teachers of the same race as the student body quite clear to their faculties. Thus white teachers frequently feel that they are unwanted and not respected in predominantly black schools.

Social class differences. Inner-city schools expose teachers to "culture shock," regardless of the race of the teacher (LeCompte, 1978, 1985a). This is because most teachers are middle-class, and new teachers are increasingly coming from middle-class backgrounds (Dworkin, 1980), but in many urban school districts rarely more than 10% of the students are middle-class.

Dworkin (1980) found that urban teachers, regardless of race or ethnicity, tend to have parents who had professional, managerial, or middle- to high-income white-collar occupations. Social class differences reflect distinctive life-styles, aspirations, expectations, and some values. Consequently, great disparities between the class and class origins of students and teachers will mean major differences in expected behaviors and styles of presentation of self between students (and even their parents) and teachers.

As noted in the previous chapter (and as we shall see in the next one), teachers perceive lower-class parents to be unconcerned with their children's education. This is because such parents do not follow middle-class models of involvement. Further, low-income, minority, and immigrant parents are often uncommunicative, sometimes because they fear or are uncomfortable and inarticulate with middle-class teachers, and sometimes because it is simply not their style to be talkative with strangers. In some instances, middle-class language usage may be off-putting to the parents, just as lower-class and minority vocabularies are off-putting to middle-class teachers. Likewise, teachers aggravate the situation by being uncommunicative or inaccessible to parents (Richardson et al., 1989; Tizard et al., 1989).

A generation ago, Gottlieb (1964) found that a major source of job dissatisfaction among white teachers assigned to inner-city schools in Chicago was that parents, children, and other school personnel seemed unconcerned about the education of the children. This complaint by teachers is still heard today (Dworkin, 1990a). Rist (1973) compared urban teachers to alienated assembly-line workers, noting that the teachers never stayed after school to discuss educational matters, but left soon after the children did. Some years ago, Orfield (1975) maintained that teaching in suburban schools was much easier than teaching in urban schools because suburban parents provided the students with the necessary resources to make up for even incompetent teaching. Thus the teachers were never faced with the possibility that they really did not know how to teach—the children came to school better prepared and the parents were available to reexplain what the teachers were unable to articulate to their classes. Finally, Ogbu (1974) noted that when middle-class teachers (regardless of race) made extra efforts to help low-income, minority children, they felt that they were shown no appreciation by either the children or their parents. In fact, the parents often complained that the teachers were so well paid (relative to the parents' own income) that they should expect nothing else.

Teacher Personality

Earlier, we mentioned Kahn et al.'s (1964) studies of personality factors associated with burnout. Dworkin, Joiner, and

Bruno (1980) further indicate that teachers who have an external locus of control are more susceptible to burnout when assigned to schools where they dislike the racial composition of the student body. Each of the studies by Dworkin (1985, 1987, 1988) found the Rotter (1966) measure of locus of control to be a significant predictor of burnout. Simply stated, Rotter proposes that there are two global generalized expectancies: internal locus of control, held by individuals who believe that they are responsible for their own actions and their own fate, and external locus of control, held by those who believe that chance, luck, fate, or destiny controls their lives. Studies generally find that working-class people, women, and racial/ethnic minorities are somewhat more likely to be externals than are middle-class people, men, and racial and ethnic majorities (Gurin & Epps, 1975; Gurin, Gurin, & Morrison, 1978; Jessor, Graves, Hanson, & Jessor, 1968; Lefcourt, 1976). There is empirically good reason for this: The stratification system and racial, ethnic, and gender prejudice and discrimination do operate systematically to disadvantage specific groups; such economic, political, and social disadvantages are externally created and occur regardless of the actions of the individuals subjected to prejudice and discrimination (see Chafetz, 1984; Dworkin & Dworkin, 1982; Feagin & Eckberg, 1980). Externals, because they feel they are usually affected adversely by events beyond their control, tend to be more pessimistic and less enthusiastic about experiences. They are more likely to assume that no matter how hard they try to effect desirable ends, someone or something will interfere and negate their efforts. They may be more compliant to the demands of autocratic administrators, but they are also unlikely to see adversity as a challenge. Internals are more likely to fight, to persevere, and to attempt to effect changes—in the school setting or elsewhere (see Gore & Rotter, 1963; Lefcourt, 1976). As noted, burnout involves a sense of powerlessness and meaninglessness, and externals are more likely to see their efforts as meaningless and to believe that they are powerless at the start. Internals believe in their own efficacy and are not a priori burned out.

Campus Demographics and Social Climate

In some instances the characteristics of the school itself affect the likelihood of teacher burnout. The locale and the size of the school represent crucial variables.

Urban schools as a special problem. Schools in urban areas are more likely to subject their teachers to stressors and hence to burnout than schools in suburban areas. However, as we shall note later, rural schools are as stress laden as inner-city schools, though the factors contributing to stress are somewhat different. Urban schools, and especially inner-city schools, are primarily populated by students who are disadvantaged in many ways. Furthermore, as members of the truly disadvantaged (Wilson, 1987), many live in communities where agencies of social support have broken down, but where there still are active agencies of aversive social control, including gangs and abusing families (see Blau, 1981; Wilson, 1987). Students lack the economic resources to purchase better education, the adult role models needed to demonstrate the value of schooling, and public investment in their future. Thus the job of teachers in the inner city is harder and more stressful than that of other teachers.

A popular misconception states that inner-city schools have more resources available to them because the per child expenditure in urban schools is higher than in affluent, suburban schools. However, this higher per child expenditure is a function of federal entitlement programs, as well as the higher cost of maintaining old and obsolescent urban buildings and providing security. Furthermore, the dollar value of parental investment in a child's education often is not considered. Thus, while the per child expenditure in a middle-class elementary school might be $3,100 per year and the per child expenditure in the inner-city elementary school might be $4,000 per year, not calculated into the formula is the value of the vastly higher parental resources that are invested in the education of middle-class children—from music lessons to tutors to books in the home to assistance with homework to home computers—as well as the substantial investments in technology, including computers, made by affluent PTAs and PTOs. It has been difficult to quantify the dollar value of an intact middle-class family in which both parents are available and able to help with school assignments and to monitor student progress. Parents who provide educational enrichment, help on science fair projects, and travel to historic sites to make history lessons more meaningful offer resources that probably explain why middle-class children forget less during the summer break than do low-income children (see Murnane, 1975).

Small schools, large schools. Yet another factor that affects levels of teacher alienation is size of school and grade level taught. Teaching high school students is somewhat less stressful than teaching either elementary school or junior high school students. Some research has suggested that small class sizes are associated with lower levels of stress (Jackson, 1968; Maslach & Pines, 1979). It might be assumed, then, that the smaller class sizes associated with elementary schools should be less stressful on teachers than the larger class sizes of secondary schools. However, it seems that smaller class sizes are associated with reduced stress primarily in comparisons that hold grade level constant. While elementary schools tend to have small class sizes, the children have the same teacher all day long, and interactions can become rather intense. Elementary school pupils tend to cry more and to expect teachers to act as surrogate parents more than do older children. Also, since elementary schools are relatively small, often having student bodies of 200 to 500 and faculties of 10 to 25, there is considerably more opportunity for the principal to monitor teacher actions, and such monitoring is often stressful. Likewise, parents are more often involved in consultations with teachers in the elementary years than later on. Dworkin (1987) reports that interactions with administrators and parents are seen by teachers as fairly powerful stressors.

In middle schools, the class sizes are larger, the greater number of faculty permit departmentalization and some level of insulation from the principal (but not from the department chair), and teachers do not interact with the same students at each class period. However, new problems emerge. In urban areas, it often is in middle schools that students are first introduced to the drug culture. Concern over sexuality becomes significant for early teens. Further, as one teacher observed, "The kids offer the unbeatable combination of bigger size and strength, raging hormones, and incomplete socialization. In short, they are animals." High school students are somewhat more sophisticated, mature, and poised, and have a better grasp of their hormones. They are also more career and future oriented. Also, especially by eleventh grade, many of the worst offenders have dropped out, leaving a self-selected group to be taught.

Enter the Principal: Administrator Behaviors and Burnout

Research in the sociology of work and occupations and in medical sociology holds that social buffering or social support can effectively reduce the consequences of job stress on morale, health, and well-being. Several investigators, including Duke (1984), Stinnett and Henson (1982), LaRocco, House, and French (1980), Kaplan (1983), Maslach (1976), Freudenberger (1974), Mattingly (1977), and House and Wells (1978), note that support from coworkers, spouses, and friends can be as effective in reducing the effects of stressors as the support of administrators. Social buffering and support function to inform individuals that they are not alone, and that others care about their welfare. As social animals people respond positively to gestures of support and love.

In his earlier study, Dworkin (1985, 1987) reported that the level of burnout and, in turn, the desire to quit teaching could be significantly reduced by the actions of the campus principal. Supportive principals—those who involve their teachers in campus decision making, seek their teachers' advice in curricular matters, and praise their teachers for work well done—are associated with significantly lower levels of teacher burnout than are unsupportive principals. Further, regression analysis revealed that when teachers were assigned to supportive principals the linkage between stress and burnout was broken, and if there was burnout, it was caused by individual factors, including the personality of the teacher. By contrast, for teachers assigned to unsupportive principals, burnout was caused by stress on the job, regardless of personality variables. It made no difference to teachers whether principals were effective or ineffective, as long as they were supportive. A supportive principal who nevertheless was ineffective in changing school climate and district policies to reduce the stressors to which the teachers were subjected was as able to break the linkage between stress and burnout as a supportive *and effective* principal who could make changes. Both supportive and effective and supportive and ineffective principals were telling teachers that regardless of the conditions at the school or in the district, and regardless of how unappreciative the students and parents were of the teachers' efforts, someone cared and considered their work to be meaningful. Since meaninglessness is central to the burnout process, such reassurances by the principal significantly mitigated burnout.

Firestone and Rosenblum (1988) also have noted the significance of principal support in building mutual commitment among students and teachers in urban high schools. Additionally, supportive principals encourage senior faculty to be supportive of more junior faculty (Dworkin et al., 1990). However, the principal's behavior is paramount. Supportive coworkers, in the absence of a supportive principal, have no effect in lowering teacher burnout.

Interestingly enough, mutual support among inexperienced teachers, in the absence of support by the principal and senior faculty, actually exacerbates burnout. In the presence of a stressful work situation, neophytes tend to exaggerate or inaccurately estimate the seriousness of the situation. Having no standard by which to judge their stressors, they rely upon expectations fostered during preservice training in schools of education. This only confirms their mutual conviction that the "reality of urban teaching" differs from the expectations they were socialized to have about teaching. They come to conclude that they were misled, and their anxieties and frustrations feed off one another. A cumulative, circular social process, exaggerated by rumor, emerges that further heightens their anxiety.

A case in point is instructive. Following the oil crunch and recession in Texas during the mid-1980s, there was a rumor at a major Texas university that some departments might have to be shut down. New assistant professors met nightly at one another's homes, working out the most dire of scenarios. Fortunately, several of the senior faculty in the department decided to approach the assistant professors and tell them that the university periodically made all sorts of dire fiscal forecasts, but that in the professional lifetimes of the senior professors, jobs had never been lost as a consequence of doomsaying. In fact, in the rare instances when departments had been closed down, the faculty were reassigned to other departments, thereby saving jobs. Fears were allayed, the process of rumor creation ended, and the junior faculty stopped trying to look for other jobs and returned to teaching and publishing. Thus intervention of a senior faculty member or a principal can soothe fears and break the cycle of anxiety and rumor.

The principal as a builder of teacher efficacy. Newmann, Rutter, and Smith (1989) of the University of Wisconsin's National Center on Effective Secondary Schools have analyzed data from the "Administrator and Teacher Survey of the High School and Beyond Study" (1982, 1984, with ongoing panel data). Based upon a random subsample of 353 high schools (including more than 10,000 teachers and administrators), the researchers demarcated the elements of school life and administrative behavior that contribute most to high levels of teacher efficacy (a sense of powerfulness), community (a sense identification with the school), and expectations regarding student learning outcomes. The authors conclude that four organizational actions that can be introduced into a school by an administrator significantly improve teacher morale: (a) enforcing orderly behavior on the part of students, (b) encouraging teachers to innovate and experiment in teaching, (c) involving teachers in the coordination of curriculum and in helping one another, and (d) increasing the responsiveness and support of administrators. Each of these is most effective when initiated at the campus level. Interestingly, staff development and in-service programs conducted at the district level seem to have no effect upon teacher morale.

In a recent study, teachers reported that on some Houston campuses the principal rarely visits their classrooms except to evaluate teacher performance (Dworkin, 1990b). Other teachers contend that some principals never leave their offices and never express interest in the human problems of their teachers. In one suburban school, the teachers contended that the principal reprimanded them in the presence of their students. Nearly half of the teachers in this study felt that if they had job-related problems the principal would be the very last person they would wish to speak to about them, and that the principal would be the least sympathetic of listeners. One-third of the teachers felt that if they were victimized by students (physically attacked or had property stolen or vandalized), the principal would attempt to cover up the incident for fear that the district would define him or her as a poor manager.

The issue of support is a difficult one. Under what conditions are attempts by a principal to be supportive seen as attempts to pry or to deny a teacher his or her sense of professional autonomy? Analyzing data from a statewide study of Minnesota teachers, Dworkin, Lorence, and LeCompte (1989) found that the combined effects of principal support, professional autonomy, freedom from community surveillance, and student body achievement accounted for the high levels of teacher morale in suburban and small-city schools and the low levels of morale in rural and inner-city schools. In the rural schools, low morale was driven by high community and administrative surveillance and a sense of low professional autonomy. The key to defining whether a principal's concerns and questions are supportive or spying lies not only in the manner in which the principal presents the support. It also depends upon the level of trust extant in the school, as well as teachers' experiences with "supportive" administrators in the past. While there is an abundance of evidence to sustain the argument that supportive principals mitigate teacher burnout, it is doubtful that principals who have been viewed with distrust by teachers will find teacher acceptance of their friendly and supportive overtures. More likely, the teachers will ask, "What is the principal up to now?"

TOWARD THE RECRUDESCENCE OF TEACHER MORALE

Given the magnitude of the burnout problem in public schools, what strategies can be implemented to rekindle enthusiasm among teachers? Some strategies are more useful than others, especially in large urban districts where thousands of teachers are affected. Figure 5.1 displays the relationship among the variables that create burnout. The proximal cause of burnout, according to most research, especially that done by psychologists, is stress. Riggar (1985) even refers to burnout as "stress burnout." The link between stress and burnout appears to be unproblematic (see Cedoline, 1982; Cherniss, 1980; Cherniss et al., 1976; Gray & Freeman, 1987; Heath, 1981; Maslach, 1978a, 1978b; Paine, 1982; Schwab & Iwanicki, 1982; Shaw, Bensky, & Dixon, 1981; Shinn, 1982; Swick, 1989; Swick & Hanley, 1983). However, individual (i.e., teacher characteristics), organizational, and structural (campus conditions) variables increase the likelihood of the experience of stress, and these in turn produce burnout. Thus most of the investigators cited above also note the essential role of organizational variables and environmental elements in heightening stress.

Social Buffering, or Yoga Isn't Practical

Much of the work on teacher burnout, and, in fact, on burnout in general, has been conducted by clinical psychologists. This means that the dominant paradigm in burnout research emphasizes the significance of self-blame and self-help in

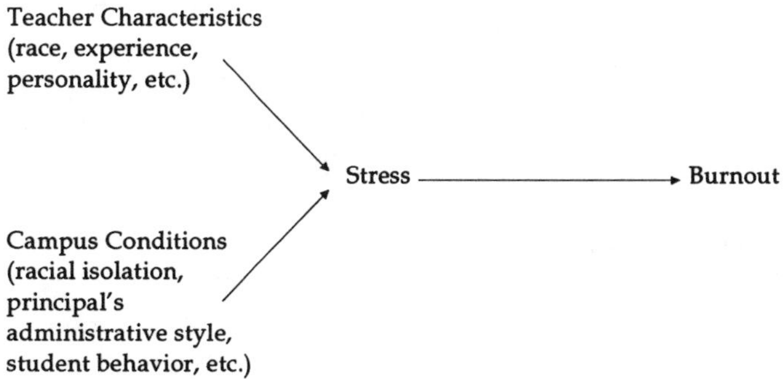

Figure 5.1 A Model for the Creation of Teacher Burnout
SOURCE: Adapted from Dworkin (1985, p. 9). Used by permission.

dealing with burnout. While there is much evidence to suggest that burnout is an individual response to stressful situations (see Caroll & White, 1982; Cedoline, 1982; Cherniss, 1980, 1982; Freudenberger, 1974; Maslach, 1976, 1978a, 1978b; Maslach & Jackson, 1979, 1982; Paine, 1982), it does not necessarily follow that the cure for burnout must or can always be individualistic and therapy based. Clinical solutions are varied, but they generally involve courses in stress management and holistic health practices (Tubesing & Tubesing, 1982), breathing and centering, cognitive reprogramming, balance exercises, and relaxation and self-suggestion (Shaw et al., 1981), as well as counseling, expansion of friendship networks, and involvement in hobbies, summer jobs out of teaching, gardening, home repairs, physical exercise, and volunteer work (Swick & Hanley, 1983). Although Cedoline (1982), Maslach (1978a, 1978b), and Cherniss (1980) acknowledge the importance of social support and organizational change to reduce burnout, they nevertheless suggest that learning to cope with stress is central. Cedoline suggests that teachers engage in "self-talk" and positive attitudes to dispel stress, involve themselves in more physical activity to generate the endorphins that lead to good feelings, chant a "mantra" and meditate daily, focus on breathing, and rely upon deep muscle relaxation, biofeedback, and autogenic training (autohypnotic suggestion).

How successful these tactics are is illustrated by the following anecdote. A suburban school district in the Houston area contracted with a local hospital to provide psychological care for teachers who were excessively stressed by the implementation of state-mandated in-class evaluations of teaching ability. A group session was set up by a clinical psychologist who knew of Dworkin's work on burnout and invited him to attend. One teacher burst into tears as she recounted the actions of her principal. She was a first-year teacher who was having difficulty with classroom management and discipline. The principal entered her classroom and told her that she was incompetent and did not belong in a classroom because she could not control her fifth graders. He then led the class in a chant, "Miss X is a dumb teacher." She ran from her classroom crying. Deep-breathing exercises and a positive mental attitude were recommended by the clinician. A sociologist who looks at structural factors might suggest instead an organizational change as well as legal or district action against the principal. An appropriate alternative might be "reprogramming" or replacement of the principal, or the institution of management skills training for campus administrators, accompanied by periodic evaluation of such administrators in terms of the level of morale of faculty. In addition, a sociologist would address the problem of class management by pairing neophyte teachers with senior, master teachers who could help socialize them into the teaching role.

The problem of scale is another difficulty associated with clinical self-help programs. If burnout is substantially a structural and organizational problem, then an individualized strategy employed in a large urban district with 12,000 teachers is much less efficient than an organizational strategy that affects the behavior of a few hundred administrators, and in turn alters the conditions that produce burnout among those 12,000 teachers.

One interesting aspect of the clinical emphasis upon self-help is that it evokes self-blame rather than system-blame models for explaining teacher problems. As we shall see in

Chapters 7 and 9, and as we have noted in previous chapters, much stress and alienation issue from administrative attempts to deflect blame away from the social system and onto the victim. Strategies that tell teachers they suffer burnout because they are unable to cope imply that it is the teachers who are flawed and that the school system will rescue them from their weaknesses. The message is effective only as long as the teachers do not talk among themselves, comparing their experiences. Once they begin to realize that stress and burnout are endemic to school systems, teacher consciousness is raised and system-blame models become more plausible. At that point collective action (including union activism) by teachers is possible. The process of consciousness development and the shift from accepting self-blame to accepting system-blame explanations for individual problems has been well documented (see, for example, Blumer, 1978; Chafetz & Dworkin, 1986; Riger, 1977; and, of course, Marx, 1959).

EDUCATIONAL REFORM AND TEACHER BURNOUT: A CASE STUDY

Frequently, educational reform means that legislatures scrutinize the activities of school districts and, in particular, the performances of teachers and students. In 1984, the Texas State Legislature passed an omnibus reform package known as House Bill 72. By 1986, several of the components of the legislation had been implemented, including the establishment of a career ladder for teachers, competency evaluations of teachers through standardized testing, periodic in-class performance evaluations of teachers, and a mountain of paperwork to be completed by teachers so as to document the effects of myriad student policy changes.

Prior to the implementation of House Bill 72 in Texas, about one-third of Houston's public school teachers could be classified as burned out (Dworkin, 1985, 1987). The most recent data, obtained from a random sample of 1,060 urban and suburban teachers, reveal that burnout rates are approaching 60%.

Presented in Figure 5.2 are comparisons of burnout rates among teachers at two different time periods. For purposes of comparability between the data sets, only burnout levels for Houston Independent School District teachers are examined. The graphing of Group A is based upon a sample of 3,444 teachers from a survey conducted in 1977; the graphing of Group B is based on the HISD subsample of 804 teachers from the survey conducted in 1987. The more positive the score, the higher the level of burnout; the more negative the score, the lower the level of burnout. The data are cross-sectional in nature, so it cannot be assumed that any given teacher will experience diminishing burnout over a span of a career. However, comparisons between the pre-House Bill 72 and post-House Bill 72 samples are instructive. In the pre-House Bill 72 sample, each additional year of teaching experience after the initial years of a probationary contract is marked with lower levels of teacher burnout among the cohorts. However, since House Bill 72, the pattern is different. What is particularly alarming is that burnout, previously most common among neophyte teachers, is now greatest among teachers with 10 to 15 years of experience. The very teachers who have had sufficient experience to master pedagogy and their subject matter report the highest levels of burnout. The semiannual in-class evaluations under the Texas Teacher Assessment System have meant that those who had come to believe that their continuing contracts and years of experience demonstrated their status as master teachers were again being evaluated as if they were neophytes. Their seniority and years of accomplishments seemed to count for nothing.

There is an additional irony associated with educational reform. In every state, educational reform has meant that legislatures establish not only goals for change, but strategies for such change. In most instances the legislation has micromanaged the school districts, campuses, and classrooms. While teacher morale is depressed when teachers feel that they have little say in the nature and content of schooling, administrators who treat their

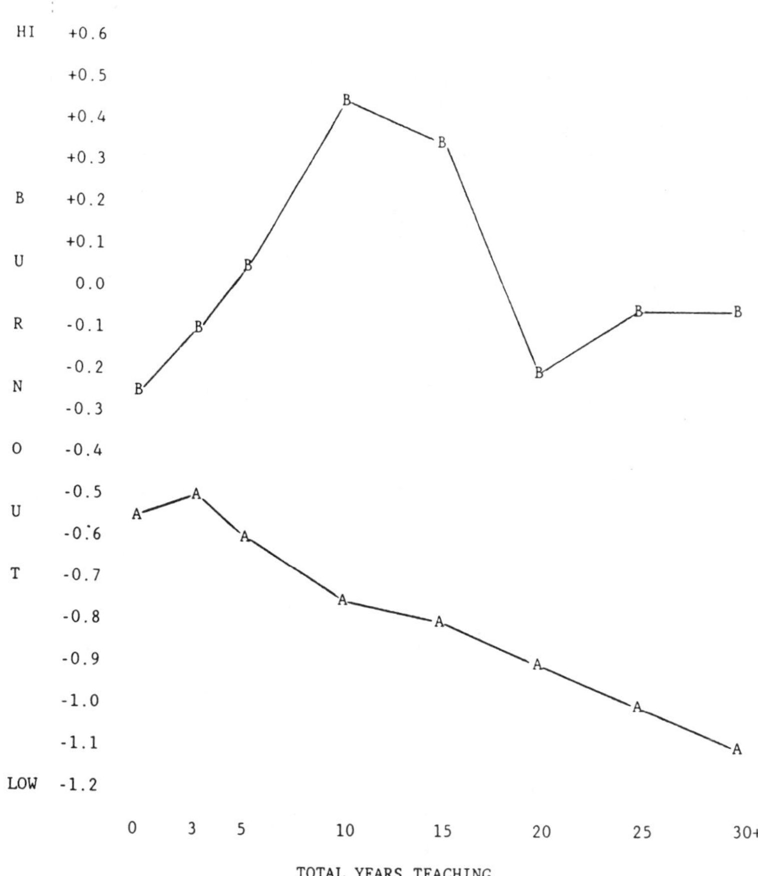

Figure 5.2 Burnout Levels Among HISD Teachers, by Years Teaching
NOTE: A = pre-House Bill 72 data; B = post-House Bill 72 data.

teachers as respected colleagues improve morale and aid teachers in coping with school-based stressors. The further management is distanced from the classroom, the more teachers will feel demoralized. Educational reform has had the effect of removing management of the classroom to the highest state levels. The effect has been a greater sense of powerlessness among teachers.

NOTE

1. In the computation of faculty turnover rates, some schools do not distinguish between voluntary turnover due to quitting and turnover due to death, retirement, maternity leave, prolonged illness extending beyond the paid sick-leave period, and short-term resignations of teachers who must care for sick relatives.

SIX

To Quit or Not to Quit

In Chapter 5 we explored the social forces that create teacher burnout. Burnout is rarely an end unto itself. Often the sense of burnout leads to intentions to leave a disliked activity or occupation and, in turn, actual quitting behavior. In many instances involving teachers, the desire to quit teaching is thwarted by the absence of career alternatives. Under such circumstances teachers are entrapped in their roles, hating their job, their students, and all with whom they interact as teachers. This chapter examines intentions to quit teaching, actual quitting behavior, and teacher entrapment. The effects of these attitudes and behaviors on individual teachers and school systems are examined. However, it is first useful to locate the desire to quit teaching and actual quitting behavior within the context of the larger sociological issue of work commitment, as theories of commitment help to inform us of the range of variables that convert burnout as an attitude into job action.

THE CONCEPT OF COMMITMENT

Public school teaching is considered by sociologists to be a "semiprofession." Semiprofessions are characterized by the facts that "their training is shorter, their status is less legitimated, their right to privileged communication less established, there is less of a specialized body of knowledge, and they have less autonomy from supervision or societal control than 'the' professions" (Etzioni, 1969, p. v). In comparison with other semiprofessions, including nursing, social work, and related service occupations, teaching has slightly lower turnover rates; however, the rate is higher than in other fields of works where women are concentrated, such as clerical occupations (Etzioni, 1969; Price, 1977). As in other professions and semiprofessions, what first attracts a person to the career is some sense of "a calling" (Lortie, 1975; National Education Association, 1983). That is, individuals choose such careers because they want to make a difference in the world; in the case of social service occupations, they want to make a difference in the lives of those on whom they practice their expertise. We frequently talk about the enthusiasm, idealism, and desire to continue in a line of activity on the part of professionals and semiprofessionals as "commitment." In turn, burnout can be seen as the loss of such commitment.

Loss of Commitment

Theories of commitment represent explanations for the absence of burnout and for the continuity of role performances. Generally speaking, commitment may be thought of as an affective attachment that an actor has to a person, object, role, or setting such that the probability of perseverance and continuance of a relationship to that person, object, role, or setting is enhanced. When coworkers and superordinates, a job or career, and a workplace are involved, we may speak of job and/or organizational commitment. Kanter (1968) provides a tripartite model of commitment, involving conformity to norms (control commitment), solidarity with coworkers (cohesion commitment), and perseverance of affiliation (continuance commitment). Kanter has cogently argued that commitment conjoins individual wants, needs, and experiences with the demands of an organizational structure (see also Porter, Steers, Mowday, & Boulian, 1974).

Beginning in the 1960s, the social sciences have offered two distinct perspectives on commitment. The first, advanced by H. S. Becker (1960) and based on the ideas of Schelling (1960), views commitment as the structural addition of "side bets," or factors external to the career or work activity that make increasingly painful the abandonment of that career or line of activity. The Becker model represents a theory of motivation in which the actor, in justifying past and/or present actions to self and to others, evokes explanations that are external to actual career considerations. Side bets are usually operationalized by such structural factors as age, race, years on the job, educational attainment (especially within a career specialty), marital status, and number of children. They have been shown by H. S. Becker (1960), Becker and Strauss (1956), and Alutto, Hrebiniak, and Alonzo (1973) to account for commitment, as indicated by attitudes toward quitting.

In the second perspective, Ritzer and Trice (1969), Shoemaker, Snizek, and Bryant (1977), and Stevens et al. (1978) have found greater support for a social psychological model that emphasizes satisfaction and solidarity as forces behind work commitment. For these investigators, factors intrinsic to the work, including a sense of satisfaction that one's work is meaningful and a feeling of collegiality with coworkers, better account for the continuance of career behavior than do accumulated side bets.

Shoemaker et al. (1977) suggest that side-bet variables may have greater explanatory power in terms of organizational commitment, while the strength of satisfaction/solidarity variables is greater in explaining career or occupational commitment. However, these authors contend that satisfaction/solidarity variables do an acceptable job of explaining organizational commitment as well. Much evidence garnered from studies of cognitive dissonance (Festinger, 1964; Janis & Mann, 1977) also illustrates that actors who invest many resources in a career (e.g., side bets) are likely to convince themselves that they also gain intrinsic satisfaction from their work and their colleagues (satisfaction/solidarity). Evidence presented by Stevens et al. (1978) has pointed to the possibility that different commitment variables play differing roles throughout a worker's life cycle. Satisfaction and solidarity may be of greater importance in attracting an actor to a career, but side bets, as they accrue, become more influential later in the actor's work life.

In her study of men and women in an industrial organization, Kanter (1977) proposes that, where blocked career mobility exists, workers tend to emphasize social relations over other factors (Ritzer & Trice's solidarity variable) as a basis for continued role relationships. In contrast, Dworkin and Chafetz (1983) maintain that in organizations characterized by very low levels of vertical mobility (not the relative immobility of Kanter's respondents), idealism, such as seeing one's work as a calling, may be a significant factor in accounting for continuation behavior. In this instance, then, immobility may heighten the significance of Ritzer and Trice's satisfaction/solidarity variable. It is apparent that the two approaches are not mutually exclusive, and there is no necessity to choose between the side-bet and satisfaction/solidarity approaches to commitment. Rather, these two perspectives may be conjoined to provide better insight into the mechanisms of work commitment, thereby providing us with a more general theory of commitment.

A Reexamination and Synthesis

Dworkin (1982) has reexamined the samples from which the side-bet and the satisfaction/solidarity models gain support, and suggests an additional reason the two models may be part of a larger whole. The studies that support a side-bet hypothesis sampled individuals in semiprofessions, including nurses and classroom teachers, while data that give credibility to the satisfaction/solidarity thesis were gathered on personnel managers and park rangers. The former group has specialized training that is not readily translatable into other occupations or industries; the latter group has greater skill translatability. That is, outside of hospital or other medical settings and schools, nurses and teachers have few salable skills. In contradistinction, the skills of the personnel manager are generalizable to other industries and/or other fields where decision making on personnel matters is involved. Likewise, the manifold skills required of a forest ranger—knowledge of forestry, agriculture, public relations, fire fighting, conservation, and some police work—suggest that this is an occupation that does not limit career alternatives. What distinguishes the two classes of occupations, and thus the relative influence of side-bet and solidarity/satisfaction variables, is the extent to which individuals in each occupation can translate their skills into other fields without substantial retraining. A high degree of overspecialization serves as a limiting factor to career alternatives. The reader may recognize that the distinction between high and low translatables corresponds closely to the distinction made by Gary Becker (1964, chap. 2) between specific and general training as investments in human capital.

Dworkin (1982) used coders to sort the various occupational roles within the school district into those that were thought to have analogues in other economic sectors and those that did not. Occupations were thus categorized as either translatable or nontranslatable, with the former facilitating easy career change and the latter mitigating career change. Teachers in the sciences, mathematics, business, industrial arts, and bilingual programs were coded as translatables, while those in elementary classes and in the humanities and social sciences were coded as nontranslatables.

Two separate analyses were conducted to discern the role of translatability on commitment attitudes and behaviors. In the first, a series of regression analyses were run comparing the relative power of side-bet versus satisfaction/solidarity variables in explaining the desire to stay or to quit teaching. Among teachers who were not translatables, side-bet variables better explained the desire to stay or to quit, while among teachers who were translatables, the satisfaction/solidarity variables better accounted for quitting or staying. Only slightly more than 8% of the nontranslatable teachers who were both dissatisfied with their jobs and wanted to quit actually did quit teaching. By contrast, three-quarters of the translatables who were dissatisfied with their jobs and wanted to quit teaching actually did quit. Dworkin concludes that the two models of commitment both play roles in accounting for the desire to remain in a line of activity, with each moderated by the degree of translatability of the teacher.

WHO WANTS TO QUIT TEACHING AND WHY?

Numerous studies have suggested that burnout is a significant contributor to a teacher's desire to quit teaching (see, for example, Cherniss, 1980; Dworkin, 1985, 1987; Jackson et al., 1986; Maslach, 1982). Many people consider teaching to be their "calling," and enter the career with the desire to make a difference in the lives of children. However, as we observed in Chapter 5, the bureaucratization of schooling, the deskilling of teachers, and the belief that nobody cares about education or teachers quickly cause their enthusiasm to flag. The majority of teachers who have burned out want to quit; however, without alternative sources of employment, many teachers remain in schools long after their enthusiasm and sense of calling have evaporated. (We shall address the matter of teachers who want to quit but cannot somewhat later, under the rubric of teacher entrapment.) The Washington, D.C.-based Institute for Educational Leadership surveyed 400 urban teachers and found seven groups of factors that depress teacher morale and heighten the desire the leave teaching. Our own research has confirmed the widespread concern of teachers with these seven issues: physical conditions of the school, safety, resources, support staff, student behavior problems, testing, and poor leadership (Corcoran, Walker, & White, 1988, p. xi).

Physical conditions. Teachers report problems with the physical conditions of the schools, including inadequate repair and maintenance of facilities and lack of space. In a study conducted in Houston, one group of teachers reported that the heating and air conditioning had been broken for two years in one of the buildings of a high school and that the principal had never investigated the teachers' complaints about the problem. The principal was mystified that there was a high turnover rate among teachers assigned to that building, but assumed that it had to do with idiosyncrasies among that group of teachers, including the replacements who also quit.

Safety and student behavior. Safety is a serious problem in inner-city schools. In fact, the Safe School Study reports that 40% of the robberies and 36% of the assaults experienced by teenagers occur on school grounds. The report goes on to note that "the proportion of public secondary school teachers victimized by theft, attack, and robbery is roughly similar to those of students." Additionally, "an estimated 12 percent of the nation's teachers have something stolen from them each month . . . and one-half of one percent of the teachers are physically attacked at school in a month's time" (National Institute of Education, 1978, p. 3). This translates to approximately 130,000 teachers victimized by robbery or theft and 5,200 teachers attacked each month across the nation. Recently, Dworkin et al. (1988) reported that more than 61% of urban teachers feel very stressed or fearful when they discipline their students in the classroom, and more than 71% feel very stressed or are fearful when they discipline students in the halls.

Resources. Urban school teachers do not have the necessary material and nonmaterial school resources to conduct their work, and often are deprived of many of the technological innovations that could make their work easier. The families of children attending inner-city schools generally cannot afford many of the requisite school supplies, and district budgets are often also too meager to provide them. Teachers in our studies have reported having to provide many school supplies out of their own money. Some teachers contribute as much as 10% of their meager salaries to supporting the needs of their students. Districts that are too poor to provide school supplies also cannot afford computers, structured instructional programs, and other resources.

Support staff. Not only is there a lack of school supplies, but there is a critical shortage of support staff. Urban teachers are expected to help children cope with a plethora of societal problems, including child abuse, drug and alcohol abuse, poverty, teenage pregnancy, and delinquency. However, there are so few school counselors in urban schools that caseloads often exceed 500 students per counselor. As such, counselors become merely paper pushers, and teachers are expected to pick up the pieces.

Testing. Districtwide testing policies have made teachers feel that they have little control over the content of their teaching. Most teachers feel pressure to teach to the test, regardless of what they believe the curricular content of their courses ought to be. While most teachers feel that they lack jurisdiction over *what* they teach, they still believe that they have control over *how* they teach when their classroom doors are closed.

Leadership. Urban teachers have little confidence in their supervisors, principals, staff development personnel, or the leadership in their central offices. Most teachers feel that central office administrators are too concerned about appeasing legislators and voters ever to care about the needs of teachers (Dworkin, 1990a).

When Louis Harris and Associates interviewed a national sample of teachers who had left teaching, they found that the combined effects of inadequate salaries and poor working conditions were the most important factors that drove teachers from schools. Additionally, respect, professional autonomy, and the quality of resources and equipment were factors they valued in their new careers (National Education Association, 1987a, p. 21).

Burnout and the Desire to Quit

Just as not every teacher burns out, not all teachers want to quit. However, most of the characteristics of burned-out teachers also fit teachers who want to quit. This is because, as studies have demonstrated, burnout is the single most important element in the desire to leave teaching. In fact, 36% of the total variance in the desire to quit teaching is a function of burnout. In two large studies of teachers in the Houston area, Dworkin (1987, 1990b) found that the association between burnout and plans to quit teaching was moderate and the causal influence fairly high.[1] Additionally, just as supportive principals break the linkage between stress and burnout, they also reduce the likelihood that a teacher will want to quit his or her job.

Factors Beyond Burnout

Other factors that affect the desire to quit teaching are those that either make the teaching job less rewarding or make job abandonment less punishing. In one study, Dworkin (1980) observed that white faculty were more likely to want to quit than black or Hispanic faculty; that younger teachers were more likely to express a desire to quit than were older teachers; that teachers assigned to campuses where they did not like the racial composition of the student body were more likely to want to quit than teachers not so assigned; that teachers who were racially isolated from the student bodies of their campuses (i.e., who belonged to a different racial group than the majority of their students) were more likely to want to quit than those who were not racially isolated; and that teachers whose parents had high-status occupations were more likely to want to quit than those whose parents held lower-status occupations.

There are other push and pull factors as well. In another study, Dworkin (1987) found that inexperienced teachers were more likely to want to quit than were experienced teachers. Teachers in senior high schools were less likely to want to quit than either elementary school or junior high school teachers. Higher salaries were associated with a greater desire to remain than were lower salaries, and desire to remain was also higher if a teacher's salary made up a major share of the total family income. Men were more likely to *want* to quit teaching than were women, although those in this study were less likely actually to leave the profession than were women.

Gender, race and ethnicity, and income, as well as non-teaching sources of income, all represent surrogate measures for alternative opportunities. Many female teachers have reported that they could always go back home and raise their children, an option rarely considered available to male teachers, whom society expects to remain in the labor force. In fact, one small study conducted by the Houston Independent School District in 1978 noted that 48% of the married, white, middle-class female teachers with young children who quit that year elected to stay at home and care for their children; almost none of the married minority teachers with young children who quit did the same. Likewise, having low wages, a factor associated with inexperience, increases the likelihood that a job outside of teaching could provide comparable income. By contrast, quitting teaching represents significant costs to minorities and individuals from working-class backgrounds. This is because they and their parents expend a greater proportion of family economic resources in obtaining college degrees and teaching credentials than do more privileged groups. Further, there is greater status honor accorded to individuals who have experienced intergenerational mobility than to those who have not; thus teachers from working-class backgrounds have experienced upward mobility, while those from professional and managerial backgrounds may be seen as immobile or downwardly mobile by entering teaching. Finally, those with privileged backgrounds are more likely to have influential friends and alternative career networks than those who do not have such backgrounds (for further clarification of these points, see Butler, 1976; Dworkin, 1980).

Racial isolation, assignment to an undesirable school, an unsupportive principal, and unruly students (whether crying elementary school students or poorly socialized junior high school students) affect burnout, which, in turn, makes continuation and further commitment to teaching punishing. In turn, the punishment exacerbates the desire to look for career alternatives to teaching. Additional push factors include excessive paperwork, especially as mandated by educational reform and the call for greater teacher accountability, the threat of competency testing, and the micromanagement of education by public watchdog groups and state legislatures, also in the name of educational reform (Dworkin, 1990b; Greater Houston Partnership, 1990; Rosenholtz, 1989).

A new study by Rosenholtz and Simpson (1990) examined six workplace conditions (factors other than burnout) in Tennessee schools to determine their relative impacts on the commitment of teachers. The conditions included perceived effectiveness in producing desired learning outcomes in students ("performance efficacy"), intrinsic pride and satisfaction with the teaching role ("psychic rewards"), relative freedom from constraints by administrators ("task autonomy and discretion"), opportunities to acquire new knowledge ("teachers' learning opportunities"), the presence and implementation of rules for student conduct ("managing students' behavior"), and supportiveness of the principal ("principal buffering"). The researchers found that the six organizational dimensions did not have uniform effects on teacher commitment; rather, the magnitude of the effect of each organizational factor varied with years of teaching experience. Principal buffering is most important for teachers with from 1 to 5 years' experience, task discretion and autonomy is most important for teachers with moderate levels of experience (6 to 10 years), and performance efficacy as well as task discretion and autonomy had the most impact on the commitment of teachers with 11 or more years' experience. This study supports an earlier observation by Stevens et al. (1978) that the factors that produce work commitment among newer employees are different in kind from those that engender commitment among more senior employees. New, idealistic teachers who are not as confident of their teaching and classroom management abilities need more support from their principals than do more experienced teachers, who demand greater degrees of professional autonomy. However, the most senior teachers want autonomy and a sense of efficacy—a sense that their work is meaningful and the investments they have made in a career have been worthwhile.

The Importance of Salaries

Finally, it is appropriate to examine more fully the effect of teachers' salaries upon plans to quit. The National Education Association (1987a) reports that low salaries are a major obstacle to attracting and keeping top teachers. A 1982 Gallup poll collected for *Phi Delta Kappan* reported that the general public thought that teachers' salaries were the main reason teachers were quitting, and urged states to address the problem (Gallup, 1982, p. 46). A 1980 Gallup poll reported that 62.2% of Americans felt that school financing, including the issue of teachers' salaries, was the public's principal concern about education (Elam & Gough, 1980).

A Metropolitan Life Insurance Company study conducted by Louis Harris and Associates (1985) shows that salaries are a major concern of teachers and that those who quit teaching often state that higher salaries were the most important pull to their new jobs. Teacher pay is an important issue in education; low teaching salaries, combined with 9- or 10-month paychecks, do discourage many from entering the career. However, among teachers who are thinking about quitting but who have not as yet left teaching, school resources and working conditions, professional respect, collegiality among administrators, and work-load factors are much more important than salary (Dworkin, 1987; Elam & Gough, 1980). Recently, an article in the *Houston Chronicle* reported that 57% of the Texas teachers planning on quitting in 1990 listed working conditions as the major factor in their decisions, while only 24% spoke of money ("Teachers' Report Cards," 1990). Although an offer of a large increase in salary is likely to lead most workers to abandon one job for another, small to moderate salary increases in the absence of the push factors (especially burnout, lack of collegial and administrative support, and the like) are not likely to have an effect. Salary has a greater recruitment effect than retention effect; high salaries can attract people, but high salaries accompanied by ill treatment cease to be an incentive to remaining in teaching.

In one study of Houston teachers the regression coefficient for the effect of salary on the desire to quit teaching was so tiny that there was not enough money in a school budget to persuade teachers who wanted to quit to remain in teaching. A pay increase of at least $18,518 was needed to produce a slight change in attitudes toward quitting (Dworkin, 1987, p. 55). What this really means is that there is little variance in salaries and much variance in the desire to quit. Thus salary differences do not account for differences in the desire to quit teaching. If there were significant differences within the range of teachers' salaries, salary might have a greater effect upon attitudes toward quitting. However, in most urban districts the range is quite narrow. Lortie (1975) has observed that teaching is one of those few professions in which the ultimate income is no more than twice the starting income. Ornstein (1980) points to the fact that during the 1970s teachers' salaries doubled, but the inflation rate rose so much that in constant dollars teachers were earning nearly $1,500 less in 1980 than in 1970.

Today it is not uncommon for new urban public school teachers to earn about $20,500 with a bachelor's degree, $21,500 with a master's degree, and $22,000 with a doctorate, and for their counterparts with 20 years' experience to earn $29,500, $33,500, and $36,500, respectively (Houston Independent School District report of salaries for 1989-1990 academic year). In some districts these represent high salaries. By contrast, salaries for beginning assistant professors in the social sciences (also with doctorates) start at more than $32,000, while senior faculty with 20 or more years' experience on average earn approximately $60,000. These salaries are all based on 9-month contracts (Dworkin, 1990b), and comparable salaries can be found throughout academia (American Association of University Professors, 1989). Starting salaries for engineers, graduates with business degrees, and lawyers are all higher than those of senior teachers with doctorates. This disadvantage of teachers with doctorates holds true even when adjusted for the fact that teachers have 9- or 10-month contracts.

One must realize, however, that teachers are not drawn to their careers in quest of wealth. In another study involving urban and suburban teachers in the Houston area (Dworkin, 1990a), teachers were asked if they would quit teaching if they were offered another job (outside of teaching) that gave them slight increases in pay, freedom and autonomy, status, responsibilities, and friendliness of coworkers. While 29.5% said that they would leave with a slight increase in pay, many more, between 54.7% and 59.1%, said that they would leave with slight increases in freedom and autonomy, status, responsibilities, and friendliness of coworkers. The differences between salary and the other factors were statistically significant.

ACTUAL QUITTING BEHAVIOR

During the 1950s the teacher turnover rate nationally averaged 17%. The 1960s and 1970s saw that percentage drop somewhat. However, the 1980s and projections for the 1990s suggest that where education reform has been implemented the percentages have risen or will rise above previous levels.

The best studies of teacher turnover follow cohorts of teachers (groups who entered teaching in the same year and are thus subject to similar historical effects). Charters (1970) studied a cohort of new Oregon teachers from 1962 through 1966. By the end of the first year more than one-fifth of the men and one-third of the women had quit. By the end of the fifth year, 60% of the men and 72% of the women had left teaching, not simply changed districts.

A series of teacher cohort studies in the St. Louis schools were conducted from the end of the 1960s through the mid-1980s (see Anderson & Mark, 1977; Mark & Anderson, 1978, 1985). Eight successive cohorts monitored between 1968 and 1975 reflected an interesting pattern. Earlier cohorts were more likely to quit than were later cohorts. Within a cohort, the rate of turnover diminished with each successive year. While more than one-third of the new teachers in the 1968 cohort had quit in their first year, less than one-fifth of the new teachers in the 1975 cohort had quit within their first year. The 1985 analysis, which traces cohorts from 1969 through 1982, indicates that about 50% of all the teachers quit within less than five years.

In the earlier turnover study by Charters (1970), women were more likely to quit than were men; however, the Mark and Anderson studies suggest gender parity in turnover rates. Earlier studies reflected a pronounced tendency among women in the early 1960s and before to remain in the labor force only until they were married. The feminist movement, growing rates of divorce and single parenthood, normative acceptance of married women in the labor market, and, most significantly, the fact that a middle-class life-style is now often plausible only for two-earner families have done much to bring female turnover rates into parity with male rates. In fact, because there still remain inequalities in job opportunities for women, turnover rates for male teachers now exceed those of female teachers.

Citing studies by Weaver (1978) and Murnane and Phillips (1981), Mark and Anderson (1985) suggest two alternative explanations for the gender differences in turnover rates since the mid-1970s. Data suggest that the teacher glut of that decade, occasioned in part by the exit of much of the baby-boom generation from public schools, may have meant that schools could be more choosy about whom they tenured and permitted to remain in teaching. An oversupply of teachers would also mean that fewer men would seek employment in a traditionally female occupation, as their chances of employment are diminished. It also means that those who elect to enter teaching may do so not because it is an easy occupation in which to find placement, but because they actually wish to be teachers. Additionally, there is growing evidence that more recent cohorts of teachers are less academically able than earlier cohorts (Darling-Hammond, 1984; Schlechty & Vance,

1981; Vance & Schlechty, 1982; Weaver, 1978). Lower academic ability may be associated with diminished chances of receiving a continuing contract, especially if there is a pool of replacements available in the colleges of education and an oversupply of teachers.

Heyns (1990) warns against assuming that teacher turnover rates necessarily reflect the permanent loss to schools of groups of trained teachers. Using the National Longitudinal Survey of the High School Class of 1972 (NLS-72) data base, a panel study that monitors some 20,000 former high school seniors, Heyns reports that "for a large number of teachers, leaves or breaks of 1 or 2 years are customary and accepted practice" (p. 131). Heyns found that 1,100 of the former high school seniors sampled in 1972 trained to become teachers (p. 129). This produced a weighted estimate of 211,000 trained teachers in the cohort, of whom 74% never entered teaching, 54% quit teaching, and almost 33% reentered teaching.

Why Intention to Quit Does Not Always Produce Quitting

It is common for teachers' unions to survey their members to determine the percentage who claim that they plan to leave teaching by the end of the current school year. If the percentages are high, the unions report to the press that, unless certain concessions are made to teachers, the districts will face insurmountable shortfalls in the supply of teachers for the next school year. The press responds by decrying that students will either be turned away from schools or that class sizes in the coming fall will be so large that educational goals will be thwarted. While it might seem that the intention to quit teaching would be an excellent predictor of actual quitting behavior, in point of fact it is not. In one study, attitudes toward quitting teaching were enumerated from a random sample of 3,444 urban teachers (Dworkin, 1987). Over the subsequent five years (the data were collected between 1977 and 1982), school district data were used to determine which teachers in the sample actually quit the district and/or teaching.

It should be noted that monitoring of cohorts of teachers for five years is typical of turnover studies. It also should be recognized that forecasting the distant future is unrealistic, and thus quitting during the five-year period neither ensures that a person might not return to teaching at some later date (see Heyns, 1990) nor mandates that someone who does not quit will never quit. Of the 3,444 teachers in the sample, 798 (23.1%) stated that they were planning to quit teaching. However, of those planning to quit, only 232 (29.1%) actually had left teaching within the five-year period. Furthermore, the obtained correlation between plans to quit and actual quitting is only .102 (Dworkin, 1987, p. 57).

There are many reasons for the weak correlation between intention to quit and actual quitting behavior. First, actually quitting a job depends for most people on having an alternative job available that offers comparable quality of life, standard of living, and psychic rewards of status and satisfaction. The role of unemployment is not an equitable exchange for the abandonment of a hated teaching job. As one teacher interviewed noted, "Teaching, even when you can't stand the students or the administration, certainly beats not eating."

As noted earlier, many teachers have skills that are limited to working with a youthful clientele and are thus not in high demand by the private sector. When teachers have amassed numerous investments or side bets in their careers and have few salable skills useful to employers outside of education, they are likely to be forced to remain in teaching. Thus the desire to quit does not explain much of the variance in actual quitting behavior. The association between intention to quit and actual quitting is symmetrical, which means not only that people who say they want to quit do not do so, but also that people who do not say they want to quit actually leave.

Over a five-year period many things can occur, including changing structural, economic, and personal factors, that can affect attitudes and behaviors. However, one relevant social structural element in the actual likelihood for teachers who said they did not want to quit to do so is a product of the demographics of the teaching population. A disproportionate number of all teachers (about 75%) are women, and many are married women whose career plans are affected by their husbands' career decisions and job circumstances. Because our society has not adequately addressed issues of comparable worth (Bose & Spitz, 1987; England, Chassie, & McCormack, 1982; England & Dunn, 1988; Wittig & Lowe, 1989), women tend to be paid less for their economic activities than men, especially if they work in predominantly female occupations (England, 1984). Therefore, married women are likely to be earning less than their husbands and, for economic reasons alone, husbands' job constraints, including corporate transfers and out-migration to seek new or better employment opportunities when the labor market becomes tight, tend to take precedence over the wives'. When one considers the fact that the advantage in family power remains vested with the husband (Blumberg, 1979; Chafetz, 1980, 1984), it is clear that whenever the husband's job situation is at odds with the wife's, this tends to mean acquiescence by the wife in quitting a school district job and moving with her husband.

There seems to be a demographic anomaly in the analysis of turnover data on teachers. The data that are based upon urban districts show that men are more likely to want to quit teaching, but that women are more likely to quit (Dworkin, 1987). The studies by Charters (1970) and those by Mark and Anderson (1978, 1985; Anderson & Mark, 1977) also reflect higher turnover rates by women than by men. However, surveys by Louis Harris (1985), Mark and Anderson (1985), and Heyns (1990) also show higher turnover rates by men than by women. Heyns's (1990) analysis of the fifth wave of the NLS-72 data found that the greater likelihood of men quitting than women can be explained by grade level. High school teachers, who are more likely to be male and "translatables," are the source of gender differences in turnover rates. When turnover rates are higher for women than for men, three factors are operative: Women have the alternative of staying at home; as noted, women are more swayed by factors that affect their husbands' jobs than vice versa; and, finally, men have a greater chance of escaping the classroom and entering administrative positions in school systems than do women.

The apparent reversal in turnover demographics may reflect a complex of factors now operating in urban society. First, career opportunities outside of teaching, nursing, and secretarial work are greater for women than they were one or two decades ago. Therefore, more of the talented women who might have left teaching elect never to enter teaching at all. Darling-Hammond (1984), Vance and Schlechty (1982), and Dworkin (1987) have noted that those individuals, regardless of gender, who enter colleges of education, become teachers, and stay in teaching come from those who score lower on college entrance examinations. Second, urban teaching is increasingly becoming a minority and minority female occupation, and will continue to be so into the next century, especially as the percentage of black males entering college is declining (U.S. Bureau of the Census, 1989). Minorities, and especially minority women, have fewer networks that can help them find alternative professional or higher-paying careers; they also sacrifice more to get to college and earn teaching credentials than do majority group members. For many, teaching represents intergenerational upward mobility (Dworkin, 1980). Third, turnover rates for white, middle-class women remain quite high in urban schools. These women are both afraid to teach in inner-city schools and dislike having to drive considerable distances from their white, suburban neighborhoods to the inner city (Dworkin, 1987). Finally, divorce rates and the numbers of single-parent families have increased over the past two decades and are highest among black women. With fewer sources of alternative income, single parents and unmarried minority women who enter teaching are least likely to quit, regardless of the job circumstances. It is thus possible to explain the anomaly in gender and turnover. Women did quit at higher rates than men, and it may be true that white, married women continue to quit at higher rates than any group. However, as more teachers experience marital breakup and as urban schools experience an increase in the minority female teaching population, aggregate statistics will show that now and into the near future men are more likely to quit teaching than women.

Additional demographic factors associated with quitting include differentials in years of teaching experience and grade level taught. Mark and Anderson (1985), Louis Harris and Associates (1985), and Dworkin (1987) report that the likelihood of quitting diminishes with years of experience. In the Louis Harris survey, 46% of the teachers who quit had less than 10 years' experience, compared with only 22% of the current teaching population (see National Education Association, 1987a, p. 21).

Grade level taught is also associated with rates of quitting. Dworkin's (1987) survey of urban teachers found that high school teachers were the least likely to want to quit and actually to quit teaching. By contrast, elementary school teachers were the most vulnerable to quitting. Three explanations for the lower turnover rates among high school teachers include that they are more likely to have advanced degrees in their specialization, thereby making for a career investment or side bet; that they are higher paid than are elementary teachers; and that high school teaching is less stressful, given that teachers do not interact with the same children all day, that they have off periods, and that the students are somewhat better behaved (see the earlier discussion on burnout and grade level). High school teachers are also more likely to join unions than are elementary school teachers (Dworkin, 1987), and union members are more likely to consider themselves to be professionals and less likely to quit (Bacharach, Bamberger, & Conley, 1990; Donnenworth & Cox, 1978; Falk, Grimes, & Lord, 1982; Fox & Wince, 1976).

Surveys of teachers who have quit the field of education reveal that quitting behavior is driven by all of the variables that affect burnout and the desire to quit teaching, including the issues reported earlier from the investigation by the Institute for Educational Leadership (Corcoran et al., 1988).[2] Teachers who quit complain about lack of administrative support; they report that they are burned out; and they speak of excessive paperwork and lack of concern about schooling by students, their parents, and even by school officials (Dworkin, 1987). Teachers who quit have a strong sense that what they are doing is meaningless and that they are powerless to effect changes to improve their lot. Teacher respondents in the Louis Harris and Associates (1985) survey for the Metropolitan Life Insurance Company shared the same perceptions. Other points made by the former teachers who were interviewed in the Harris survey are that salaries are inadequate, working conditions are poor, supplies and resources are inadequate, and the occupation is not respected. The National Education Association (1987a) adds that low salaries and 9- or 10-month contracts have caused many teachers to have to moonlight to supplement their incomes. The NEA cites a Department of Labor survey finding that male teachers are more likely to have to moonlight than any other group of workers in any occupation (Stinson, 1986). While the average rate of moonlighting for all employed workers in the United States is 5.4%, male teachers have a moonlighting rate of between 16% and 19%, and the percentage of women who moonlight is increasing.

TEACHER ENTRAPMENT: A DOUBLE BIND FOR SCHOOLS AND TEACHERS

Earlier we observed that the percentage of teachers who want to quit teaching is several times greater than the percentage of teachers who actually do quit, even when one allows teachers five years to find other careers. With each additional year a teacher remains in the public schools, side bets and other investments build up to make actual quitting more and more costly and problematic. When teachers indicate that they intend to quit and then do not, we may describe them as potentially entrapped. When they make efforts to leave, but remain in teaching anyway, we have evidence of actual entrapment.

From the study of a random sample of 3,444 urban teachers (Dworkin, 1982), we noted that slightly over 29% of those who wanted to quit did so. Thus about 71% could be termed *potentially entrapped*. That study did not assess the percentage of teachers who made attempts to quit—that is, the percentage of *actual entrapment*. However, the newer data, collected to assess the impact of educational reform on teachers in urban and suburban schools, did measure actual entrapment (Dworkin, 1990b). Nearly 37% of the teachers sampled indicated that they had attempted to leave teaching, but had failed to find alternative careers. In some instances the teachers would have had to abandon their educational investments or undergo significant retraining. Becoming a salesclerk was an example of the former, while entering a new profession or semiprofession, usually after a return to a university, characterized the latter. A total of 56.3% of all teachers in the sample felt that they would need retraining in order to have new careers that paid at least as well as teaching, even though nearly all of the teachers felt that teaching did not pay well. For other teachers the exigencies of the labor market and their spouses' jobs prevented them from leaving.

Entrapment represents a problem for both teachers and school districts. It is a human problem for the teacher, as there are many personal, emotional, and psychophysical costs associated with the continuation of a line of work that is disliked, or even hated. It is an organizational problem for schools for several reasons. First, it becomes all the more difficult for districts to introduce programs aimed at helping children to learn more effectively and not drop out of school when they must rely upon unenthusiastic teachers to implement those programs. As discussed in earlier chapters, students who drop out often feel that their teachers do not care about them; for students assigned to teachers who hate their jobs, but are entrapped, this is no misperception. Second, teacher entrapment exacerbates staffing problems. School districts that count on turnover to balance budgets through the replacement of higher-paid teachers with lower-paid new teachers discover that some of the teachers they might like to see quit do not.

Entrapment in an Era of Teacher Shortages

We have observed that turnover rates among teachers are higher than in many other occupations in which women are concentrated, although somewhat lower than in some other semiprofessions. Studies by Mason (1961), Pavalko (1965, 1970), Charters (1970), and Mark and Anderson (1978, 1985; Anderson & Mark, 1977) note the relatively high turnover rates among new teachers. This has been a problem for decades. In fact, the issue of teacher turnover has been a topic of discussion by the U.S. Office of Education since the 1960s and even by Willard Waller in the 1930s.

During the late 1970s and very early 1980s, when the baby-boom generation was no longer in public schools, but before urban districts had to become preoccupied with youthful refugee populations from Latin America, the Caribbean, and Asia, some researchers were concerned with strategies to reduce the teacher glut by prolonging the number of years that preservice teachers remained in colleges of education (Stinnett & Henson, 1982). In fact, the supply of public school teachers exceeded demand by 88.7% (National Education Association, 1983), and districts spoke of declining shortfalls in the supply and demand of teachers. At that point, the National Education Association, in an effort to protect its membership, urged that districts calculate supply and demand in terms of "quality education," which factors in the need for smaller class sizes, special education and bilingual education teachers, the temporary replacement of teachers with substandard skills who could return to college to retrain, increases in the number of courses offered by schools, reduction of the number of teachers misassigned relative to their specializations, and the demands created by nursery school, prekindergarten, and kindergarten programs. Using their measure of "quality education," the NEA predicted a shortfall in the 1980s of 38.5%.

National studies issued during the 1980s, including those by the National Commission on Excellence in Education (1983), the RAND Corporation (Darling-Hammond, 1984), the Carnegie Forum on Education and the Economy (1986), the Holmes Group (1986), the National Science Foundation (1984), and the National Education Association (1987b), decried the coming shortage of teachers (especially those with translatable skills such as those in the sciences and mathematics) that will continue into the next century. The National Education Association (1987b, p. 25) cites one of the most complete of the state studies, California's PACE (Policy Analysis for California Education) study, which projected a shortfall of 167,000 teachers in that state by 1994-1995.

When there was an oversupply of teachers, teacher entrapment created some difficulties for schools, but the exit of translatables could be overcome by the recruitment of new faculty. Districts could be very choosy about their replacements. However, with teacher shortages, schools must often do without replacements for teachers who quit at the same time they must contend with some portion of the teaching population who are entrapped. They are in a double bind. Some portion of the teachers they want to keep leave and cannot be replaced, and some portion of the teachers they would like to have leave stay, and districts cannot afford to encourage their departure because of the absence of replacements.

NOTES

1. The obtained correlation between burnout and plans to quit teaching is between .59 and .60, while the *b* value for the effect size of burnout on plans to quit (an estimate of the causal influence of burnout on plans to quit) is .81 and .85. The *b* values can be read as follows: For each unit of increase in burnout there is more than four-fifths of a unit of increase in the desire to quit teaching.

2. A caveat must be invoked when one studies employees who quit and then asks them to explain their decisions. Reliance upon retrospective histories often means selective perception. First, individuals who have already quit are likely to need to rationalize the correctness of their actions and to blame job conditions or their employers for leading them to quit. They are also likely to remember only the bad things that happened. Second, when former employees speak about how unsupportive their superordinates and coworkers were, it is difficult to establish the directionality of the causal arrow. Did lack of support cause them to dislike their jobs and quit, or did they dislike their jobs first and then read lack of support into the actions of their fellow employees? These questions are impossible to answer without longitudinal analysis—something that has never been done in studies of turnover.

SEVEN

Alienation and Schools

Our explanation of the continued problems in schooling utilizes the concepts of structural strain and alienation. That is, our theory posits that macroscopic changes such as those discussed in Chapter 2 make demands for change in the form and content of all social institutions, including schools. If the institutions lag significantly behind the macroscopic changes, individuals will be unsuccessful in attaining either the career and life goals that they set for themselves or the goals that the institutions hold are attainable through conformity with norms espoused in the institutions. Eventually, individuals come to recognize that the failure they experience is due to flaws in the institutions rather than personal shortcomings. Depending upon opportunities, individuals may elect to reject the institutions and the normative systems that support them—they may give up on the institutions.

We begin our theoretical approach by describing the two central problems that define the core of this book: (a) the specification of structural and organizational factors that weaken the fit between schooling in the United States and the goals and needs of students and teachers, hence creating strains; and (b) the mechanisms and processes by which students and teachers come to realize that schools fail to meet their expectations or facilitate the attainment of their goals, hence producing alienation from school. It is tempting to explain teacher and student outcomes differently. After all, teachers voluntarily enter schools as participants in a paid labor force; students are mandated to attend school and are not paid for their work. However, we believe, as do Firestone and Rosenblum (1988), that teachers and students influence each other. Further, we have seen in Chapters 3 through 6 that teachers and students similarly conclude that schools fail them because nobody cares. Their sense of alienation derives from feelings of meaninglessness and powerlessness. Thus, while slightly different variables make up the constructs we use to explain why teachers burn out and quit and students tune out and drop out, the constructs themselves are nonetheless the same. These constructs all speak to the alienating forces operating in American education.

ALIENATION THEORY: A GENERAL INTRODUCTION

The concept of alienation has been of central significance in the social sciences and has been evoked frequently to explain individual and collective reactions to a vast array of social problems. When applied to individual behavior, alienation frequently is viewed as a perceived disjuncture between expectations with regard to a role or an activity and actual experience within that role or activity. Although not inherently functionalist in nature, because alienation theory can point to contradictions in the social structure, the most widely proposed functionalist model of disjuncture has been termed *strain theory,* and is best represented by the work of Robert Merton (1968).

The Genesis of Strain

In Merton's conceptualization, structural strain issues from a gap between culturally prescribed goals and structurally or institutionally available means to attaining such goals. The gap is perceptual and real. That is, cultural goals are universals and are inculcated in the socialization of societal members. However, access to the necessary means for attaining the goals is not universal; it is stratified, or differentially allocated across the social structure. In fact, the concept of stratification implies both the scarcity of means and resources for attaining such means and an invidious evaluation of those who are found lacking in both means and resources. Individually, the personal experience of such disjuncture is manifested in a range of emotions from rage to despair. Behavioral reactions range from routinized behavior to deviance. The image of the worker who mindlessly plods along doing his or her work represents one extreme, while norm-violating behavior, and even crime, represents the other.

However, linking these reactions to their cause has been difficult. Just as educational researchers could not initially identify the links between cultural difference and educational disadvantage, sociologists have struggled to articulate a series of translation mechanisms in their conceptualization of strain and alienation theory. One problem is the manner in which values and acceptable means are specified and understood. Another difficulty involves the specification of the process by which individuals come to recognize that there are disjunctures between goals and means. A third hindrance is that the investigator must identify elements that lead individuals to conclude that the source of strain is within the social order or within personal failure—that is, the mechanism that leads to system blame or self-blame.

Recently, Farnworth and Leiber (1989) have offered a new operationalization of strain theory in their study of the factors that account for juvenile delinquency (and presumably other forms of juvenile deviance, including, perhaps, even dropout behavior). These authors note that Merton's original conceptualization assumed that cultural goals were universally held and that access to the means of achieving those goals was differentially allocated within the social structure. A wide array of social scientists have raised serious questions about the universality of goals, although Farnworth and Leiber cogently observe that pecuniary goals are probably widely held. Those who have tested the Mertonian model on school-aged youth and found it lacking have tended to operationalize the disjuncture between goals and means in terms of educational aspirations and expectations, because young people—especially lower-income youth—often have only vague career aspirations and little idea of the education necessary to attain the jobs they desire (Coleman et al., 1966; Moreno & Dworkin, 1988, 1989). Strain theory based upon educational goals and attainments would have predicted higher rates of delinquency among youth whose educational goals have outstripped their ability to attain such educational goals. However, Hirschi (1969) and Liska (1981) have each observed not only that delinquents often have educational goals commensurate with their educational attainment, but that those young people whose goals for education are higher than their actual attainment are no more likely to be delinquent than young people with nondisjunctive goals and attainments. Alternatively, it is possible that deviance can be found among those youth whose educational attainments and educational aspirations are equal if the individuals do not value education, if they believe that education is irrelevant as a route to attaining valued goals, or if the content of educational training is not career directed.

In their analysis, Farnworth and Leiber (1989) argue that an appropriate test of strain theory should be the link between a desired goal (such as upward mobility, money, the good life, steady employment, satisfying work) and the means to such a goal (such as access to college or the acquisition of skills in school that can produce a good-paying job). That is, they argue against previous researchers who have looked at the perceived gap between educational aspirations and educational expectations as the true source of alienation. They do so because the earlier approach ignores goals and aspirations and assumes that individuals can specify the intervening conceptual linkages between schooling and careers—for example, that students would observe that doing well in school enables them to acquire requisite cognitive, communicative, and quantitative skills that they will be able to use in the future to be successful in some unspecified activity, rather than saying that doing well in school gets them a good job. While education may actually function that way, few students use such a view in their preparations for the future.

The match between goals and means to goals that is used to describe student behavior is equally viable in describing teacher actions. Teachers enter a career in teaching for many reasons, including that it is a relatively secure, paying job, it provides a sense of fulfillment, it permits one to work with children, it allows one to continue in school, it may provide one an opportunity to become occupationally upwardly mobile relative to one's parents, and so on (see Lortie, 1975, for an itemization of other motives to enter teaching). While teaching might also prepare a person for parenthood—or convince him or her that parenthood is an inappropriate choice—it is not useful to evoke such a means/access to means model to explain why teachers quit their jobs. Likewise, considering that teacher entrapment is prevalent because teachers have few salable skills to permit them to enter other career lines without retraining (see Chapter 6), teaching ought not be considered a route to other goals. The means-ends schema permits the exploration of the extent to which the organization of schooling facilitates or impedes the attainment of any of the stated goals of teachers.

Reference Groups

How is the awareness of disjunctures between goals and means communicated to individuals? For an answer we need to turn to reference group theory to inform models of social strain. Reference group theory also suggests that a significant linkage exists between the social constructions and definitions that emerge from student-teacher interactions and the likelihood that students and teachers will fail or succeed in school.

Reference groups are made up of individuals or groups of individuals that a person knows, or knows about, who serve as role models, frames of reference, and standards of judgment and comparison in the formation of attitudes, images (including self-images), and decisions to act. Reference groups can even be models of inappropriate action (Francis, 1963, calls these "anti-models"). Three functions of reference groups have been isolated (see Hyman, 1942; Kelley, 1952; Merton & Kitt, 1950; Shibutani, 1955; Stouffer, Suchman, Devinney, Star, & Williams, 1949). Reference groups serve a *comparative function,* in which individuals compare their situations with those of referent others and decide whether they are better or worse off. Alternatively, reference groups can serve a *normative function,* in which reference group members reward or punish individuals to maintain conforming behavior. Finally, they perform a *gatekeeping function,* whereby access to new roles and statuses is controlled by the reference group. The concept of reference groups is useful in accounting for the three transmission mechanism problems of strain theory. Reference groups help to provide mechanisms that communicate goals and access to goals, mechanisms that communicate disjuncture, and mechanisms that attribute blame to the individual or deflect such blame to the social structure.

The three kinds of reference group functions produce distinctive perceptions about one's social world. Comparative reference groups permit individuals to determine whether or not they are advantaged or deprived relative to other individuals. That is, when individuals compare their experiences and positions with others and discover that others are relatively advantaged, they become more aware of personal deprivation and may feel anger and frustration. Different comparative reference groups will produce different perceptions. For example, when minority or low-income students compare their school experiences with majority and middle-income students, and discover that they have had more pejorative treatment by teachers, lower grades, and less rewarding school experiences, they come to ask whether school is really just for majority or more affluent students, not for them. By contrast, comparisons with like-status individuals may produce a perception that everyone gets treated the same way in school.

The perception of relative deprivation and the anger that follows can be focused or enhanced by normative and gatekeeping reference groups. These groups define appropriate expectations for individuals of different statuses. In a sense, they enforce sumptuary norms—norms about appropriate behaviors, aspirations, expectations, and styles associated with different social classes or other hierarchical social groupings. Reliance upon dominant groups and higher socioeconomic status groups for explanations of relative deprivation may lead one to conclude that the advantaged are simply smarter or that they work harder. Interaction with other disadvantaged individuals may lead one to assume that the system gives preferential treatment to people who enter school from privileged backgrounds. In essence, normative and comparative reference groups help one to create self-blame or system-blame explanations for school failure. Teachers tend to blame students' disadvantaged positions on the students' own shortcomings. Self-blame permits teachers to say, "If at first you don't succeed, try, try again," or to criticize students for failure with statements such as "When *I* was in school, I worked hard." Ginsberg and Newman (1985) report that a majority of all new teachers they interviewed believed that children fail because they are lazy, not because they are disadvantaged relative to others. Of course, a few decades ago, before they learned that it was not fashionable, teachers blamed the poorer performance of disadvantaged and minority children on their biologically inferior genetic backgrounds. Others used the cultures of minority group children to explain their poor performance. Dworkin (1968) interviewed several teachers in Los Angeles who reported that if they punished Mexican-American children whenever they spoke Spanish, they would be able to free them from their culture and the children would then succeed in school.

Teachers clearly can serve as a significant reference group, although their impact may not be as great as that of parents and peers. However, the content of teacher messages to children varies in part with their expectations for their students, as we saw in our discussion of the studies by Rosenthal and Jacobson (1968) and Rist (1970, 1973).

Before finishing our discussion of reference groups, we would like to address a final element of strain theory: its emphasis on contextual variables, particularly as they affect the influence of reference groups. Similar messages from reference groups may have different effects in different settings; likewise, different messages may have similar effects in different settings. Thus messages from parents, teachers, or peers about hard work in school will be effective or ineffective depending upon how well integrated and articulated the school, home, and community are.

The work of Coleman and his associates over the past decade represents a case in point. Using national data sets from the National Center for Educational Statistics's (1982, 1985) ongoing High School and Beyond study, initiated in 1980 (from which the best assessments of attitudes of dropouts have been enumerated), Coleman and his associates have attempted to understand why achievement is higher and the dropout rate is halved in parochial and other private schools compared with public schools (Coleman & Hoffer, 1987; Coleman et al., 1982). After controlling for numerous structural variables that permitted them to discount obvious explanations, the Coleman team found two categories of variables that explained the differences: those referring to activities within the school and those referring to relationships between the school and the community. First, compared with public school students, private and Catholic school students took more honors-level course work, were assigned and completed more hours of homework per week, were absent less from school, were more supportive of discipline in school and more often thought that the teachers were fair and interested in them, and were more supportive of norms against absenteeism, cutting of classes, student. fighting, and students threatening teachers.

The second category of variables that Coleman and his associates found were those that denoted social context differences between private and public schools. Summoning up alienation theory and the traditions of Durkheim (1933) and Weber (1947) with reference to solidarity and social integration, the investigators hold that what really makes Catholic and private schools more effective is that they exist in a "functional community" of often primary group relationships. Parents know their children's friends and teachers as whole individuals, not as incumbents in restricted roles; teachers know the children and their parents in the same fashion; and the children know their own parents' friends. Such a social network makes for a sense of solidarity and functional interdependence, often unified by a common religious ideology. As a consequence, teachers and parents serve as mutually supportive agents of socialization. When schoolwork is assigned, parents ensure that it is completed, even if they are unable to assist in the completion of the assignments. The messages are the same from each reference group, but, more important, because the groups are embedded in a common social context, the student is likely to interpret the meanings of the messages in the same way, whether delivered by teachers, parents, or even classmates. That is the central contextual element that links reference group effects with strain theory. Reference groups effectively communicate messages of self- and system blame, and in so doing they provide the necessary transmission mechanisms to make strain theory heuristic.

ALIENATION AND GIVING UP ON SCHOOL

It is our contention that alienation theory can provide us with an understanding of the forces that compel students and teachers to abandon schools, either by becoming student dropouts and faculty who quit teaching or by becoming in-school student dropouts and burned-out teachers. Central to the concept of alienation is a sense of a gap between expectations and experiences, or between potentials and objective realities for individuals and groups. However, scholars debate the experiential or social psychological aspects of alienation. Are deprived individuals aware of their deprivation, or are there powerful structural and societal mechanisms that blur the awareness? These divergent views can be posed in the question raised by the French scholar Touraine (1971): Is alienation "a sensation of deprivation or a deprivation of sensation"? (p. 75).

Like Seeman (1959, 1967, 1975), we assume that individuals are at least minimally aware of the gap between expectations and experiences. We further hold that reference groups or other actors who shape attitudes are often required to convert felt dissatisfactions of teachers and students into awareness of the sources of strain that produce gaps between expectations and experiences. Seeman has reviewed the classic statements on alienation from several theorists, extracting defining elements from each. He concludes that alienation reflects feelings of powerlessness, meaninglessness, normlessness, isolation, self-estrangement, and cultural estrangement.

Views of Alienation

Alienation as *powerlessness* comes from Marx's belief that entrepreneurs, who neither labor nor create value, expropriate from workers the means and products of production and the right of decision making over the process of production. For Marx, loss of control over one's labor, loss of autonomy, and being denied ownership of both one's work and the product of one's labor signify the essence of alienation.

Alienation as a sense of *meaninglessness* comes from Mannheim's conceptualization of the domination of "functional rationality" over "substantial rationality." Mass society (Selznick, 1951; Shils, 1963) and bureaucratization of society result in the creation of systems of organizational efficiency in which individuals have decreasing access to information upon which to base their actions. Consequently, "the individual is unclear as to what he ought to believe—when the individual's minimal standards for clarity in decision-making are unmet" (Seeman, 1959, p. 786). Individuals are uncertain of both goals and the appropriateness of action (means) to achieving such goals. As such, individual actions, while potentially meaningful to societal elites who are aware of larger purposes of action, appear to be random to the individuals engaging in them.

Alienation as *normlessness* derives from the condition Durkheim defines as *anomie* and the variant developed by Merton. Under conditions of normlessness rules are either inoperative, such that following rules will not achieve the goals to which one aspires, or nonexistent, such that the individual can turn to no rule to guide action. For Durkheim, anomie occurs under conditions of rapid social and political change, in which the societal norms that adequately regulated expectations and appropriate actions collapse. For Merton, anomie occurs when there is a disjuncture between societally prescribed goals and structurally available means, such that individuals are unable to attain desired goals through legal or acceptable means. A series of adaptations occurs, ranging from the acceptance of goals and rejection of means to goals (deviance, or innovation) to rejection of both goals and means (retreatism) and all combinations of means-goals options in between.

Nettler (1957) and Dean (1961) conceptualize alienation as *isolation*. They portray the alienated individual as one who is alone and who rejects the actions and beliefs valued by society. The individual is a stranger, unconnected and apart from his or her society. Camus's image in *The Stranger* (1946) is definitive; the protagonist, Marceau, comes to see himself apart from his society and even his own existence. In Marceau's case, the sense of isolation was intertwined with an equally strong sense of the meaninglessness of human society.

Seeman's fifth form of alienation, *self-estrangement*, is defined by Fromm's *The Sane Society* (1955). In this form of alienation individuals are, by the nature of their work or their social roles, forced to act and present themselves in ways that are foreign to them—as objects or instruments of themselves. They come to see their actions and role performances as distinct from their believed nature. Being forced to do things that are alien to one's being, to behave as if one were a different person, one with whom one is uncomfortable, defines this form of alienation. It is as if the roles one plays force one not to be oneself. The current popularity of books on self-awareness and self-discovery reflects a growing conviction that complex, bureaucratized social life estranges us from our "real" selves.

Several years after his initial conceptualization, Seeman (1975) offered a sixth form of alienation, *cultural estrangement,* in which the individual is forced to separate him- or herself from the central values of his or her group or society. In some instances cultural estrangement refers to a sense of rejection of the values of the core culture. The emergence of the counterculture in the 1960s exemplifies some aspects of this form of alienation.

Blauner (1964), Mottaz (1981), and others have shown that powerlessness and meaninglessness statistically provide the most powerful explanation for negative work attitudes. Seeman (1975) has maintained that self-estrangement is the most often studied dimension of alienation. Mottaz (1981) constructed and found support for a minitheory that effectively links these three dimensions. He holds that technology, bureaucratization, and its incumbent organizational structure and task fragmentation separate workers from control over their work and diminish their sense of their contribution to its final product. Alienation theory tends to view human labor as a significant source of personal fulfillment for people. Deprived of evidence that they produce anything, and lacking control over that product, workers fail to see their place in the larger scheme of production. Their work cannot be fulfilling if they cannot control, own, or even identify within a larger context what they produce. Since work time represents a major component of workers' daily activities, it is easy to see how workers come to feel that what they do is unrelated to their own image of themselves and their intrinsic worth. Work becomes a time when the individual suspends awareness and becomes an automaton. Only after work hours can one return to human existence—too exhausted to enjoy it. Blauner (1964) and Kanter (1977) hold that when work becomes meaningless and self-estranging, workers seek only pecuniary and social relational rewards at work rather than the rewards associated with a job well done.

The above-mentioned view of work best fits the mindless tasks of the assembly-line worker; however, bureaucratization, the fragmentation of work, diminished control, and lack of autonomy are pervasive in most workplaces in complex societies—even in those where "educational work" is done. Teachers rarely are able to exercise control over curricula, student bodies, or school policies; huge classes in huge educational "factories" prevent them from knowing many of their students. Teachers thereby cannot identify the products of their labor. Further, the confinement of teachers to their classrooms isolates them from one another (Jackson, 1968; Lortie, 1975). And low salaries provide teachers with little compensation for their lack of fulfillment.

Students, too, have little control over their academic lives. Their course work is prescribed and their input on its content is not welcome. Many students see little reason for their courses or assignments, and cannot envision how schooling will help them achieve their goals. Further, large schools mean that students are relative strangers to most teachers and other members of the student body. Thus contemporary schooling can be dehumanizing for both students and their teachers.

In Chapters 4 and 5, we described the sense of alienation that characterizes many American students and their teachers. In the next few paragraphs we shall summarize how the elements of alienation that students and teachers feel fit within the context of Seeman's categories.

Teachers and students believe that they lack sufficient power to change conditions in school so as to give them a sense of efficacy and control over their lives. Because of their sense of powerlessness, both believe that what they are doing is meaningless. Students cannot understand what schooling will do for them, and in some instances they recognize that their educational training is not convertible into any desired outcome or attainment. Teachers feel that their activities in school have no real purpose and that what they attempt to teach is falling on deaf ears. Teachers also believe that many tasks associated with the teaching role are inane, including serving as parent substitutes, paper pushers, and monitors of reform-mandated accountability schemes. In some instances, students can see no connection between what they are asked to learn and the skills needed for jobs, goals, and resources they wish to attain. In other instances, it is clear to students that even people who graduate from school are relegated to jobs that they hate. As observers of social reality, they conclude that schooling has little or no association with desirable goals. In fact, for many children in inner-city schools, the only successful and satisfied people they do see are those in deviant careers that require "street smarts," not success in school.

Both teachers and students believe that many campus and district rules, as well as rules legislated by state governments, are unrelated to the actual tasks of teaching and learning. While there might be overregulation in many areas of education, teachers and students also believe that there are no clear norms regulating the most important aspects of schooling. This creates a condition of normlessness. For example, there seems to be no formula that explains how going to school can be converted into desired learning goals or career goals. Students maintain that counselors cannot tell them how to get into college or whether their course work will lead to certain jobs. Teachers contend that there is little information available on how testing is related to achievement. Finally, teachers and students complain that excessive bureaucratization of education, with its accompanying multiple layers of authority, leads to role conflict. This common complaint is one of the significant factors contributing to teachers' sense of burnout (Schwab & Iwanicki, 1982).

The history of American education has been one of consolidation of school districts and dramatic increases in the size of student bodies. Between 1930 and 1990, during which time the population grew substantially, the number of public school systems in America decreased from more than 130,000 to approximately 15,000 (see Ornstein & Levine, 1981, p. 390). Urban areas produced campuses with enrollments as high as 2,000-3,000 in elementary schools and 5,000 in high schools (LeCompte & Dworkin, 1988). The result is that teachers no longer can be expected to know their students and students often know only a small percentage of their classmates. All of the conditions that typify the alienating mass society are present. Individuals feel alone and detached from groups that traditionally provided nurturance, meaning, predictability, and identity for individuals. For many students, not only the school but also the family and other societal institutions have ceased to provide an anchoring point. Students feel that teachers are uninterested in their welfare, and are only interested in drawing their paychecks. Teachers believe that administrators, other teachers, parents, and especially students lack concern about both student learning and the demands placed upon teachers. National surveys suggest that the public *is* concerned about the schools, but unwilling to trust teachers.

A sense of cultural estrangement also afflicts actors in school. Students often reject the dominant values prescribed by their teachers and schools. They complain that schools expect them to conform to alien expectations. Teachers bemoan the fact that they have to fake being enthusiastic and concerned about teaching in ways they disapprove in order to satisfy evaluators (LeCompte & Dworkin, 1988). All are forced into an unreal presentation of self for the benefit of the bureaucracy.

THE GAP BETWEEN EXPECTATIONS AND EXPERIENCES

As we have noted, alienation reflects a gap, disjuncture, or contradiction between what is expected and what teachers and students believe actually occurs. In education, powerlessness is increased by the gap or disjuncture between the decision-making power needed to facilitate teaching and learning and the ability to exercise such power to implement decision making. Educational bureaucratization and educational reform have created a chasm separating policy formation from policy implementation, such that frontline participants (students and teachers) are disempowered. Teachers often observe that they have little or no control over the methods of teaching they can use or the content of the material they must teach (Duke, 1984; Dworkin, 1987). Curricula, textbook selection, course content, and even style of presentation increasingly have become the province of district school boards and state boards of education, leaving teachers and students with little or no say in these matters.

Meaninglessness results from a gap between the activities of schooling and what these activities are intended to produce. Teachers and students do not know why they do what they do, except that it is mandated by the state, the district, or the principal. Nobody can specify which long-term goals the activities are directed toward. Teachers teach to standardized tests and students learn the material on them not because high performance on the tests will lead to success in later life, but because test scores are an end unto themselves, demanded by voters who support or attack school bonds and school boards on the basis of aggregate performance on standardized tests (Dworkin, 1987).

Normlessness is created by the gap between rules and the understanding of their function. Students and teachers often believe that rules are created capriciously; they cannot explain why things are done. Often rules appear to exist only to ensure that students and teachers recognize their lack of influence—to keep students and teachers in their place (see Dworkin, 1990b).

Isolation and estrangement also are consequences of gaps. Massive schools prevent even campus elites from having much impact on daily events in school (Olson, 1963). Yet, lack of elite domination does not produce democratization or the transfer of influence to nonelites. To the extent that school is an unrewarding activity for both teachers and students, both engage in a kind of clock-watching. The school is a mindless factory in which students enter, age like cheese, and leave. Time in school becomes a period to suspend reality and one's sense of a real self—like alienated assembly-line workers or entrapped clerical workers (Blauner, 1964; Dworkin, Chafetz,

& Dworkin, 1986; Kanter, 1977). Students really begin their day when school ends and they can pursue jobs or social activities that connect them to material and nonmaterial goals, including interpersonal relations. Teachers also begin their day when school ends and family life begins or when they can attend postgraduate courses that will help them escape the classroom, either as school administrators or in new careers away from public education.

What Are the Essential Elements in the Gap? The Case for Students

Earlier we summarized the Farnworth and Leiber (1989) approach to strain theory. This argues that the individual's sense of alienation is a function of how large the discrepancy between personal goals and the likelihood that such goals will be attained is believed to be. Students attend school for many reasons, ranging from career aspirations to parental pressure. For example, if one were to enter a high school or junior high school counselor's office, one of the first things one would see would be posters that promise careers in business or in the military, or announcements about college opportunities. When teachers speak to students about the future, they speak of careers and colleges. Public schools promise lifelong opportunities to students who do well; they often point to the career outcomes of their successes. Neither the "advertising" nor the schools' very frequent failure to deliver on access to college or good jobs is lost on the students.

Nevertheless, a further gap is created by the excessive caseloads of inner-city school counselors. Overwork makes counseling inadequate and creates the perception that both counselors and teachers are inattentive to the needs of students. This situation emphasizes a distinction between what schools *expect* students to know and do and what the students are *willing* to do and *believe is necessary* to achieve career goals. All too often, inner-city youth underestimate the levels of education needed for professional occupations. They know few professionals other than their teachers and counselors, who are too busy to provide them with the needed information.

Dworkin and Caram (1987) asked a sample of 235 inner-city minority junior and senior high school students how much education they needed to reach their career goals. The answers suggested that these students saw only a weak link between schooling and careers, or, at least, that their counselors and teachers had not discussed careers with them. More than 20% believed that to become a doctor or lawyer one needed only to finish high school. About 4% believed that finishing high school was not required in order to become a professional. Another 7% thought that a college education was needed to become a hairdresser or cosmetologist. The level of ignorance about career education, which rivals that found by Coleman et al. (1966) a generation earlier, suggests that inner-city teachers and counselors continue to fail in addressing important issues of career education in their schools (see Fine, 1987; Firestone & Rosenblum, 1988). The next year, Moreno and Dworkin (1988) queried a sample of 502 students from the same backgrounds as the previous sample about their career plans and the amount of education needed to attain them. While three-quarters of the students had career goals, 68.7% of the sample were either unable to answer the question about the level of education needed or sufficiently vague in their answers to suggest that they were uncertain about the connection between level of schooling and career choice.

The Vocabulary of Dropping Out

Exploring a previous analysis of the National Longitudinal Survey of Labor Market Experience Youth Cohort (1979-1982 data base), Mann (1987) observed that 51% of the males and 33% of the females who dropped out of school gave school-related reasons for dropping out. Students cited bad grades and uncaring teachers, and said that they did not like school (pp. 4-5). In Chapter 4, we cited studies that clarified what "disliking school" means. Rumberger (1983), Deyhle (1989), Hess et al. (1987), Holley and Doss (1983), Fine (1987), Fine and Zane (1989), McLeod (1987), Powell et al. (1985), Valverde (1987), and Williams (1987) all report that students find school boring, that they can see no valued outcome from their school experience. That is, school *is* meaningless and they are powerless to effect changes that would make it more meaningful. Schoolwork, especially the remedial work that is often assigned to "at-risk" students, is boring and appears to have no connection with those aspects of life that both students want and schools claim to help to deliver: careers, jobs, money, self-confidence, respect, freedom, and so on.

Part of the reason schools lack meaning for students is that their curricula are out of step with the labor market, as we noted in Chapter 2. Students do not receive the career counseling or training they need because overworked and burned-out faculty and staff cannot accommodate students with diverse backgrounds and destinations. Urban schools were originally designed to provide basic academic training to a large number of students who would be absorbed into a labor-intensive and growing manufacturing sector and a still-viable agricultural sector. Even students who failed in school could be absorbed into farm labor or blue-collar jobs. But, as we have indicated, the labor market no longer performs this function.

Vocational programs—often reserved for the disadvantaged—also are anachronistic in that they are usually stocked with technologically obsolete equipment more suitable for a labor force from the 1950s than for today's high-tech marketplace. Where the service and manufacturing sectors increasingly will need skilled labor who can handle "smart machines" (Zuboff, 1988), the schools' response is to continue training students in outmoded technologies. Science is almost absent from elementary school instruction; labs in most urban and rural high schools use techniques and equipment more appropriate to the early 20th century than the beginning of the 21st.

CREATING A SENSE OF ALIENATION IN TEACHERS AND STUDENTS

As discussed in Chapter 1, the conditions that made schools "work" in the 1950s are generally absent today, especially in urban areas. Information about rates of child abuse and abandonment, unemployment of adults, teenage pregnancy, delinquency, and the often-publicized failure of American industry and schools is not lost on students. While students have not necessarily read the works of Easterlin (1987), Bluestone and Harrison (1987), Toffler (1970, 1981), and others, they are aware of two things: First, theirs is a generation not likely to outdo their parents in acquisition of wealth; second, many of the adult role models around them are either unhappy in their work or have found apparently lucrative work outside of legitimate employment—the kind of employment that the schools claim to prepare them to enter.

For many children teachers are presented as possible role models, demonstrating the payoff for hard work in school. However, those same teachers are burned out, underpaid, dissatisfied, either hostile to or uninterested in their students, in debt, and scapegoated by the larger society, the press, the business community, elected officials, and all who seek explanations for why student do not learn.

What Are the Essential Elements in the Gap? The Case for Teachers

Throughout Chapter 5 we described elements of the gap between expectations and aspirations for teachers. There are two aspects to this gap: One is the discrepancy between expectations engendered during preservice training in colleges of education and actual experiences in classroom settings; the other is the discrepancy between the degree of autonomy expected as a professional and the actual amount of autonomy granted to teachers as semiprofessionals.

Idealism is a frequent factor in recruitment of individuals into professions (see especially H. S. Becker, 1960; Dworkin, 1982; Stevens et al., 1978). For many individuals the decision to choose education as a career derives from a sense of "calling." People are attracted to teaching because they like to work with young people, because they are perceived as providing a "special and important service" (Lortie, 1975, pp. 26-33).

In the survey of Houston urban and suburban teachers discussed in Chapter 5, early idealism affected the decision to enter teaching. Nearly 65% of the respondents indicated that they first decided to be teachers when they were students in public schools. More than 40% had wanted to be teachers since their preteen years. They spoke of wanting to make a difference in the lives of children and to work with people. Some even reported specifically feeling that because of their special talent with children, they felt a calling to become teachers.

The content of training in colleges of education fosters this idealism in teacher recruits. Education students are provided with two tools that are intended to serve them in their chosen careers: ideological tools, which define as essential the shaping and molding of young minds, and methodological tools, or pedagogy, to accomplish the task. The ideology holds that teaching is a special profession; the teacher's task is to shape the beliefs, attitudes, and knowledge base of the next generation. Further, teaching is defined as valuable and valued for education students, who generally function in an environment where parents, children, and the community share those values. Some of our graduate students have reported to us that the preservice and practice teachers they have supervised begin teaching with the belief that their pupils are eager to learn, grateful for the opportunity to be liberated from poverty through education, and love their teachers because their teachers love them. In fact, familiar with a modicum of psychological theory, many preservice teachers believe that resistance to education and offers of help by teachers signifies that children are actually calling out for help and love. Thus, armed with enthusiasm, the preservice teacher may interpret every student act—even active revolt—as a reinforcement of his or her own ideology (see Kozol, 1967; McLaren, 1980).

However, contradictions between the training of teachers in colleges of education and the conditions encountered in public schools severely attenuate the idealism of teachers. As noted in Chapter 5, a vast array of social pathologies in urban schools reduce the autonomy and sense of control of teachers. A few of the more salient ones include high student-teacher ratios; children who come to school distracted, unenthusiastic, ill prepared, and sometimes ill fed and ill clothed; and district bureaucracies and state legislative mandates that permeate even the micromanagement of classrooms, requiring teachers to document the effects of educational policies and reforms with excessive amounts of paperwork. Further, policies that preselect textbooks and determine course content and even the style of instructional delivery likewise remove control from teachers. Teachers are rarely told much in advance that field trips, in-service programs, or other interruptions to the teaching routine are to occur (Duke, 1984). Under desegregation mandates, teachers also have no control over which schools they are assigned to or when they may be assigned to another one.

There is a disjuncture between the new methodologies created and taught at colleges of education and those permitted by school boards, district administrators, and principals, most of whom are committed to tried-and-true—and often outmoded—techniques (Cherniss et al., 1976). Because teachers must interact with a multitude of students, parents, colleagues, and administrators, each of whom has different problems and makes different demands, teachers have to make quick, personalistic responses to individuals with unpredictable problems. However, because many of their interactions have implications for school policy, teachers are rarely permitted to make the "command decisions" that circumstances require. Rather, permission and counsel must be sought and decisions must work their way down the hierarchy. Meanwhile, the teacher is blamed by the client (student or parent) for being uncaring, inept, or unwilling to make decisions. The movement toward greater student and teacher accountability has compounded the problem by escalating the number of forms and reports a teacher needs to complete, and hence the number of superiors and offices to which the teacher is held accountable. This concatenation of work load has not been accompanied by an increase in the amount of time teachers have to complete the paperwork. Thus one source of alienation for teachers is the realization that the ideology and methodology they received in colleges of education have little utility in most large urban school districts.

A second alienating gap is that between the expectation of respect and autonomy that is thought to accompany professional status and the lack of respect and autonomy that characterizes the status of most urban teachers. Critical theorists, including Apple (1979, 1986), Bartholomew (1976), and Ginsburg (1988), have argued that the central problem teachers face is that their occupation has been subjected to systematic deskilling. Over the years, autonomy, decision making, and even control over what constitutes pedagogical knowledge have been taken from teachers by elites who fear either the incompetence of teachers or that teachers will impart to children of nonelites the necessary information, knowledge, and skills to make them effective competitors for scarce resources. While such a conspiratorial view of elite motivations may be questioned, it is nonetheless true that a perceptual gap exists between the amount of professional autonomy preservice teachers expect to have when they begin teaching and the actual level of autonomy they do have once they begin their teaching careers.

Some of the deskilling of the teaching profession is a consequence of a "behavioristic revolution" in curriculum and pedagogy at colleges of education. What is taught to aspiring teachers has been fragmented, modularized, and compartmentalized into measurable skills and behavioral objectives. It so completely separates learning from practice that education students are often unable to generalize what they have been taught from setting to setting (Ginsburg, 1988). Many teachers complain that their training in colleges of education prepared them for teaching situations that do not exist (LeCompte & Ginsburg, 1987).

It has been our perception that deskilling often promotes categorical logic, in which individuals, including education students and practicing teachers, tenaciously hold on to slogans without critically evaluating their relevance or implications. During the heyday of the competency-based teacher education movement in the 1970s, one of the authors served as a consultant to a staff-development office of a large urban school district. Experienced teachers were assigned to new faculty as mentors to reduce the turnover rate among new teachers. The senior teachers and the new teachers were given modularized instruction on multiculturalism. The modules warned the teachers against racism and sexism in instruction and reading assignments. Armed with a new resolve to purge education of bias, they concluded that all literature that had implicit or explicit bias should not be taught. English teachers in the program decided to drop Chaucer because of sexism and Mark Twain because of racism; they supplanted these writings with banal and inoffensive readings they themselves developed, thereby contributing to the cultural illiteracy of the student body.

Another consequence of the deskilling of teachers has been the self-fulfilling prophecy it has imposed upon recruitment. We assume that teachers are inept and that only the least able will become teachers. Next, we pay teachers poorly, give them little control over their subject-matter content and the operations of their schools, and do not encourage principals to consider them as colleagues. Finally, we are surprised that the best and the brightest elect not to become teachers! Recently, Frymier (1987) bemoaned the fact that bureaucratization and distrust have made for the "neutering of teachers." What is needed are "reskilling" strategies that will return professional status to teachers (Bennett & LeCompte, 1990; Ginsburg, 1988).

Why should teachers be deprived of their autonomy? Public education is very big business. It often represents the largest segment of a state's budget, and in some states involves billions of dollars. Schools receive the lion's share of local property tax dollars. Nevertheless, as we saw in Chapters 1 and 5, the public has lost considerable confidence in the ability of schools to deliver on their promises. It has become unlikely, then, that the public and their elected and appointed officials will grant teachers, whom they view as representative of a failed educational system, the level of autonomy they have come to expect as professionals or semiprofessionals. Even recent calls for more localized control of schools, at the level of the district rather than at the level of the state, have been met with resistance. Recently, the Houston Independent School District's Task Force on Restructuring (1990) released a "declaration of beliefs and visions" that calls for substantial decentralization and the placement of decision making at a level as close to the students and teachers as possible. The state board of education responded by noting that such decentralization would result in myriad school policies and the absence of any control—which surely would trigger a panoply of countervailing state and federal regulations.

Autonomy and self-regulation are interdependent and crucial for the status of an occupation. Occupational groups that do not support and press for self-regulation, with emphasis upon collegial control in defining roles and the parameters of work, are likely to be subject to regular intervention by outsiders who define standards for appropriate conduct in the execution of their work. Such intervention also questions the right of the practitioner to make judgments on the job. Thus an occupational group that does not self-regulate, especially if it utilizes considerable public funds, will be regulated externally. Such external regulation will often involve the micromanagement—excessive intrusion by school administrators into the routines of teachers—of the daily work activities of individual practitioners, which further attenuates autonomy.

The relative absence of autonomy among public school teachers is not unique to their occupation, however. Etzioni (1969) and Sarason (1977) note that increased bureaucratization and economic pressures have caused many professionals to lose some degree of autonomy, thereby creating a gap between the level of autonomy expected by neophyte professionals and what is actually present. Even as distinguished and respected a profession as medicine has experienced a considerable diminution in professional autonomy over the last 20 years. For example, combined pressure from hospitals—to regulate the flow of patients and utilization of bed space and expensive equipment—and from insurance companies—to reduce the expense of medical payments to their policyholders—have led to the creation of "diagnostically related groups" (DRGs). Control over the length of hospital stay and extensiveness of treatment is driven by formulae generated actuarially, rather than by an individual physician's decision. Thus, while teachers are not alone in their sense of diminished autonomy, their level of autonomy was lower to begin with. The extent to which they now can control their work is even less than in many other professions and semiprofessions.

Changing Demographics

Apple (1989) is accurate in associating low teacher autonomy with the fact that teaching is predominantly a female occupation. The relatively lower status of women in the United States (see Chafetz, 1984) and the even lower status of the minorities who make up an increasing percentage of the teaching populations and student bodies in urban schools (see Dworkin, 1987; Dworkin & Dworkin, 1982; Hodgkinson, 1985) help to ensure the lack of autonomy accorded teachers.

Another demographic factor that has accelerated the change in teacher status since the 1950s and ensures the diminished autonomy of educational practitioners is the increasing level of education in the general population. In the late 1940s and early 1950s, when many of today's more experienced teachers were in elementary school, only a little more than one-half of all students graduated from high school (National Education Association, 1967). In fact, in 1940, only 24.1% of the adult population 25 years and over were high school graduates, and by 1950, the proportion of high school graduates 25 years of age and over was only 41.1% (U.S. Bureau of the Census, 1964, p. 113). Only 10% of the adult population 25 years and older had attended

Table 7.1 High School Graduation and College Attendance Rates for All Adults, 25 Years and Older, by Race: 1940-1985

	Total Population	*White*	*Black*	*Hispanic*
1940				
high school graduate	24.1	25.8	7.6[a]	N/A
one or more years college	10.0	10.7	3.2[a]	N/A
1950				
high school graduate	33.4	35.4	13.2[a]	N/A
one or more years college	13.2	14.0	5.1[a]	N/A
1960				
high school graduate	41.1	43.2	20.1	N/A
one or more years college	16.5	17.4	7.2	N/A
1970				
high school graduate	52.4	54.6	31.5	32.1
one or more years college	21.3	22.4	10.3	11.0
1980				
high school graduate	66.5	68.8	51.2	44.0
one or more years college	31.9	33.1	21.9	19.6
1985				
high school graduate	73.9	75.5	59.8	47.9
one or more years college	35.7	36.5	25.9	19.5

SOURCE: U.S. Bureau of the Census (1964, Table 146, p. 113; 1986, Table 198, p. 121).
a. Until the 1960 census, blacks were placed in the category "Non-White" along with other racial groups.

as little as one year of college themselves, while about 24% had graduated from high school. As a consequence, most teachers were better educated than the parents of their students (U.S. Bureau of the Census, 1964, p. 113). However, by 1985, more than 35% of the adult population 25 and over had attended at least some college, and nearly 74% had graduated from high school (U.S. Bureau of the Census, 1985, p. 121).[1] Since the 1950s, the proportion of parents who have attended college has increased dramatically, from about 10% to more than 35% (U.S. Bureau of the Census, 1986). Parents now have a claim to much of the same expertise that teachers offer. (Table 7.1 presents the changing percentage of the population who completed high school and went on to college, displayed by race.)

Declining Autonomy

One aspect of professional autonomy depends upon the recognition that the professional practitioner has a special expertise, generally achieved through higher education. However, in many states undergraduate education majors often take no more than introductory-level academic courses outside the college of education. As a consequence, they may not be as well educated as their arts and sciences college counterparts—whose children they will someday teach. Teachers may have considerable difficulty in defending a claim to professional autonomy if they cannot show special expertise relative to parents or present themselves as better educated than the parents of many of their students, especially in suburban schools.

A valued expertise that creates a legitimate claim to autonomy also creates social power. That is, possession of special information and valued skills creates a legitimate claim to authority and gives one the right to impose one's will upon others. Teachers with this authority, for example, have more success in getting parents to ensure that their children behave in school or do their homework. However, when their expertise is in doubt or when they are no better educated (and perhaps less well educated) than others in the community, practitioners must rely upon persuasion and considerable expenditure of personal resources to gain compliance. Teachers must prove to a doubting public that their actions are correct and based upon substantial knowledge in order to obtain compliant behavior. When evidence is sufficient to indicate that the schools are failing and test scores and dropout rates are at undesirable levels, it becomes that much harder for teachers to persuade parents that their assessments, not to mention their expertise, are legitimate.

The socialization of professionals in graduate schools or of teachers in colleges of education is still based upon a model of autonomous professionals who rely upon self-regulation and subscription to a formalized code of ethics laid down by their professional organization. Preservice teachers are taught to expect that if they hold teaching credentials, they will be welcomed as valued professionals by students, parents, and administrators. However, in reality, bureaucratic accountability and the increasing magnitude of organizations means that rules and regulations take precedence over individual judgment. Teachers are not respected, and in some instances they are distrusted, especially if they are racially or culturally different from their students.

As we stated in Chapter 6, teaching tends not to attract the best and brightest recruits. Teacher candidates tend to be drawn from the lower scorers on standardized college entrance examinations. Further, teaching is often a default career among college students, even among its primarily female adherents. This adversely affects the recruitment of males and majority group members. The situation is worse in central-city schools, where low-income, minority-dominated student bodies adversely affect teacher recruitment and retention (see Haberman, 1989; National Institute of Education, 1976; Ogbu, 1974; Orfield, 1975).

All of these factors contribute to the low status of teachers, which, in turn, makes voters and legislators more reticent to pay teachers competitive salaries. However, the condition of teachers could be ameliorated if the elements of professional status were altered. In the next chapter we shall offer our suggestions for redressing the status problems of teachers.

THE PROCESS OF GIVING UP ON SCHOOL

In the previous section we suggested that the sense of alienation experienced by students and teachers comes from the recognition of a gap between what they have been led to expect from life in school and what schooling actually offers. In the final section of this chapter we shall describe a process model that attempts to explain student and teacher behaviors in terms of a sense of alienation. This process model represents our view of how teachers and students come to perceive that schools are the source of their dissatisfaction; they believe that leaving school will remove that dissatisfaction and redress some portion of their alienation. Our model describes how individuals decide that schooling is not worth the investment of time, effort, and resources.

Our model for giving up on school is based upon research on deviance and delinquency, although we do not maintain that those who quit school are necessarily deviants or delinquents. Nevertheless, giving up on school does violate common expectations and norms attached to student and teacher roles. Some years ago a concept called "drift" emerged in the deviance literature. According to this concept, individuals are not assumed to endorse norms that condone or are supportive of deviant behavior; rather, they simply do not endorse norms that are opposed to deviant behavior. Thus when circumstances make conventional conformity difficult, individuals tend to drift toward deviance. However, once they are engaged in such behavior and are labeled as deviants, alternative modes of action become less likely, and they continue to drift toward a deviant life-style (see Matza, 1964; Short & Strodtbeck, 1959; Sykes & Matza, 1957). A variant of the drift approach was proposed by Hirschi (1969), Briar and Piliavin (1965), and Glaser (1978), who held that deviance occurred when individuals are freed from social controls against deviance. In general, loosening of social constraints occurs because the individual is not emotionally attached to social support groups that stress nondeviance. In some instances, a sense of betrayal by that social network accompanies the drift.

For drift to occur, students and teachers must cease to be constrained by the social and normative bonds that prescribe conforming behavior. They must conclude that norms prescribing staying in school are inoperative and that sanctions against rule violations are less punishing than the costs of rule conformity. How does the normative hold that keeps students and teachers committed to schooling deteriorate? Functional and conflict theories both address the classic Hobbesian question of how order is possible. The former generally emphasizes socialization and the development of consensus; the latter stresses coercion and surveillance, although critical theorists do speak of hegemonic domination.

Effective normative control over the actions of individuals, when such actions are not backed by legal sanction, requires a belief on the part of the individuals that the norms are morally right, desirable, and appropriate (Durkheim, 1958). While it is true that even norms codified into law and backed by legal sanction must be seen as right, desirable, and appropriate in order to reduce deviance, such laws have the backing of the legitimate use of force by the state to secure behavioral compliance. However, assent to norms that regulate professional behavior or the adequate performance of individuals in arenas not strictly enforced by the state requires a greater degree of moral persuasion, which, in turn, is dependent upon the actors' belief that the prescriptions are correct. Here professional ethics and societal urgings to strive harder come into play. However, once the moral correctness of the normative prescriptions is questioned and individuals come to question whether conforming to rules is in their own best interest, acceptance of the norms becomes problematic. Individuals then can drift into more norm-defying behaviors. In schools, once teachers and students come to question the value of compliance with norms that prescribe dedication and hard work in school, they may engage in increasingly deviant behavior, ranging from failure to do assignments or prepare for classes to frequent absenteeism. Such behaviors have two consequences: (a) They evoke negative labeling on the part of others who remain committed to the norms, and (b) they permit the individual to redefine his or her role and self in terms of such deviations.

If we integrate the ideas of strain theory presented earlier with the concept of drift and the loosening of social constraints, we can generate a distinctive theory of giving up on school. The commitment to schooling is based upon the promise of schooling: economic rewards and occupational goal attainment. Public schools and colleges of education assure their students that what they learn in those institutions will assist them in securing future opportunities and future desired rewards. Students are told that schooling is a prerequisite of good jobs and a life-style equal to or surpassing that of their parents. Students also are told that schooling will make them better citizens, or full participants in their society. Preservice teachers are told that the skills and ideology they acquire in colleges of education will help to make them effective teachers; subsequently, they will be rewarded by knowing that they have made a difference in the lives of their students. As we have described in previous chapters, these "tellings" most frequently prove false or misleading.

For many minority students the situation is worse. They are subjected to a paradoxical double set of attitudes about schooling (Mickelson, 1990). They endorse an "abstract attitude" that schooling is a route toward upward mobility and a better life more often than do majority group individuals (Coleman et al., 1966; Cricklow, 1986; Mickelson, 1990; Ogbu, 1978; Patchen, 1982; Sleeter & Grant, 1987), but they also accept a "concrete attitude" that people like themselves are precluded from attaining such rewards through education. Endorsement of abstract attitudes leads one to speak in general of the benefits of education, but endorsement of concrete attitudes leads one to realize that such goals are probably unrealistic. For minorities, these concrete attitudes reflect perceptions of what Ogbu (1978) refers to as "job ceilings," or observable and experiential limits to attainments of members of one's own group (the structurally supplied means to goals). Many minority students value education and at the same time attain low grades, fail, are retained in grade, and drop out of school, all the time believing that success depends upon educational achievement. Even those who have left school may continue to accept the general promise of education, while believing that they, or their group, are precluded from such a realization—as evidenced by their own experiences of school failure and isolation.

Teachers likewise discover that they work with unenthusiastic students, unsupportive administrators, and unconcerned parents. They are underpaid and burdened by the paperwork mandated by educational reforms instituted by public and government cries for school accountability. Convinced that nobody cares and that regulations and an impersonal bureaucracy prevent them from doing their job, they become demoralized. They turn cold and impersonal toward their students (an essential symptom of burnout as conceptualized by Maslach, 1982), thereby reinforcing their students' belief that nobody cares. Their students fail to respect them or to do their assignments, and may even subject them to physical and verbal abuse from which they may not be protected by their administrators. Thus teachers and students mutually reinforce a belief that the promise of schooling is a lie. When they see people with less dedication and sometimes even less education finding better-paying and more fulfilling jobs than teaching, eventually they too give up on school.

As the rewards of schooling appear to evaporate for both students and teachers, the moral and normative justifications for commitment to schooling also evaporate. Like the individual freed from controls against deviance, students and teachers become unable to justify continuing in such a punishing setting.

Firestone and Rosenblum (1988) have noted the significance of social attachments to the building of commitment to schooling. Social attachments within an institution are one measure of commitment to the institution. Recently, Finn and Achilles (1989) observed that dropouts from school are less socially located in school than are nondropouts. They participate in fewer activities and have relatively fewer friends than do nondropouts; they identify with their schools less than do those who remain in school. Further, in Chapter 5 we noted that social support, especially by the principal, is a significant element in reducing burnout and increasing commitment to teaching among teachers. In short, social solidarity within school helps to mitigate withdrawal from school. Of course, one may argue in reverse: In anticipation of giving up on school, an individual may abandon a supportive social network.

A variant of the social network view might suggest that as schools fail to meet one's expectations, alternative networks and reference groups begin to define nonschool means to attaining desired goals. Such reference groups are always present, but their messages are rejected until (a) sufficient evidence exists that going to school has no payoff, and (b) pressure from the reference groups becomes a salient alternative to commitment to school. Employers, gang members, and even parents who need children at home to do chores have self-serving reasons for luring children away from school; they send messages that define school as the problem, rather than the solution. Former teachers who have gone back to universities or who have secured better-paying jobs with less stress may be the source of such messages to burned-out teachers.

The resulting drift away from school may be a not so subtle push-out by teachers, counselors, and principals whose actions suggest that they would be just as happy if the students or teachers left (Deyhle, 1989; Fine, 1987; Fine & Zane, 1989; Fordham & Ogbu, 1986; McDermott, 1987). In one large inner-city school, neophyte teachers reported that the principal told them that 80% of his new teachers quit each year and that "it suits him fine, because there are plenty more where they came from" (Dworkin, 1984).

Experiences students have of early academic failure reinforce their lack of fit in school. They enter school unprepared, have few economic or academic resources upon which to rely, and see no reason to work harder, especially if they do not understand the hidden curriculum (Friedenberg, 1970; Jackson, 1968; LeCompte, 1978). Their behavior initiates a process of negative labeling, which accelerates drift. Students begin to seek gratification through avoidance of class work, including tuning out. Anthropologists studying dropouts have called this process the "construction of failure" (Erickson, 1984), a process participated in mutually by students, teachers, and school staff. Construction of failure precludes future school success because labeled students are tracked to mindless remedial classes, where they learn even less or are ignored. Eventually, many drop out, relegated to unemployment or underemployment in the secondary labor market. Even students who believe in the benefits of education often see no evidence that schools will deliver on their promises.

Among teachers, the sense of meaningless and normlessness comes with the shattering of initial idealism and false expectations fostered in teachers' colleges. Teachers assume that they will be treated as autonomous professionals whose students are eager to learn, but the reality is quite different.

The Intersection of Teacher and Student Alienation

It is our contention that a common set of structural variables produces both teacher and student alienation. We have argued that schools have lagged far behind the changing economy and sociopolitical conditions in the United States. As a consequence, schooling has fallen out of synchrony with society. Technological changes, changes in the sectors from which jobs flow, demographic changes in the school-age population and in the cohorts of teachers available to school districts, as well as the legitimate demand by previously ignored groups for influence in the society have all made the school systems that appeared to work well in the in 1950s fail in the 1980s and 1990s.

Why have dramatic changes such as these affected teachers and students similarly? After all, students are not adults and are not in the labor force. By contrast, teachers are both adults and in the labor force. Furthermore, each group has tended to blame the other for its problems. The answer requires a new conceptualization of teachers and students. Teachers and students can be seen as terminological dyads, reflecting complementary roles. Without teachers there can be no students, and without students, a teacher has no one to teach. While this fundamental fact may seem obvious, little research in education has examined the mutual dependency of teachers and students. One exception is Firestone and Rosenblum's (1988) conceptualization of the commitment process in urban high schools. They hold that when teachers lack commitment to students, teaching, and their particular campus, they produce

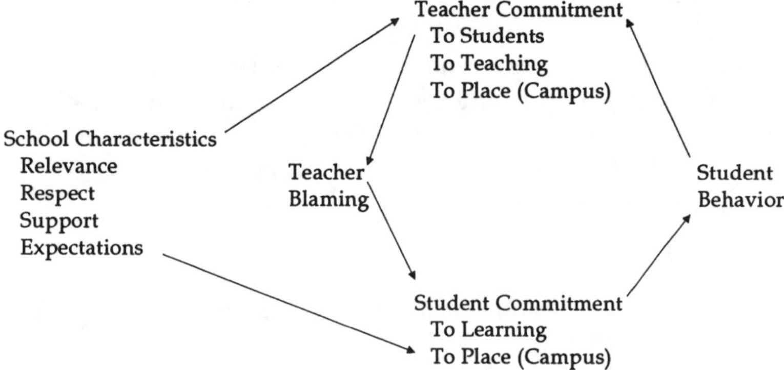

Figure 7.1 Firestone and Rosenblum's Model of the Dynamics of Teacher and Student Commitment
SOURCE: Firestone and Rosenblum (1988, p. 286). Copyright 1988 by the American Educational Research Association. Reprinted by permission of the publisher.

a rhetoric of teacher blaming (teacher labeling) that affects student commitment to learning and to the school. In turn, student commitment affects student behavior, which completes a circle by affecting teacher commitment. Teacher commitment is further affected by school characteristics such as school relevance, respect levels, support, and expectations; school characteristics also affect student commitment. The result is a cumulative circular social process that either heightens commitment on the part of students and teachers or deflates it (see Figure 7.1).

NOTE

1. We rely on statistics on college attendance rather than college graduation to compare with teachers over the time periods because many teachers in classrooms during the 1940s and 1950s had gone to normal schools, obtaining only two years of college themselves. Additionally, it should be recognized that the data are for all persons 25 years of age and over and will also include people who are well past the age at which their children would still be in school. Age-specific breakdowns of educational attainment are available from census reports only since 1970. However, interpolating back from these data

and from estimations of prior censuses suggests that in 1950, approximately 19% of adults between the ages of 25 and 44 had attended college, even if for as little as one year. In 1960, 21.8% of adults of childbearing years had some college experience; by 1970, more than 27% had attended college. Finally, by 1980, a total of 32.2% of the adults between the ages of 25 and 44 had attended college for at least one year.

EIGHT

Giving Up on School: A Process Model

In the previous chapter we surveyed the literature on alienation theory and its variant known as strain theory. We applied these theoretical orientations to account for the condition of schooling in the United States experienced by teachers and their students. We noted that both students and teachers perceive gaps between what they had expected from the school experience and what they actually have encountered. Students expected that school would be instrumental in helping them achieve their material goals, and teachers expected that they would be autonomous professionals given the opportunity to impart knowledge to eager students. Both found the school experience irrelevant and unrewarding. In this chapter we utilize the concept of strain theory to develop two process models for giving up on school: one that accounts for the awareness of strain and one that addresses the factors that convert strain into school outcomes, including teacher quitting and student dropout behaviors.

In three prior investigations, one of the authors described a model designed to account for the manner in which macrostructural changes in society affect the attitudes and behaviors of individuals and groups, including disadvantaged groups (see Chafetz & Dworkin, 1986; Chafetz, Dworkin, &

Dworkin, 1975; Dworkin & Dworkin, 1982). In those models a construct known as "global factors" established the conditions within a society that defined the operating parameters for social organizations, institutions, and interpersonal relations. Global factors, which we discussed in detail in Chapter 2, represent the general categories of demographic and distributive shifts that affect all groups in a society by dislocating populations, altering the division of labor, disrupting the operations of a normative order, and influencing such elements as population size, state of the economy, level of technology, and availability of natural resources. Global factors also include what Persell (1977) refers to as "the societal structure of dominance" (p. 151), or the stratification system, including the hierarchy of groups and rewards available to such groups. The organization of institutions in the society reflects conditions of these global factors, and when conditions change, institutions either change also or fail to provide the society with role incumbents capable of performing the manifold tasks within the society.

Disjuncture between the workings of the institutions and organizations in the society and the condition of the global factors produces market problems—labor markets are not supplied with enough or the right kind of workers; workers are unprepared to perform new kinds of tasks; school systems do not meet the needs of new labor markets. In some instances, privileged groups continue practices that maintain their own status while rendering their society less able to compete with others. Similarly, educational policies designed to train lower-income children to become industrial workers become dysfunctional when the service sector is expanding at the expense of the manufacturing sector. These dysfunctions produce structural strains that eventually are experienced by individuals. Under some conditions individuals may not recognize the contradictions—or strains—or may define their experiences as personal failings. After all, in the United States societal norms lead people to attribute their misfortunes either to lack of effort (Merton, 1968) or to chance, fate, or bad luck (Shaw & Constanzo, 1970). The old advice "If at first you don't succeed, try, try again" obviates evoking system blame or looking for contradictions within the social structure, and especially those contradictions deriving from conditions as distant from personal experience as disjuncture between global factors and social institutions.

How, then, do people come to evoke system blame? More precisely, how do teachers and students come to conclude that the structure of schooling is at fault? The model we offer is borrowed from conflict approaches to consciousness as first explicated by Marx (1959) in the essay "Eighteenth Brumaire of Louis Bonaparte." Marx asked whether the peasants could be considered a true class as long as they were isolated from one another in rural areas. His answer was that they could not become a class for themselves (*classe fur sich*) until they were concentrated together in factories and factory towns by capitalists and began to discover their common plight and common class enemy. The specific constructs for our model come from Dworkin and Dworkin (1982) and Chafetz and Dworkin (1986). The model proposes that changes in global distributive factors, especially demographic and economic changes, alter organizational variables, which include the ways in which groups relate to one another. Distributive change produces organizational change, which produces interpersonal or social psychological change as individual attitudes and behaviors become inconsistent with new forms of group relationships. These social psychological changes are a result of differences in group and individual experiences within organizations. Reference groups serve to inform and transmit interpretations of these experiences into new ideologies that may attribute the cause of these changes either to the social system or to failings within the individual. Figure 8.1 portrays the model that describes the workings of global factors on awareness.

In the model, *global factors* create *structural strains* and alter *organizational relationships* (e.g., place new demands upon major societal institutions, including the organization of work, the family, and education). If the organizations change to accommodate the changed realities, they are likely to produce

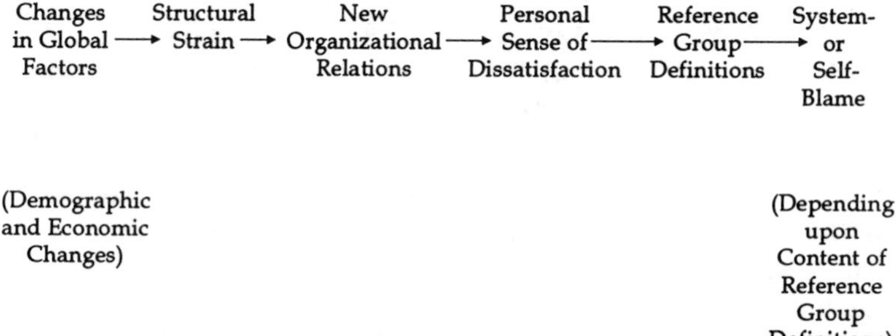

Figure 8.1 The Process of Awareness of Global-Factor-Induced Strain

displacements and disruptions in the lives of individuals. If they do not change, the organizations are increasingly less able to meet the needs of the populace, and the failure of these organizations is likely to produce displacements and disruptions in people's lives. Given normative explanations that deflect blame away from the social structure, the proclivity of individuals is to look for evil persons, or bad luck, or personal shortcomings to account for their disrupted lives. *Reference groups* may help individuals to understand their plight by evoking either system-blame or self-blame interpretations. As Chafetz and Dworkin (1986) argue, however, reference groups themselves have vested interests that can be enhanced by one or the other interpretation.

Figure 8.1 presents a very general view of the process by which global factors affect consciousness among individuals. The model incorporates macro-level structural variables into the process of individual consciousness (a micro-level concept). As developed by Dworkin and Dworkin (1982) and Chafetz and Dworkin (1986), the model requires some additional specification, especially with regard to the kinds of reference groups that provide system-blame versus self-blame interpretations. As noted earlier, there are three kinds of reference groups relevant to attitude formation: comparative, normative, and gatekeeping groups. Comparative groups provide a frame of reference by which individuals can determine whether they are relatively advantaged or disadvantaged. Normative reference groups specify appropriate expectations for people and control the knowledges, beliefs, and behaviors that Bourdieu and Passeron (1977) call "cultural capital." Gatekeeping reference groups establish barriers to access to opportunities, specifying what one must do to acquire desired goals and then granting the means to achieve such goals.

Thus when teachers and students discover that the promises of school are not being met for them—that is, teachers discover that they were ill prepared to work in a system in which they had little autonomy and little respect, and students discover that people neither care whether they learn nor believe that their education will lead to career and economic goals—alternative reference groups come into play. If teachers compare their status and rewards with those of other teachers and not with other college-educated professionals, they may conclude that they are no worse off than others; if students who are failing compare their experiences with like-situated students, they may come to believe that poor performance is normal and to be expected. If, however, teachers and students, respectively, compare their own status with that of economically or academically more successful groups, they are likely to conclude that they, themselves, have a problem, and that they, themselves, are relatively deprived.

This does not, however, establish the locus of blame. If teachers turn to school administrators or even to college of education faculty for interpretation of their felt relative deprivation, they are likely to be urged to upgrade their skills, to try harder; they may even be told that they are not capable of becoming effective teachers. Likewise, students seeking interpretation from teachers, counselors, school administrators, and even parents are likely to be told that they must study harder and become more motivated to do well in school, or may be shown a standardized test that suggests they do not have the ability to do well in school in the first place. By contrast, groups outside of the school are more likely to locate fault inherently in the schools, suggesting that "administrators really don't care about teachers," or "teachers are not out there to help you anyway," or even that doing well constitutes "acting white" (Fordham & Ogbu, 1986).

Response by educators to the impact of global change in the distributive and organizational sectors of society, as well as the economic and demographic reality of schooling, as we shall see in Chapter 9, has been to make small adjustments rather than to engage in holistic restructuring. As a consequence, the situation worsens as teachers and students are increasingly ill prepared to perform the tasks required in the changing society. The result is the sense of alienation and resignation described in Chapters 3 through 6.

However, not everyone fails in school and not everyone gives up on schooling, even if they feel dissatisfied with their experiences. Thus macro-level variables, as specified in Figure 8.1, cannot account for individual variations in school outcomes for students and teachers. The macro-level variables need further modification to accomplish that task, as we see in the next figure. Figure 8.2 presents a refined model of the factors that lead people to give up or not give up on school. The model combines elements of many theories generated for macro-level analysis—labeling theory (Bowles & Levin, 1968; Braun, 1976; Clifton, Perry, Parsonson, & Hryniuk, 1986; Cooper, 1979; Dusek, 1975, 1985; Haller & Davis, 1981; Oakes, 1985; Rist, 1970; Rosenthal & Jacobson, 1968), status attainment theory (Sewell, Haller, & Ohlendorf, 1970; Sewell, Haller, & Portes, 1969; Sewell & Hauser, 1975), reference group theory (Hyman, 1942; Kelley, 1952; Merton & Kitt, 1950; Shibutani, 1955; Stouffer et al., 1949), reproduction theory (Bernstein, 1970, 1977; Boudon, 1974; Bourdieu & Passeron, 1977; Bowles & Gintis, 1976; Ginsburg, 1988; Giroux, 1983; Persell, 1977), and credentialist theory (Collins, 1971, 1974, 1979). It is strongly within a conflict paradigm; it posits that the inability of institutions to adapt to changes in global factors is the source of the strain that produces alienation from school. However, it is unique in that it also incorporates these theories into a microsystem model that accounts for individual school decisions and outcomes.

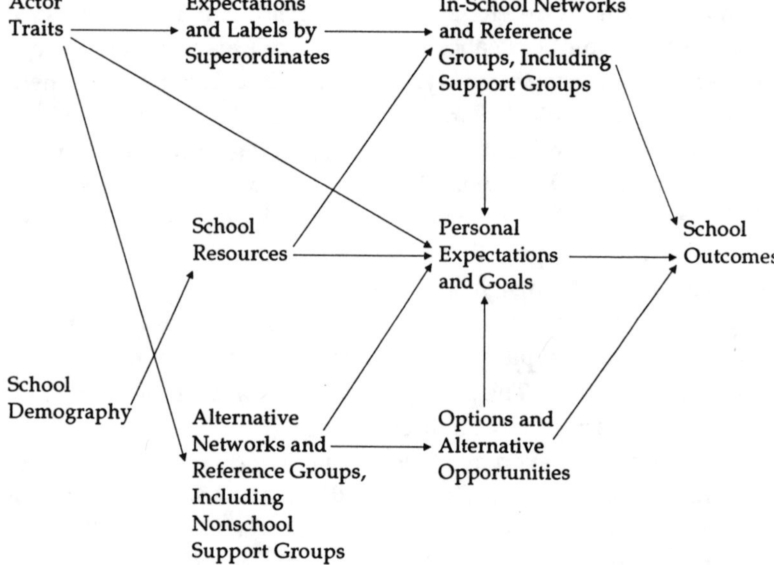

Figure 8.2 Microsystem Model of School Outcomes for Teachers and Students

The model begins with some of the elements of the status attainment model. It posits a significant role for *actor traits*, or the background variables that individuals bring to the school setting, including race and gender for students and teachers, social class and parental resources for students, and years of experience and academic attainment for teachers. These establish conditions that affect individual commitment, predispose responses by others, and influence coping and survival prospects. In our model they reflect both the resources of individuals and the ascribed and achieved characteristics that evoke responses in others. Two other blocks of variables include the constructs *school resources* and *school demography*. The former include those economic, political, and social factors that permit schools to offer quality education and enrichment to students and a less stressful environment for teachers. Thus affluent schools with supportive parent organizations are better able to compensate for educational disadvantages of their less affluent students. The equivalent for teachers is schools in which teachers are not required to supplement school supplies with their own funds and in which parents and parent organizations support teachers, agree upon common strategies for school effectiveness, and volunteer to participate in the school, thereby forming an "effective community" (Coleman & Hoffer, 1987).

School demography includes such variables as grade level, class size (and campus size), the racial and social class makeup of the student body, and the percentages of students who are performing below grade level. Such variables address several of the sources of stress that make the work of teachers more difficult. They speak to the likelihood that teachers will be isolated in terms of race and class, and they suggest the extent to which student diversity and the scale of the student body will make effective teaching and learning possible, despite resources.

In our model, school resources are affected by school demography in two ways. First, more affluent suburban schools with middle-class student enrollments can rely upon more favorable tax structures to supply needed material resources. Children in such schools also bring with them the economic advantages of their high social class status and the accompanying parental investments in their education. Second, the public is more often willing to invest in schools that have a history of producing civic leaders and successes in the past. In accordance with credentialist models, resource investments are most likely to accrue to those schools that produce future elites and students who resemble current elites and business executives than are schools with fewer exemplars of success. Simply put, the corporate sector is much more willing to invest in its own kind than in people whose success is more problematic.

Another block of variables describes *expectations and labels by superordinates,* including teacher expectations of students and administrator expectations of teachers. These expectations and labels are usually created in response to ascribed characteristics of the actors (actor traits), and interactions around them often create self-fulfilling prophecies—or construction of success or failure. They do so through differential behavior on the part of the superordinates that facilitates or inhibits opportunities to learn or to advance on the part of students and teachers. The expectations and labels also affect the content and nature of a wide range of social support networks, which we have termed *in-school networks and reference groups, including nonschool support groups.* These serve as role models for in-school success or failure, providing assistance in gaining access to school roles, coping strategies, and information. We know that dropouts report having fewer social networks in school than do nondropouts (Finn & Achilles, 1990) and that teachers who are burned out and who quit report having fewer support groups in school than do those who remain (Dworkin, 1990b). We also know that burnout is lower and stress is less likely to lead to burnout and the desire to quit teaching among individuals who have supportive administrators and colleagues (Dworkin, 1987; Dworkin et al., 1988, 1990).

The next block of variables is *personal expectations and goals.* These variables summarize the career and educational goals of students and teachers; they represent both the aspirations that people bring to school settings and those engendered in school—either in public school or in colleges of education. They may be as nebulous as wanting to do one's best or become rich, or as specific as becoming a master teacher on the career ladder or getting into a college and entering a specified occupation. Actor traits affect personal expectations in that they specify levels of motivation and ability that students and teachers bring to school. Likewise, school resources specify the extent to which material and nonmaterial goods and services are likely to be available to the individuals to achieve goals. Most important, however, are conducive expectations and labels and in-school networks, as they help focus goals, grant personal access to resources, and even supplant existing goals with new ones. Obviously, they also work to inhibit access, as teachers and administrators play significant roles as gatekeepers.

Strain theory argues that in the absence of legitimate means to goals individuals may seek alternative means, especially if the goals are attainable elsewhere and the individuals have access to opportunity structures and networks (Cloward, 1959). Alternative networks and reference groups outside of school suggest *options and alternative opportunities* as well as redirect personal expectations and goals. These networks provide support and even suggest new means and goals. They also may provide actual options to attaining goals. Thus reference groups from off the street may provide access to illegitimate means to wealth, should that be a goal. Reference groups of ex-teachers or of other college graduates may provide information and career leads outside of teaching for teachers whose in-school networks have frustrated access to career goals in teaching. Of course, actor traits may facilitate access to such alternative networks. Middle-class students who are alienated from school may have fewer street resources upon which to rely than do working-class students. Teachers whose networks of friends are primarily made up of other teachers may also have fewer paths to alternative careers than those with friends outside of teaching. Likewise, economic conditions in the community will affect access to counseling programs and goal-attainment alternatives. Thus the model should be placed within the larger economic context of the global factors about which we spoke earlier.

The dependent construct is *school outcomes,* which includes enthusiasm for teaching versus burnout for teachers and school commitment versus tuning out (in-school dropping out) for students under conditions of the absence of alternative networks and options. It also include dropping out and quitting teaching for students and teachers, respectively, in the presence of alternatives. Realize, however, that the presence of alternatives and networks need only be perceptual. Whether or not viable alternatives are actually present is less important to the decision of teachers and students to leave school than is the belief that something better is out there beyond the schoolyard fence.

We propose, then, that both in-school and out-of-school reference groups play significant roles in creating feelings of dissatisfaction, translating such dissatisfaction into self- or system blame, and suggesting strategies to attain goals or create new goals on the basis of the locus of blame. Teachers, parents, and school administrators are most likely to encourage students to evoke self-blame to explain failure. Administrators do the same to teachers who are having difficulty coping with their work. On the other hand, the street, other students, and some social agency practitioners are more likely to look at system-blame models. Nonteachers, ex-teachers, and other well-paid, college-educated reference groups are likely to encourage teachers to evoke system blame for their difficulties. If teachers, parents, and administrators provide resources and assistance in goal attainment within school, the likelihood of dropping out, burning out, or quitting is reduced. By contrast, support from nonschool sources may provide opportunities to achieve goals out of school. Not all of the means to goals need to be thought of as deviant. Many colleges and universities have retrained teachers to enter new lines of work, and many proprietary schools have offered skilled trades to high school dropouts. However, whether a teacher remains in school, burned out and hating the students, or quits and enters a new career depends upon economic and social opportunities. Reference groups out of school often provide access to and information about such opportunities. Likewise, whether a student remains an in-school dropout by tuning out or actually drops out of school often depends upon the pressures imposed by out-of-school reference groups.

The elements of the model we have offered are affected differentially by the components of alienation described by Seeman (1959, 1967, 1975). We suspect that a sense of meaninglessness and powerlessness in school is most affected by the superordinate labels and the actions of in-school reference groups. Supportive teachers and administrators are known to reduce levels of burnout and alienation among students and teachers alike. Isolation is heavily a function of in-school networks and reference groups and may compel an individual to seek the support of out-of-school reference groups, if available. School resources and school demography are likely to determine whether superordinates are willing to bend rules and whether rule obedience is likely to have payoffs. Thus the interplay among resources, superordinates, and reference groups is likely to affect normlessness. In turn, all of these factors come into play in creating a sense that schooling is central or foreign to one's being—that is, a sense of estrangement or engagement.

Our model suggests that there are numerous elements that come into play in determining whether a person will give up on school. Experiences, goals, opportunities, alternatives, and, most of all, reference groups determine the algorithm that leads the individual to embrace school with enthusiasm or give up. Some of these factors are under the control of school policy and staff; others must be addressed in larger social, political, and economic arenas. In Chapter 10 we shall identify these different kinds of factors and offer our not too modest suggestions to exploit the model's potential in preventing teachers and students from giving up *in* and *on* school.

NINE

Why School Reforms Fail

A central problem in school reform is that few of the reforms that will be detailed in this chapter address the central concern in this book: the alienation that leads to burnout and quitting behavior. This is because few actually alter the patterns of power and control inside school, and none have much power to alter powerful social, political, and economic factors outside the school. Sarason (1971) states that innovative curricula and pedagogical approaches that reduce alienation by attempting to get students involved in their own learning—such as problem solving and discovery learning—necessitate structural changes at the level of the classroom in how teachers and children relate to each other. It is precisely these relationships that remain untouched by current educational reforms (cited in Puckett, 1989, p. 282). Newmann (1981) has argued for institution of reforms designed to improve the performance of students by reducing alienation: increasing student participation; building in voluntarism and more diffuse and extended relationships among students and teachers; establishing clear, consistent educational goals; making institutions of manageable size; and integrating school roles with the work world. He suggests that school reforms can be evaluated in accordance with the degree to which they reduce alienation—the factor to which he attributes primary blame for poor student performance. We reproduce his array of programs and their respective evaluations in Table 9.1 because it not only summarizes some of the most common forms of alternative programs for at-risk students, but illustrates the degree to which their ability to reduce alienation is limited, at best.

Newmann (1981) points out that

> the good news is that none of the reforms seems likely to contradict any of the guidelines [leading to a reduction of alienation] and each . . . seems . . . to promote at least one. . . . The bad news is that no single reform is likely to be consistent with more than three guidelines, and that almost half the cells are filled with (?). (p. 557)

This means, he tells us, that some of the reforms also have the potential to violate individual guidelines against alienation (p. 557). Given that, we must look to new approaches that do not. Doing so, however, requires taking into consideration changes in the societal context of schools, and developing explanations for why and how these changes alter the lives that students and teachers lead in school. This is because the global factors outlined in Chapter 2 have so altered the world in which we and schools live that the repeated "cycles of reform" so common in the past no longer will serve to remedy the kinds of problems we will outline in this chapter.

Tyack and Hansot (1984) give four explanations for the failure of school reform: (a) attacks on the American social philosophy positing that public education is a public good; (b) what the authors call the "politicization of education" during periods of retrenchment, or a more open ambivalence about actually achieving greater equality and the value of compensatory social services for the poor and minorities; (c) overambitious reformers who promise effects for their programs that cannot be realized; and (d) real areas of deficit in the schools. We find this to be a useful analysis. In this chapter, we will examine how various reforms have attempted to improve performance of teachers and students. We first discuss

Table 9.1 Ratings of the Extent to Which Reforms Implement Guidelines for Reducing Alienation

	Guidelines								
	Vol. Choice	*Clear, Consis. Ed. Goals*	*Small Size*	*Partici-pation*	*Exten. and Coop. Roles*	*Integ. Work*	*Totals* +	*Totals* ?	*Totals* /
Schools within schools	?	?	+	?	?	?	1	5	0
Specialized schools	+	+	?	?	?	?	2	4	0
Alternative schools	+	?	+	+	?	?	3	3	0
House system	?	?	+	?	?	/	1	4	1
Personalized advising	?	+	/	?	?	/	1	3	2
Flexible scheduling	+	/	/	/	?	?	1	2	3
Individualized programming	?	+	/	+	?	?	2	3	1
Prosocial conduct	/	+	/	?	+	/	2	1	3
Participation in governance	+	?	/	+	?	/	2	2	2
The basics	?	+	/	/	?	?	1	3	2
Career-vocational education	+	+	/	/	?	?	2	2	2
Challenge education	+	?	/	/	?	+	2	2	2
Community-based learning	+	?	/	/	?	+	2	2	2
Totals									
+	7	6	3	3	1	2	22		
?	5	6	1	5	12	7		36	
/	1	1	9	5	0	4			20

SOURCE: Adapted from F. M. Newmann (1981, p. 558). Harvard Educational Review, 51:4.
NOTE: Vol. Choice = Voluntary Choice; Clear, Consis. Ed. Goals = Clear, Consistent Educational Goals; Small Size = Small Size; Participation = Participation; Exten. and Coop. Roles = Extended and Cooperative Roles; = Integ. Work = Integrated Work; + = reform likely to result in practice that promotes the guideline; ? = reform could be implemented in ways that promote or contradict the guideline; / = reform largely irrelevant to the guideline; no basis for assessing potential promotion or contradiction.

the standards used to determine whether or not schools are successful. We will look at reforms that have been tried and why, given the theoretical framework that informs this book and the evaluative standards usually applied to schools, the reforms have had limited utility. Second, we evaluate so-called no-cost reforms. Third, we discuss the mismatch between clients and program characteristics, indicating that what schools do for dropouts does not meet their needs. Finally, we discuss reforms that actually have exacerbated the problems they were intended to solve. Our purpose in this critique is to demonstrate how the very act of trying to solve problems of alienation can actually create them, because it makes even educators who have the best of intentions and skills feel as if their efforts are meaningless and ineffective.

Educational reform movements, whether in the United States or elsewhere, are stimulated by dissatisfaction with both specific school activities or functions and social conditions that it is believed the schools can, or should, correct. We shall argue in this chapter that educational reforms fail for a number of reasons. First, they often have been held accountable to impossible standards for social reformation. Second, they have tended to be short-lived and underfunded. In both cases, because they have failed, they exacerbated alienation of educators, who were left feeling powerless to effect change and as if their efforts were useless. They foster cynicism, because teachers know that reforms come in waves. Many teachers simply lie low and wait out innovations that they find unworkable or philosophically repugnant. Third, particularly with regard to instruction, many reforms exacerbate the low achievement and poor student self-esteem they seek to ameliorate. Reforms also seldom change dynamics at the heart of pedagogy—patterns of teacher-student interaction—nor do they change the top-down flow of power and control in schools. Finally, many reforms really are directed at, and are most appropriate for, the children of middle America, not those most at risk. As a consequence, they have little effect on target populations and increase the sense that educators are powerless to solve their own problems.

It is probable that schools cannot by themselves create a good and equitable society, but rather that schools are good and equitable where society itself is good and equitable. We do believe that it probably is within the power of the United States to create good schools for all children, schools that are humane and interesting places for children to acquire basic cognitive tools and to become competent and critical thinkers. However, doing so may not eliminate poverty, reduce unemployment, or strengthen the national economy. Far more stringent action than school reform would be needed to accomplish these objectives. In fact, much school reform may hide a conservative agenda to avoid the possibility of more far-reaching social change, changes that would involve redistribution of wealth and elimination of entrenched privilege (Giroux, 1988a). The failure of both the Right and the Left to accomplish their educational agendas probably has increased a sense of social disenfranchisement, because neither has been able to implement change in schools and their effects. In the pages that follow, we examine some of the reasons reform programs have failed to meet expectations.

INAPPROPRIATE STANDARDS TO MEASURE SCHOOL EFFECTIVENESS

School failure is in part a function of how success is measured. At the school level, excellence comes to be defined in terms of (a) overall scores on standardized tests, (b) the number of students who graduate in four years, (c) the number of students—graduates or not—who find jobs, and (d) the number of students who go on to attend college, whether or not they graduate from college (LeCompte & Dworkin, 1988, p. 146). Unfortunately, in the past few decades public schools in the United States have been found wanting on all of these standards, and, as a consequence, reforms intended to improve performance have been adjudged defective.

Why Do Schools Fail to Meet the Standards?

A number of explanations have been advanced for the failure of schools to measure up; some of these are discussed in turn below.

Test characteristics. Test scores have declined in ways that cannot be explained in terms of changes in the characteristics of the student body (O'Neill & Sepielli, 1985). Some of the declines can be explained in terms of the tests themselves. First, the tests and how they are scored have changed. Lower rates of passing are created when "cut scores," or the lowest passing levels, are raised to reflect concerns over excellence. Another test artifact—still unexplained—is the reduction of differences in test scores between males and females. This can be attributed not to improvement in the performance of females, but to a decline in male scores in reading, language arts, and composition. Since women traditionally score lower than men in math, overall test scores of males have moved closer to those of women. Why male scores have declined still is unknown.

The standardized tests upon which schools—and students—are assessed also have been pegged to minimum competencies in reading, mathematics, and sometimes writing. While some urban schools have demonstrated remarkable increases in student performance, they have often done so on these basic skills tests, which assess only the most *minimum* of competencies. Administration of tests and how they influence instruction also affects performance; test scores can be "cooked" by teaching to the test. When this happens, test scores rise because teachers teach nothing but what is to be tested. While it is appropriate for teachers actually to teach children the material upon which they will be assessed, improvements in test scores may not necessarily reflect improvements in the amounts of knowledge students have acquired.

Graduation and employment. We pointed out in Chapters 1, 2, and 4 that students are not graduating, going on to higher education, or finding employment in the numbers desired. The consequently increased rates of dropping out and unemployment are considered measures of school failure. A further issue not often addressed by basic skills reforms is that the kinds of skills needed in higher-level employment are often not just the basics, but privileged intellectual skills and behaviors. In addition, specific organizational and curricular practices in schools, such as ability grouping and tracking, labeling, and placement in special programs, also act to deprive poor children, young women, and minorities of experiences that impart social skills and value orientations necessary for success in desirable occupational sectors (Apple, 1979; Aronowitz & Giroux, 1985; Bernstein, 1977; Bourdieu & Passeron, 1977; Gouldner, 1979).

Educational need and public support. Educational needs in the United States are seriously out of sync with public, or at least legislative, willingness to assume responsibility for their costs. Further, there is little consensus over how, and in what manner, educational needs should be met. For example, in 1988, the courts in Texas declared unconstitutional the state's practice of using property taxes to finance schools. In a special session of the Texas State Legislature during March 1990, an odd coalition of conservatives (who believed the bill too expensive) and minorities (who believed it offered far too little) defeated a multimillion-dollar educational spending package that was to replace the property tax. At the time of publication of this volume (mid-1991), the issue remains unresolved.

Penny wise and pound foolish. The United States simply does not value children and education as highly as public rhetoric would indicate. One of the highest accolades that policymakers can give to a proposed program or innovation is that it will require no additional funds. The War on Poverty, which attempted to address the larger social problems underlying school failure, brought a substantial amount of incentive funding into the public schools. Subsequent disenchantment with the impact of the War on Poverty—fueled in part by an unwillingness to spend enough or to wait long enough for results—has led to a series of new reforms whose primary cachet seems to be that they are characterized by decreasing levels of funding. The logic seems to be that since increasing funds to schools did not end poverty, we need not continue wasting money on the poor.

NO-COST REFORMS

Publication of *A Nation at Risk* (National Commission on Excellence in Education, 1983) and other commission reports critical of the performance of U.S. schools was followed by various less costly and more modest moves to increase "excellence" in education by altering the curriculum and raising standards. In the 1990s, so-called no-cost reforms are in vogue. The most popular of these emphasize various forms of organizational restructuring and decentralization, parent responsibility, and appeals to higher values, morality, and hard work. No-cost, we submit, is almost universally a recipe for an ineffective program.

The High Cost of "No-Cost"

Perhaps among the most important fallacies of these programs is the illusion that they are, in fact, less costly. We believe that they are costly indeed, if only because they are ineffective and divert attention from other, more serious, efforts at change. Their critics suggest that some of these programs—such as choice plans and district decentralization—actually can produce sharply negative results, including increased racial and economic segregation in the schools (Daniels, 1989). Further, these proposals do little to solve many of the concrete and oppressive internal problems that alienate students and teachers from school.

Decreasing levels of funding are the norm in educational programming because they are tied to legislated or agency funding cycles. Because government budgets operate on one- or two-year cycles, projects that actually succeed in obtaining as much as three-year grants are considered to be unusual. Results always are expected in less than the three-year period, despite the fact that research on educational innovation indicates that results usually are not evident until after the three-year budget cycle is over—by which time the program has been judged unsuccessful and funding has been discontinued (Corwin, 1973; Whitford, 1986). On the assumption that external funds are to be used only for start-up of programs, agencies also tend to give less than was requested and to reduce funding each year. Innovators thus find themselves in a continual funding shortage when local funding is not allocated to make up the difference.

Decreasing levels of funding contribute to the cynicism and alienation of teachers, who know that innovations will not be around for long. Since special programs usually are not continued with local funds, short-term gains made as a consequence of innovative programs will not persist when the programs are gone. For example, a New York elementary school that began a crash emphasis on reading three years ago instituted a two-hour-daily after-school tutoring program taught by four experienced teachers for its lowest-achieving students. In one year, the percentage of its children who read at or above grade level rose from 36% to 60.4%, and its ranking among schools rose by one-third. However, in the following year the after-school program was cut back to two days a week because it received a smaller grant for the second year. The principal now worries that next year, the school again will fall into the ranks of low-achieving schools—and probably now wonders if all the effort was worth it (Berger, 1990).

Reforms Predicated Upon the "Quick Fix"

A recent analysis of reform movements in several states by the Center for Policy Research in Education shows that, during the 1980s, state legislatures did indeed initiate an unprecedented number of educational reform-related bills and task forces. Most popular were "quick fixes," including salary increases for teachers, mandates for higher standards for student promotion and retention, establishment of more selective standards for entering the teaching profession, and raising of graduation standards and cut scores for exit examinations. These are the types of reforms most likely to be put in place and to remain, in large part because they involve modest programs that disrupt the existing system very little and whose dynamics and resource requirements are familiar and comfortable to school personnel ("Modest Gains," 1989).

At the same time calls are being heard to make preservice teacher training programs more rigorous, reformers also advocate alternative, quicker, and cheaper ways to circumvent even traditional teacher preparation programs. These programs diminish the value of efforts (and credentials earned) by people have who participated in more time-consuming traditional programs. For example, New Jersey "solved" its chronic shortage of qualified teachers by instituting a program of alternative certification. Any college graduate can be hired on a temporary certificate, and then, after a year's supervision and a year's successful teaching, become state certified. New Jersey now has a surplus of teacher candidates, and other states are considering adopting New Jersey's procedures (S. Thomson, quoted in "Learning Conditions," 1989). There is, however, considerable controversy over the degree to which teachers provided by such alternative systems are as qualified as teachers who traverse traditional university-based programs (Haberman, 1987; Kirby, Darling-Hammond, & Hudson, 1989; Lutz & Hutton, 1989).

More difficult to implement, less likely to persist, and more prone to dilution have been those reforms that involve conflicts of interests or complex or ambiguous solutions, such as assessment of practicing teachers and implementation of career ladders (Fuhrman, Clune, & Elmore, 1988; "Modest Gains," 1989). Where these programs have been implemented, they have often become co-opted, serving to reinforce the status quo. This is what happened to a career ladder program in Utah; teachers who already were at the top of the pay scale simply became the master teachers, and other teachers were arrayed downward according to seniority (Malen & Hart, 1987). In other cases, as in the well-conceived—and well-received—Fairfax County merit pay scheme, school board-mandated cuts in the types and levels of incentive pay that had been promised to teachers led to bitterness and what appears to be loss of trust in the superintendent who initiated it (Fiske, 1989).

Avoiding Expense by Shifting the Cost of Reform

Cost-free reforms are popular because they reduce the level of public ambivalence for funding educational programs by shifting the cost of school improvement away from taxpayers. One solution is to let private schools provide an elite stream for more privileged sectors of the population. Private and parochial schools also provide considerable relief to public schools in certain urban areas, but do so at the expense of "creaming" affluent and white children out of the public schools. Other solutions make parents more responsible for the type of schools their children attend and the amount of instruction they receive at home. Still others shift costs to the corporate sector in the form of programs such as school-business partnerships, executives on loan for teachers and tutors, and job training programs.

Parent involvement programs. Parent involvement programs transfer responsibility for student performance to the child's home. They have three dimensions. The first, and most typical, form of parent involvement sees parents as emissaries of, and adjuncts to, the school. These programs are premised on the assumption that the performance of children will improve if parents reinforce school activities at home. School responsibility is limited to progress reports to parents and admonitions to help students and to make sure they do their homework and turn it in on time. However, as we have indicated, schools are relatively ineffective at communicating with parents and often sabotage them.

These programs also are effective only with certain segments of the population. Most limit their efforts to bringing more parents to school on special days when teachers are freed for conferences by dismissing children. These ignore the fact that poor and working parents may not only be unable to get away from work and travel to school for the meetings, but also are handicapped by having to find child care for children who are home on conference days. Second, as we have noted, while teachers find it easy to inform parents of satisfactory progress or to complain to them about behavior problems that disrupt classroom activities, they are less prone to inform parents when their children are beginning to fall behind academically. They are quick to attribute poor performance to problems in the home and to resist explanations that fault teacher behavior or the quality of instruction. As a consequence, parents—especially those whose children are not doing well—frequently are the last to learn that their children are in trouble, after the report card comes (Goldenberg, 1989; Stern, 1987; Tizard et al., 1989).

Programs that go further involve evening conferences, sending teachers out on "house calls," and enlisting parents as tutors for their children. At their best, these programs concentrate on teaching parents how to teach their children. Some programs actually supply parents with instructional materials and give them training in how to use them. One of the most innovative—and unfortunately short-lived—programs of this type was "Computers Can," which was instituted by the Houston Independent School District with Chapter I funds and sturdy computers donated by a local company. After taking training from school staff in how to use it, parents could check out a computer and take it home for their children. The premise was that even in disadvantaged homes, where purchase of a computer was absolutely impossible, both parents and children could become computer literate. These programs, especially the tutoring programs, are rare, and most customarily have been included as part of federally funded compensatory programs. When funds are cut, they disappear.

Parent involvement programs facilitate blaming the victim because they shift the responsibility for education from school systems to parents. Parents are seen as culpable if they do not make wise decisions on behalf of their children. Regardless of their resources, it has become increasingly popular to make parents fiscally and legally responsible for their children's school performance. Some Houston judges, for example, have fined parents of children who were habitual truants and then jailed them if they did not pay the fines (Warren, 1990). Wisconsin—which also makes parents responsible for the financial support of the children of their own teenaged children—has created a statewide program that cuts welfare payments to families whose children exceed 13 unexcused absences from school in a semester. However, the program has proven to be ineffective in keeping children in school, at least in Milwaukee County. Only 28% of the county's teenagers affected by the program returned to school and were still there after two months ("On Welfare and Truants," 1990). Further, the consequences of cutting off welfare payments or jailing parents may work to the further disadvantage of other children still under the care of the punished parents.

Voucher systems. Another way to transfer the cost of school reform is to encourage market forces to run bad schools out of business. The assumption is that if parents are allowed to choose schools for their children rather than being forced to send them to the school closest to home, the best schools would flourish and market forces would make poor ones close for lack of enrollment. Critics argue that choice systems will benefit only the affluent, and will act to segregate schools further by race and class, since poor parents lack both the information to make effective choices for their children and the resources to transport them to schools outside the immediate neighborhood. Bad schools in the poorest neighborhoods will, in fact, not be driven out of business, but will persist because they are the only viable alternative for people in those areas. Additionally, voucher systems may create a boondoggle for proprietary schools. If the widespread lack of scruples and poor instruction that characterize many proprietary vocational schools in the 1980s and 1990s is any indication, schools may profit substantially while student-clients—especially the most vulnerable students from minority and inner-city areas—gain little.

Parents as board members. Finally, in some districts, such as the Chicago Public Schools, parent involvement means that parents now are elected participants in the actual governance of schools. We will discuss this form of involvement later, in the section on school reorganization and decentralization.

Tapping the Corporate Sector

These programs emphasize the relationship between the school and its business community. Like parent involvement programs, they are based upon the assumption that getting local businesses and institutions involved in school affairs will stimulate both the quality of schooling and the performance of students. Bailin (1990) defines three categories of school-business partnerships: "adopt-a-school" programs, programs for at-risk students, and "systemically oriented" programs such as the Boston Compact (Hargroves, 1987), which establish very elaborate, almost contractual arrangements between school districts and the business community. These lay out specific goals and objectives for businesses and schools and often imply systems of evaluation and monitoring of compliance. One of their major objectives is to elicit supplementary resources and services for schools. These resources usually involve the promise of training and jobs for students who maintain adequate academic records and who undergo training by the company involved. They also can include soliciting volunteers to serve as adult mentors, role models, and tutors, and as actual classroom teachers in specialty areas such as computer programming and the sciences. While they can generate a great deal of interest in public schools, they often have little substance, are preceded by too little discussion, and establish no real consensus between the parties on the goals of education. Most have failed to set up systems of accountability or evaluation. As a consequence, most really fail to initiate much reform or to serve at-risk students, even in the area of providing employment. The Boston Compact, for example, failed to produce anywhere near the number of jobs the school district had been promised—or needed—for disadvantaged youth. Critics of these programs also argue that they not only produce too few jobs, but those they do create involve short-term, dead-end employment that does not articulate with future professional careers. Many also cream, serving not the most disadvantaged, but those students who need only a little help to be successful (Hahn & Danzberger, 1987).

These programs also share a disability with parent involvement programs: Schools are suspicious of outsiders and try to restrict their participation to only those activities that can be carefully controlled, monitored, and rendered nonthreatening. All of the programs described above serve as little more than a Band-Aid for the most pressing problems of education; their failure only increases alienation by making change seem more impossible.

MISMATCHES: PROGRAM CHARACTERISTICS THAT DO NOT MATCH AT-RISK STUDENT NEEDS

Most reform movements really are directed at and are most effective for middle-class students, not those most in need. This is because the United States has a two-tiered form of education, structured in accordance with the perceived socioeconomic origins and destinations of the students it serves (Haberman, 1987; Resnick & Resnick, 1985):

> One, endowed with resources and talent, serves middle-class and affluent white youth. The other system is a pauper's system. . . . The second system, in which most of America's poor children are educated, has been largely overlooked in the current wave of educational reform. (Hahn & Danzberger, 1987, p. 3)

In addition, some curricular innovations that work well for affluent students do not work at all, in the same way, or as well with minority students or the poor (Delpit, 1988; Reyes, in press; Richardson et al., 1989). Several researchers have found that interactive teacher-student narratives, one of the most highly touted practices for teaching reading and writing, are ineffective ways to help Hispanic elementary school children increase their vocabulary in English, construct better sentences, or write more elaborated texts (Cummins & Miramontes, 1989; Reyes, 1990). Skills-based instruction, which is heavily dependent on phonics, can confuse and even retard the development of English-language facility among elementary-level language-minority children (Richardson et al., 1989). And the same decontextualized, skills-based instruction, which degenerates into the "teaching of lists," retards understanding of complex concepts among high schools students (McNeil, 1986, 1988b, 1988c). Still other reforms, like increasing the number of children retained or the amount of homework and parental involvement, are out of sync with the realities of the lives of many poor families and their children and actually contribute to disillusionment and dropping out.

Programs Do Not Match the Needs of the Population

We believe that current emphases in dropout prevention fail to address the characteristics of a population as heterogeneous as the at-risk, alienated population of schoolchildren in the United States. They meet the needs of only a segment of the at-risk population; they are not appropriate for the "gentrified" potential dropout (students who are academically able but alienated, those who are from the middle classes or who aspire to middle-class employment) or for the increasing numbers of very young dropouts who are too young for the job market or GED programs. Further, with few exceptions, they constitute a boring and inadequate educational experience that manufactures failure.

Perhaps more important, the programs are not congruent with what makes schools acceptable to many dropouts and at-risk students. First, most of these students do not want to be singled out, isolated, and stigmatized. While many of them do not want to return to their home schools, it is because their experiences in their homes schools were so unpleasant, not because they want to be segregated with other dropouts. Some students want their "special schools" to have school spirit, pep rallies, and sports teams, just like ordinary high schools (Compton, 1983). And they want parity of esteem with other schools—diplomas, not GEDs, if possible, and class work and training that leads to real jobs, not dead-end minimum-wage employment.

Reforms Do Not Provide Adequate Nonacademic Support

Many young people know that if they are to stay in school, their most pressing economic and socioemotional needs must be met before they can cope with their academic problems. Young women do not drop out of school because they are pregnant; they drop out because they cannot find safe, accessible, and affordable day care for their infants (Hess & Green, 1988; Holley & Doss, 1983). Young people who must help support their parents and siblings—as well as their own children—during economic hard times must have flexible school schedules; for most, the few available night high schools are too far from their homes to make attendance possible. Sometimes simple rigidity in transportation schedules makes it difficult for students to stay in school. Pregnant teens, mathematically gifted children, or children with physical handicaps may find that the only programs appropriate for them are located across town, far from the bus route. A child whose parent has no car may live too close to school to be eligible for free transportation, but may be afraid to traverse the dangerous neighborhood between home and school on foot. Students who are abused, neglected, or in poor health, and those who have personal, emotional, or psychological problems, need appropriate medical and mental health services.

Programs advocated to address these problems include professional counseling; peer group support networks and peer counseling; counseling for drug and alcohol abusers and children who are victims of sexual and other forms of abuse; and medical clinics with special emphasis on prenatal care, contraception, and sexually transmitted diseases. These programs founder on the reefs of insufficient funding and lack of consensus over the purposes of schooling.

Reforms predicated upon more individual attention for troubled students and more and better counseling are a joke when, as we have noted, most schools lack support staff such as social workers, counselors, and nurses. Elementary schools typically do not have counselors; those in middle and senior high schools typically serve 400-450 students and can be assigned as many as 700 (Corcoran et al., 1988, pp. 26-27; Powell et al., 1985; Sarason, 1971).

Empowerment. Special notice needs to be made of programs that seek to improve retention to graduation by empowering students. These programs are highly individualistic, devoted to improving school performance by improving the self-esteem of students. Their primary focus is on getting poor and minority students to become critical thinkers and to be aware and appreciative of their class and cultural heritage. Many are built around reading and writing programs; some, like those modeled on the Foxfire programs (Puckett, 1989; Wigginton, 1985), involve innovative and creative community-based out-of-school experiences. The problem is that they do not address the structural problems that underlie individual problems; they can leave supposedly empowered students "all dressed up, with no place to go."

Locking the Barn After the Horse Has Fled

Most intervention programs offer too little and begin too late—after the process of a student's alienation is well begun or the student actually drops out. Once students are no longer enrolled, intervention is infinitely more difficult; most of those who leave cannot be tracked down. Hahn and Danzberger (1987) call these students "estranged" (p. 51); they are youths on the outside who often have failed both in and out of school. The cost of recycling these students is tremendously high, and rates of success with them are extremely low.

Programs that do bring dropouts back into school have their own problems. They are too brief—usually no more than 10-12 weeks—to provide training for meaningful employment, especially since their clients often need substantial remediation in basic academic skills before they can even begin actual job training. They usually do not provide support services, such as day care and transportation, that clients need in order to participate in the programs. Further, most of the employment they do provide consists of dead-end or entry-level jobs from which clients find it impossible to move into positions that permit them to support their families. Those who seek an alternative in proprietary programs often find very high tuition charges and very little training. In fact, financial abuses by private technical and vocational schools constituted a near scandal in the 1980s (Berger, 1989; Fine, 1986).

Even the most well-established programs fail to serve those most in need of help. The number of dropouts joining youth programs such as the Job Corps or those established under the Job Training Partnership Act has declined. In large part this is because programs elevate their success rates by a creaming process that enrolls only the most promising youngsters—those who can read and write, who have not spent a great deal of time on the streets, who are motivated, and who have no criminal records (Hahn & Danzberger, 1987, p. 51). While this assures high levels of job placement, and hence continued program funding, it means that the only people served are those who need minimal training and who, for the most part, might be able to find jobs on their own.

Discussions of school reforms usually begin—and often end—with a consideration of at-risk students; they very quickly are transformed into attempts to do something about dropouts. However, not all at-risk students are, or ever will be, dropouts. More important than consideration of dropouts, we believe, is the great majority of students who are not dropouts, but who *are* alienated. They must be reached before they find dropping out to be a viable alternative to going to school. To do this, a whole new approach to schooling, its purposes, and the content and delivery of instruction must be developed, one that no longer is tied to mere employment and that provides meaningful and challenging cognitive experiences to all children.

REFORMS MAINTAIN THE BASIC STRUCTURE AND OFTEN MAKE THINGS WORSE

Many of the most highly touted reforms and curricular innovations have contributed to falling standards for many schools and to widespread perceptions of failure. In this section we discuss some of those that have been most problematic.

Reforms "Dumb Down" the Curriculum

Reforms in education can act to "dumb down" the level of instruction to the barest minimum by gearing the curriculum to basic skills and the lowest levels of cognitive operations. This deprives students of opportunities to master the skills they will need to succeed in more advanced studies and professional careers. Dumbing down began as a reform designed to assure mastery of skills and make instruction more accessible to slow learners. The first move was to create extensive "basic," non-college-preparatory and remedial programs to upgrade the skills of students who were falling behind or for students who were not deemed able enough to entertain aspirations for college. In an attempt to teach the children "where they are" and to link instruction to "realistic" student aspirations, educators adjusted the scope and complexity of the curriculum in any given subject area, gradually diluting it to make it more "accessible" to children. The effect is the creation of a vertical curriculum (Powell et al., 1985), in which entire programs of courses at different levels are created and populated with students according to their perceived ability levels. This has led to considerable inequity in curricular offerings from school to school, in that entire schools become oriented to basic or remedial instruction.

Teaching down to the minimum means not only teaching at a lower level, but emphasizing or actually teaching fewer subjects. As a consequence, students who barely pass exit competency tests as seniors may in fact be graduating with, at best, eighth-grade skills, because that is the difficulty level of the tests. Similarly, the mania for passing tests causes teachers to give short shrift to nonbasic skills, such as science, written composition, and social studies. Thus what sixth graders cover in math in one school may be far different—and much less advanced—than in other, more affluent schools across town. Some high schools may offer insufficient courses in science, foreign languages, and mathematics for graduates to be eligible for admission to top-level universities. This perpetrates a fraud on children, parents, and communities; more and more children *appear* to be doing well at the same time that they are learning less and less.

Reforms designed to rationalize, standardize, and teacher-proof the curriculum have expedited the process of dumbing down. They divide subject content into sequences of discrete, isolated skills and proficiencies, each of which must be mastered before the student is allowed to move on to more advanced work. Children spend most of each day in drill and practice on decontextualized skills. They read sounds, not words and sentences, long passages, or books. They lose track of the sense of a story because their attention span is calibrated to factoids and sound bites. Their work is boring, not only because it has little connection with their lives inside or outside of school, but because they do not understand what they are doing. Even technology designed to facilitate instruction can impede it. As scientist Alvin White of Harvey Mudd College describes it:

> The more computer power we have the less students know what they're doing. The promise is that we can spend more time on the underlying ideas [by using]

calculators. But in my experience, the time is spent showing them more buttons to push. ("Calculus," 1988)

These approaches lose sight of the forest because they teach only about individual trees; they work particular hardship on at-risk students from linguistically different or less affluent backgrounds (Cummins & Miramontes, 1989; McNeil, 1988a, 1988b, 1988c; Reyes, 1990; Richardson et al., 1989). Overall, dumbing down is a consequence of school reform gone haywire. Its effect is that cognitive skills of high school graduates appear to have declined so much that new college and job recruits must undergo substantial remedial work before they can be effective workers or students.

Reforms Fragment Instruction

Departmentalization of instruction and pullout programs also contribute to increased fragmentation of schedules and decreased instructional time for at-risk students. Students lose time in instruction each time they move from their home classrooms to pullout teachers' rooms and get resettled for instruction. Departmentalization, advocated because it facilitates teaching children in homogeneous ability groups and focuses on areas of teacher expertise, may actually accelerate the alienation of at-risk children. This is because at-risk children seem to do better when they have just one teacher with whom they can become more intimate, rather than a group of specialists throughout the day. Children in lower ability groups also get fewer minutes of instruction and more often are taught by aides rather than classroom teachers. Sometimes, being at risk itself requires special organizational skills; a great deal of mental effort is required of at-risk elementary children just to remember where and when they have to be to keep up with their complex "remedial" programs (K. P. Bennett, 1986; Richardson et al., 1989).

Children are not the only people adversely affected by the rationalization and fragmentation of curriculum; contemporary curriculum reforms generate an immense amount of new paperwork for teachers. Not only does it seem that more material must be covered in a semester—the value of which many teachers question—but new instructional management systems and the preoccupation with administration and grading of tests generate an avalanche of paperwork that contributes to the hectic pace of classroom life and diverts teachers' time away from work with individual children (Apple, 1986; McNeil, 1988c; Richardson et al., 1989).

Reforms Do Not Improve Inadequate Working Conditions for Teachers

As noted previously, many of the innovations proposed are irrelevant or impossible for poor schools and districts. We have noted that funds often do not go to those most in need. Further, funds that are available often are not for the items needed most. Especially in urban areas, but characteristic of schools in many other areas, working conditions for teachers and students are so poor that they would not be tolerated in any other skilled profession (Corcoran et al., 1988, p. xiii). When schools are short of everything from textbooks to toilet paper and chalk, when necessary equipment such as photocopying machines and even ditto machines are broken and no funds are available for their repair, when the buildings have broken plumbing, leaking roofs, and peeling paint for lack of funds for preventive maintenance and repairs, teachers and students become demoralized. "Sometimes I feel like I'm coming into a garbage can," said one teacher (Corcoran et al., 1988, p. 14). Under these conditions, computer literacy programs are a luxury. Appeals to excellence, such as raising standards by raising test scores, are a fraud if intensive remediation is not offered so that students can acquire the higher levels of skills they are expected to exhibit. The situation is aggravated by lack of space; even in newer school buildings—and the majority of schools in the United States are approaching 50 years old—teachers often do not have their own classrooms, sufficient storage and activity space for students, or enough working space to prepare for their classes or meet with students individually (pp. 14-16).

A final issue is class size. While research has yet to establish definitively the relationship between class size and pupil achievement, one thing is clear: Teachers feel more competent when they have smaller classes.[1] They have more time to devote to individual children, and they feel more in control of both the management of their students and their course preparations. Large class size constitutes yet another form of substandard working condition that current reforms have done little to address; since this is one of the most pressing needs teachers feel, failure to address it makes them feel that their deepest concerns will never be heard.

Reforms Have Not Changed the Level of Administrative Support Teachers Receive

One of the key elements in how much alienation teachers feel is the degree to which they perceive themselves to be supported by their administration and believe that they can exercise their own professional judgment with regard to what and how they teach (Dworkin, 1985, 1987). However, few if any of the recent reforms seriously challenge existing conditions or styles of leadership and control within buildings. In fact, a leading critic says that reforms that propose to empower teachers, replace hierarchical structures with peer group control, or accord professional autonomy to teachers are "ludicrous intellectually but devastating in their political and policy consequences. . . . They are tantamount to prescribing the HIV virus to cure AIDS. The only question is how long the patient can survive these misguided prescriptions" (Lieberman, 1989). Reforms usually exact a price, including mandates for greater teacher accountability. These, in turn, necessitate less supportive and more evaluative roles for campus administrators, which contributes to disenfranchisement, a diminished sense of professional autonomy, and subsequent burnout for teachers.

Reforms Must Be Implemented With the Existing Educational Team

One of the real problems with school reform is implementation. Reformers tend to forget that all of the changes, whether curricular, organizational, or psychosocial, will have to be implemented with virtually the same instructional and administrative staff that existed prereform.

In-service training. All reforms are predicated, implicitly or explicitly, upon the notion of in-service training for teachers. Yet in-service training usually is provided only for new teachers or elementary school staff. As we have pointed out, however, most teachers think very little of the workshops and training services they are provided. Outside consultants come in with a standardized dog-and-pony blitz that may or may not be relevant to the most pressing concerns teachers have. Even when the training is perceived as useful, it has little or no impact on morale and none on levels of burnout. Perhaps this is because little follow-up is provided to help teachers implement what they have learned. As one of the authors was told by a teacher at a recent workshop: "Those big guys, they come in here with their canned remarks, and they all talk so LOUD! It's like they are trying to sell used cars. And they don't listen. Then they leave, and we aren't any better off than before."

Resources for in-service training and workshops are limited. Teachers usually cannot get time off for anything other than district-sanctioned—and usually district-run—in-service training. Even then, they cannot leave their classrooms unless substitutes are found, and resources for hiring subs are limited. To save money, districts often use a "trickle-down" model for disseminating information that resembles that old party game "telephone." An expert is hired to train district personnel—at best one per school, but usually limited to a few central office curriculum advisers—who then train building-level personnel, who then teach the district teachers what they have learned. Information is supposed to trickle down to the classroom teacher, but by the time it gets there, much of it has been diluted or distorted. In any case, the teachers who get the training second- or thirdhand never enjoy the immediacy and excitement of meeting and questioning experts during an actual workshop. They are left with little free time to learn how to do what they are supposed to do, and even less for follow-up or on-the-job training.

Removing incompetence and rewarding merit. One reform that addresses the flat pay scale of teaching is the institution of "combat pay" for teaching in difficult schools or neighborhoods. This has been used in a very few districts. Some districts also pay premiums to teachers in critical subject areas, such as math and science, where teacher shortages exist. Yet another reform, merit pay for exemplary teaching, has had a checkered career. Merit pay has been advocated since the 1920s; Cubberley supported it as a tenet of scientific management, to reward good teachers and weed out "dolts." The idea has resurfaced repeatedly since then, each time with the same unresolved problems. First, schools cannot define what they mean by *merit*. There is little consensus as to what constitutes good teaching or how to measure it. Second, merit pay is not an effective incentive for everybody, and it is especially ineffective for professional activities, like teaching, that do not involve piecework. Still another problem has been the interdependent nature of teaching; it is difficult to isolate the effects of any individual teacher (Johnson, 1984).

A number of reforms have been suggested to create a hierarchy—or career ladder—of merit for elementary and secondary school teachers. The same proposals also address the issue of how to get rid of teachers who are not competent. Both types of reforms are difficult to execute. They have become increasingly controversial, and teacher organizations have been unwilling to sanction them. Where career ladders actually have been implemented, authorities have been accused of subjective execution and co-optation; merit has simply been equated with seniority (Malen & Hart, 1987). Punishments for lack of competence more often have not been implemented. They have included a loss of pay raises or "step increases," being required to undertake remedial instruction, being put on probation, and dismissal. Rarely has the last step been taken.

Problems in Improving the Competence of Teachers

While some reforms call for improving the performance of existing teachers, still another involves how to get more highly qualified teachers into classrooms in the first place. Following the publication of a number of reports decrying the state of teacher education in the United States (Carnegie Forum on Education and the Economy, 1986; Holmes Group, 1986; National Commission on Excellence in Education, 1983), a wide variety of enhancements to existing teacher training programs have been proposed. These include regional "teacher centers" or "academies," which would serve as centers for staff development and training of teachers; associated with universities, but not controlled by them, the centers could draw upon university-based personnel for support and staff.

More rigorous teacher assessments and evaluations and competency tests also have been implemented, at least in some degree, in most states. One of the most popular suggestions to increase teacher competence has been to increase the number of years a teacher spends in training. These programs create the same problem nurses have: All nurses are paid approximately the same, whether they are two-year A.A.-degree nurses or four-year B.A.-degree nurses. Similarly, teachers with five-year B.A.s probably will not get paid more for knowing more, even though they will incur higher opportunity costs. Moreover, in times of teacher shortage, additional training is of little benefit because districts desperate for personnel relax their standards and hire people with minimal credentials, simply to fill empty classrooms. All of these reforms are imposed from above; teachers have little say in how they are run and what standards they use, and teachers themselves have little voice in policing their own profession. Nor do they seem to want it.

Another reform—discussed briefly in Chapter 5—involves using a human relations approach to make teachers more sensitive to the needs of their students. It most often is used with administrators who are trying to do better with teachers, but also is used with teachers trying to do better with students. Many focus on cultural issues, helping teachers to appreciate the backgrounds of their students, but others simply work to help teachers handle conflict better and love children more.

Still another approach widely advocated by critical theorists involves the "empowerment" of teachers, whereby teachers become viewed not as passive public servants, but as "transformative intellectuals" (Giroux, 1988b; Gitlin & Smyth, 1989) actively involved in investigating and questioning existing patterns of authority and control in schools and society. Implicit in this approach is that as teachers work to become transformative intellectuals, they also will work to improve their teaching—that in fact the act of doing so in itself enhances teaching competence. These ideas are, however, limited to grass-roots and building-level activity, and remain naive in the face of institutionalized bureaucratic resistance to change.

Reforms Try to Change Instruction and Performance by Changing School Organization

Another approach to school reform is to change schools by changing school structure. The most popular approaches are decentralization, or breaking up large schools and districts into smaller but identically structured units; parental control, which combines decentralization with reserving places on elected school boards for parent representatives; school-based management, or shifting most of the responsibility for hiring and firing personnel, deciding upon curricula, and dispensing of funds from the central office to the building-level principal; "restructuring" schools, or giving an increased measure of control over activities in schools to teachers and students; and breaking up larger schools into small, self-contained "houses" or units. The major issues are (a) the size of the unit; (b) the degree of control over budgets, hiring, and what is to be taught permitted to each unit; and (c) how permeable each unit is to influence by lower-level participants—parents, teachers, students, and building-level administrative and support personnel.

Reform at the district level: Decentralization. Decentralization really is a phenomenon of large urban school districts. It focuses on the bureaucratic structure of governance and control in school districts and attempts to change schools by first attacking nonresponsive, alienating, corrupt, top-heavy, and expensive bureaucracies. It begins with organizational restructuring, usually by decentralization of central school district authority. It employs a somewhat romantic rhetoric, often assuming that small is beautiful, or, at least, more beautiful than big. It also represents a reversal of the school consolidation movement, a "reform" that reduced the number of school districts precipitously in the last 50 years (Tyack, 1990).

Supporters of decentralization argue that the movement for consolidation may have been counterproductive; even when per pupil expenditures and socioeconomic status are taken into account, smaller districts promote achievement of their students more efficiently than do large ones. This may be because administrative staff can be closer to and more aware of citizen and parent preferences, teachers can be more involved in decision making, home-school relations can be more intimate, and the absence of administrative complexity and multiple bureaucratic layers promotes more efficiency in operation (Bidwell & Kasarda, 1975; Turner, Camilli, Kroc, & Hoover, 1986; Walberg, 1989). Supporters also believe that decentralization will reduce bureaucratic cost, especially if administrators are returned to lower-paying jobs and their support staff fired. Economic reasons and a top-heavy, self-serving administrative structure were primary factors in the radical court-ordered decentralization of the Chicago Public Schools in 1989 (Hess & Addington, 1990).

On the other hand, critics argue that decentralization of districts could cause fragmentation of systems, and, to the extent that district boundaries reflect ethnic divisions, it could also result in resegregation. The experience of decentralization in New York, whose 32 subdistricts were larger than most city school systems (Wilkerson, 1989b), has demonstrated that rather than eliminate abuse, it can simply shift the locus of corruption downward. Pending investigations, members of several local school boards were suspended over charges of corruption, squandering of funds, creation of unnecessary jobs, and racial, religious, and political favoritism in filling jobs (Lee, 1989a).

Chicago's decentralization is extreme; whereas New York's local districts could not fire or transfer principals and principals maintained tenure, Chicago has given near-absolute power to the smallest possible unit, the 540 individual neighborhood schools. Tenure for principals has been abolished, and locally elected school boards, dominated by parents and with control over the hiring and firing of principals and teachers, now set policy for each of the schools in the district. The experience raises questions as to how a school district can train parents—some of whom are not high school graduates, many of whom have never voted before, most of whom are hostile to the school district, and none of whom have ever run an organization—to get along, make decisions, resolve conflicts, and build teams (Wilkerson, 1989a).

Decentralization at the building level: School-based management, restructuring, and participative models. School-based management programs focus upon delegating to individual school principals—and sometimes teachers, parents, community members, and the student body—decision-making power that formerly was held by the superintendent and the school board. Their purpose is to increase creativity and responsiveness to local needs. The logic is, "So you think you can do a better job? Okay, you're in charge!" These programs often are built around retraining of teachers to assume team leadership, development of peer review programs and professional accountability, transformation of principals into instructional leaders while many of the business aspects of school administration are transferred to business managers, institution of school-community advisory panels, and a variety of school improvement plans (Hess, 1991). Despite a great deal of enthusiasm about this kind of reform, it does not yet seem to have been widely adopted. Obstacles include difficulty in sorting out budgets, increased costs of staff time required by decentralized purchasing and personnel activities, lack of wholehearted support from central administration, and ambivalence over delegation of critical areas of responsibility, such as hiring and firing of personnel, standards for students, and curricular innovation (Lindquist & Mauriel, 1989). Critics also argue that school-based management can be effective only when it utilizes that rarest of commodities, a gifted administrator, and that it can introduce unacceptable levels of variability in performance among schools.

Reforms involving organizational restructuring, some form of school- or site-based management, or increased professional autonomy and empowerment of teachers have called for the development of collegial and participative decision-making frameworks at the school level. Many implicitly borrow from "Japanese management theory," which develops collaborative models in which all participate and all are rewarded, rather than the competitive "rational" model, which gives big rewards to a few people and weeds out the rest (Peters & Waterman, 1982). Suggestions have included quality circles, peer assistance, career ladders, teams, departmentalization, and teacher councils. It has been particularly difficult to legislate these kinds of programs, because they require both willingness on the part of administrators to delegate power in traditional realms of administrative authority and readiness and ability on the part of teachers to lead.

Teachers' ambivalence about these programs stems from their suspicion that the programs are designed, at best, to facilitate acceptance of decisions that management has already made. On the other hand, some teachers clearly view such proposals as ways to gain more professional control over the profession. A particular obstacle to implementation of such programs has been their lack of specificity regarding areas of responsibility. They have been notable in their failure to specify the types of decisions in which teachers are expected to become involved or the types of involvements required of them (Conley, 1989). They give little attention to the degree to which power at the departmental or building level trickles up to, or has any influence over, policy in the central office or state legislature, where decisions most affecting what teachers will do and how much they are rewarded actually are made. They also have failed in providing sufficient release time for teachers to take on any additional tasks (Corcoran et al., 1988); teachers who want to be empowered, it seems, must do so on their own time.

A final type of reorganization involves reducing the size of the student body served in any given unit. In most cases, this does not involve building new schools, but rather dividing large buildings and using innovative scheduling to create semiautonomous schools-within-a-school. The primary purpose of such reforms is to increase intimacy among students and between teachers and students; typically, students are taught by a team of teachers assigned to their unit. Because each of the teachers sees each child every day, instruction can be coordinated, and educational programs can be managed on a more or less case-by-case basis. This innovation, which is commonly used for school-within-a-school magnet programs, is widely believed to increase participation rates among at-risk students, and is one of the most frequently mentioned antidotes to the oversized, impersonal, factorylike urban school.

Except for building-level programs, the effect of organizational reform on teachers is an open question, and can depend upon how far down it reaches. The impact of these reforms on achievement is unknown, especially given that the effects cannot be expected to be evident for some time to come, and that, like many educational reforms, they are not targeted at the one issue by which their success typically is measured—pupil achievement.

Changing the organization of curriculum. Other organizational reforms involve the structure of the curriculum. One involves providing special programs for children in trouble. Curricular organization for at-risk or special-needs children involves identification and isolation. Notwithstanding a continued and heated debate over the efficacy and dangers of "labeling" children, the practice endures as a necessary prelude to placement in programs designed to "meet their needs." The result is that labeled children are isolated from other children in special programs that are geographically distinct from other students—whether they are "pullouts" or located in different buildings and classrooms.

Earlier, we noted how programs designed to help slow learners ossify, trapping their clients forever in a slow track, rather than bringing their performance up to the point where they can move into regular, on-grade-level instruction. While all are supposed to be content oriented and geared to the skill levels of the students, the distinctions among remedial, vocational, and enrichment streams actually work to obscure the real knowledge that labeled children have and to retard their achievement. These distinctions preserve them in instructional programs geared to the lowest skill levels, rather than comprehension, critical thinking, and synthesis. What tracking does is increase gaps between high- and low-achieving students; it creates slow learners who are trapped on the lower levels of an ever-proliferating "vertical curriculum" (Lee & Bryk, 1988; Oakes, 1985; Page, 1989; Powell et al., 1985).

Furthermore, as we have noted, the fact that schools focus on the college bound to the exclusion of anyone else makes it difficult to obtain resources, much less establish parity of esteem, for programs for non-college-bound students (Bishop, 1989). Since schooling is designed only to move the fortunate few on to college as expeditiously as possible, those students who are not college bound—in most schools the majority of the enrollment—are made to feel irrelevant.

Institutional Inertia: The Mousetrap Resists Reform

Finally, reforms founder because of organizational inertia and resistance. Schools often greet reform initiatives with a "circle the wagons" mentality impervious to change initiatives. Others engage in sabotage of change, especially of reforms that attempt to improve intercultural understanding by granting parity of esteem to nontraditional ways of teaching or viewing the world. Killing the messenger of change by "silencing" students (Fine, 1987), parents (Stern, 1987; Tizard et al., 1989), and teachers is common; those who protest are often viewed as troublemakers and forced to leave the school (see, for example, Kohl, 1967; Kozol, 1967; McLaren, 1980; Puckett, 1989). What then, can be done? And how can schools be forced to respond to their changing cultural and demographic conditions? In the final chapter we address the issue of alienation head on, describing its origin in organizational dynamics and suggesting some possible avenues for innovation in schools.

NOTE

1. Finn and Achilles (1990) indicate that dramatic reduction in elementary school class size—to 10-15 students per class—does improve achievement significantly. However, such large reductions would be financially impossible for most school districts.

TEN

Conclusion: Some Modest and Not So Modest Proposals

One of the recurrent themes in American culture is the bipolar tension between distrust of government on one hand and the desire for public solutions to social problems on the other. Calls for privatization often follow on the heels of widespread discontent with public institutions; we see this theme in the move to contract out the construction and administration of prisons to private entrepreneurs, to make systems of public transportation and communication "pay for themselves," and to make the administration of schools and their recruitment patterns subject to putative "market forces," such as voucher systems and district-wide enrollment. Solutions such as these can be called private solutions to a public problem, an approach we clearly eschew. We believe that the private and quasi-private solutions for education's ills proposed by conservatives and the radical Right—including home schooling, voucher systems, lowering the age for compulsory school attendance, raising graduation standards, and providing tax credits for parents whose children attend private schools—violate deeply held American cultural ethics. From both educational and sociological perspectives, the private solution to public education can be only a partial one.

We want to make clear our firm commitment to universal and public education. Whether that commitment derives from an egalitarian—if romantic—desire to promote the general welfare and to facilitate individual economic mobility or from a more Hobbesian concern with social order and the assimilation of the culturally and economically different, schooling as an institution for socialization and societal mobilization can be effective only if all members of the youth cohort are forced to experience a similar set of enculturating conditions. This does not mean, as we shall argue, that all students should experience exactly the same kind of school. The one-size-fits-all solution is one of the primary reasons all extant attempts at school reform have had less-than-satisfactory outcomes. It does mean providing challenging and flexible educational experiences for all students, education that is geared to acquisition of a common battery of inquiry skills.

Because private solutions are, by nature, exclusionary, societal institutions such as schools should operate under societal control, however loose that might be. Like the private and parochial schools often touted as models for effective schools, private solutions exercise triage; they work best for the least disadvantaged or injured student (Hess, 1986). They are subject to the same problems illustrated by research on "teachable groups" in the late 1950s and 1960s. These studies demonstrated conclusively that children did learn much more effectively when they and their teachers mutually chose each other; however, more than 25% of all children and teachers never were chosen by anyone. Like private schools, teachable groups appear to "work" because, among other things, they involve only those teachers and students who are most mutually congenial. Public education, however, does not have this choice. No longer can we exclude students nobody wants to teach—who now constitute the 25% of any given cohort of students that does not complete high school—and the inestimable number of in-service teachers with whom nobody wants to study. The reader will not, therefore, find such solutions advocated in this book.

We premise all of our suggestions upon the following assumptions:

(1) A child's education should not be stigmatized by derogatory labels or implicit disparity of esteem.
(2) Curricula should not be stratified into advanced, college prep, "ordinary," and remedial streams, because this contributes to labeling and disparity of esteem.
(3) Education for every child should be individualized and case managed.
(4) School schedules and facilities should be organized to make it possible for today's children to attend, regardless of their need to work, to fulfill their own parenting responsibilities, or to be provided special services.
(5) Teachers and students should have adequate materials and working conditions.
(6) A child's success in school should not require two resident parents and a nonworking mother.
(7) Similarly, a child's success in school should not be predicated upon the help of able parents.
(8) The assumption that better education can be had for less money should be rejected.
(9) Pedagogy should not be decontextualized, fragmented, and narrowly skills based. Just as the whole child is taught, so also should the whole subject, the whole curriculum, be taught.

AN EXCURSION INTO UNPOPULAR COMPLEXITY

We have chosen an unpopular way to talk about education in America: We have presented both the problems and the solutions as extraordinarily complex. Much of what we have reported in the preceding pages is neither new nor surprising to many readers. The titles of two recent modest booklets, *Dropouts in America: Enough Is Known for Action* (Hahn & Danzberger, 1987) and *School Dropouts: Everybody's Problem* (Ranbom & Lewis, 1986), summarize our feelings. They make it clear that they promise nothing new: "Taken individually, none of the program proposals and policy recommendations represents a fundamental break with examples that can be found in existing programs" (Hahn & Danzberger, 1987, p. 63). The authors of these two works state that schools are everybody's problem, and that many good ideas about how to start solving the problems already have been developed. However, they share our feeling that the current popular revulsion against public spending—and taxation—militates against certain kinds of change. We also believe that the widening gap between rich and poor, documented in Chapter 2, has increased widespread public denial of youth problems in particular and education in general in the United States. Thus we hope that what *is* new about our call to action is that it delineates how bad the problems are.

We have indicated in the preceding chapters that education in the United States is in a virtual state of emergency. We feel that the situation many American children experience in their homes and neighborhoods and the conditions that confront their future are devastating. Furthermore, the conditions under which teachers are expected to teach and children are expected to learn are catastrophic. As we have argued, consciously or unconsciously, policymakers perpetuate a state of willing ignorance about the state of American public education, the conditions in which American children live, and the causes of these conditions. Such ignorance facilitates the perpetuation of "quick fix" simplistic problem solving; its results are sufficiently devastating that it verges on criminal collusion to avoid consequential change. Nevertheless, consequential change in educational institutions and the array of expectations surrounding them is of the utmost necessity. Change in the social and economic context in which educational institutions are embedded has taken U.S. society light years beyond the organization and operation of contemporary schools. These changed societal factors act as external or "independent variables" to which schools, willingly or not, are causally linked, but over which they have little control. To ignore these factors is to render schools increasingly dysfunctional and to render their participants increasingly alienated. It also permits policymakers to ignore systematically the impact of external factors and encourages them to persist in trying to solve problems by manipulating those school- or micro-level variables over which schools do have control.

What, then, should be done? At this point it will be helpful to discuss societal perceptions of the correspondence between schools and the structure of opportunity.

TIGHT, LOOSE, AND NONEXISTENT COUPLING BETWEEN SCHOOLS AND SOCIETY

As we have pointed out elsewhere, the "linkage of education with jobs and exit from poverty is indirect and at times tenuous" (LeCompte & Dworkin, 1988, p. 135). Yet what schools have preached—and what teachers, students, and their parents have been encouraged to believe—is that schools and society are tightly "coupled" and solidly interrelated, especially with regard to education and occupational opportunities. This type of relationship, were it to exist, would justify belief in the argument that if children work hard and achieve success in school, and if teachers are competent and carry out their job of instruction effectively, children will be rewarded in the occupational structure and teachers will garner the respect of the community.

Considerable research on both the internal organization of schools and their connection to local, regional, and national institutions suggests that, contrary to the tightly coupled hypothesis, the schools/society relationship does not operate so smoothly. Schools really are characterized by loose coupling (Corwin, 1973; Herriott & Firestone, 1984; Marrett, 1990; Meyer & Rowan, 1978; Weick, 1976; Wilson & Corbett, 1983). Marrett (1990) defines the issue of coupling in organizations as follows:

> In loosely coupled systems, events are related, but the events remain identifiable, although they are linked physically or logically. The components of such a system carry out tasks that are relatively independent. Tightly coupled systems are woven together in either of two ways: through interdependent tasks or a formal authority structure. (p. 76)

By contrast, loosely coupled systems permit a considerable degree of autonomy among members.

For school systems, loose coupling means that direct supervision and control are difficult to achieve. Both the geographic dispersion of supervisory staff and the "autonomy of the closed door" (Lortie, 1969) that protects teachers and staff from surveillance contribute to their structural looseness. Moreover, the public cannot regulate the schools directly. Public directives—which themselves are couched in vague policy statements—must be filtered through various interest groups and community organizations, transmitted to accrediting and regulatory agencies, and implemented by periodically elected boards of trustees, whose ability to manipulate the actual operations of schools and classrooms is indirect at best. Tangible linkages are tenuous among the activities of schools—what they teach—and both public desires and individual aspirations of teachers and students. The public desires social control and economic welfare; teachers and students desire public esteem and job satisfaction on one hand and personal challenge and tangible occupational attainment on the other. These are not linked aspirations. Often whether or not a teacher finds a good placement and whether or not a student experiences training and career placement commensurate with his or her talent are governed more by chance than by express design. However, schools do achieve a degree of coherence despite loose coupling because they rely upon the common commitment of staff to an agreed-upon set of goals to ensure quality control over the product. This kind of autonomy and commitment often ensures that the organization will adapt to the needs of clients (students).

While schools in general are characterized by loose coupling, many specific schools, especially those in the inner cities and economically devastated rural areas, are characterized by no coupling at all (Marrett, 1990), and hence little adaptation to student or teacher needs. There is little agreement over organizational goals, and commitment of teachers is often too minimal to ensure any kind of quality control. Marrett describes many of these schools as "uncoupled" (p. 78); in them, there is no promise at all of a connection between the labor market and what is taught in school. Lack of societal opportunity leaves teachers with no realistic reward whatsoever that they can hold out to students who want to succeed. And intractable and corrupt bureaucracies reinforce the total lack of connection among components of the system; they make it impossible for any attempts at reform to "trickle down" to the individual schools and classrooms (Hess, 1991). These conditions are, in fact, one of the catalysts for radical school decentralization of the kind begun in 1989 in the Chicago Public Schools.

Coupling at the Micro Level

The metaphor of coupling has significant heuristic value beyond the microsystem of school organization. In the previous chapters we have discussed the range of problems that produce in schools, teachers, and students a sense of alienation and failure to deliver on promises. Provided that there are shared educational goals and professional commitments to realizing such goals, loose coupling at the campus level, or even at the district level, is preferable to tight surveillance and the loss of student and teacher autonomy. However, many of the so-called failures of schooling are attributable to the lack of coupling between schools and social and cultural conditions in the larger society. As we have noted, these include myriad changes in the labor market, family structure, national and global economies, and the breakdown of institutions of social control in the society.

Schools are expected to solve all social ills that befall children, while still utilizing instructional organizational and managerial patterns designed for a different, earlier, and far more limited set of purposes. Critics of schools have variously used the tight coupling argument for their own purposes, calling for improvements in school performance by increasing "accountability," or tightening up of these same obsolete systems at the micro—or within-school—level.

Neo-Marxist critical theorists have argued deterministically that tight coupling leads schools to act as agencies of cultural and economic reproduction. Political conservatives in the United States also have embraced the argument and wedded it to a nouveau social Darwinism that calls for policies—such as earlier school-leaving ages, enhanced graduation standards, and increased job and vocational training for the so-called non-college bound—that cull academic failures out of the educational system early. Critics also have called for increased "teacher-proofing" of curricula, competency testing, and monitoring.

We submit that these approaches, however varied in their philosophical origins, have the effect of increasing entropy *within* school systems without linking schools more tightly to the external factors—what we earlier called independent variables—that really have made schools obsolete. Calls for tighter coupling have simply concentrated on tightening patterns of control *within* and *between* internal components of the schools, rather than on linking those internal components to components of the larger society external to school systems. The resulting practices breed an alienating organizational pathology as severe as the chaos and demoralization of a completely uncoupled system. They also confirm the prediction of critical theorists that schools actually act to restrict opportunity, continually reproducing the existing structure of economic and class domination.

In Chapter 7, we proposed alienation or strain theory as an explanation for teacher burnout and quitting and student tune-out and dropping out. This approach posits the existence of a gap between the expectations about school and teaching created in the society and actual opportunities to achieve such expectations in the real experience of the public school. In short, a dichotomy between goals and means to attaining goals has been created, just as posited by Merton (1964a, 1964b), Farnworth and Leiber (1989), and other strain theorists. In general, tight coupling implies that means and ends are conjoined; loose coupling posits that goal attainment may be more difficult; uncoupling assures that goals and

Table 10.1 The Impact of Coupling on Educational Practice and Socioeconomic Structure

	Level of Analysis			
	Microsystem (Schools and Classrooms)		*Macrosystem (Socioeconomic Structure)*	
Coupling Level	*Practice*	*Consequence*	*Practice*	*Consequence*
Tight	Imposition of uniform policy and practice guidelines; possibility of both rigidities in practice and administrative surveillance instead of support; micromanagement of daily activities; inflexibility in addressing idiosyncratic student needs	Decreased autonomy, innovation, and commitment among teachers; failure to meet special needs of students; may lead to uniformity of student product, but on limited objectives; higher rates of teacher burnout and student dropout	State-centralized human resources planning; consensus on labor and training needs and employment opportunities; planned, tracked, and vocationally oriented curriculum, administered and coordinated by state or federal authorities	Inelasticity in response to technological shifts in labor market needs; intermittent and situational periods of under- and unemployment; attempted goodness of fit between educational training and careers; highly stratified educational and career opportunities
Loose	Some imposition of uniform policy, but with opportunities for autonomy in practice, innovation, and realization of individual goals; administrative and instructional leadership provided consistently;	Increased autonomy, innovation, and commitment among teachers; development of individualized educational programs; lower rates of teacher burnout and student	Diversification of instructional delivery and philosophy among schools; consensus on labor market and training needs; cognitively oriented liberal arts and humanities curriculum, coupled with	Considerable goodness of fit between educational and occupational opportunities; education for career flexibility and change; close articulation with changing technological nature of labor force; higher levels

	flexibility in curricular offerings, with emphasis on cognitive and critical thinking skills	dropout; higher rates of student success	experiential, mediated, and situated pedagogy	of public satisfaction with schools
Uncoupled	No uniformity of policy or practice; support and surveillance random or nonexistent; curricular offerings disorganized and unstructured	Anarchy in classrooms; innovation and commitment treated with indifference; educational outcomes dependent on chance or personality factors; high rates of teacher burnout and quitting behavior and student dropout	Diversity in instructional delivery and philosophy among schools, but without consensus on educational or labor market needs; considerable class, ethnic, and gender stratification and rigidity in curricular offerings; no external or centralized guidance in instructional delivery or philosophy	Random connection between schooling and employment opportunities; high levels of public dissatisfaction with schooling; skill needs of labor market poorly articulated with educational training

means toward achieving goals are unlikely to be related, unless by chance alone. This is not to suggest that coupling always should be tight. While organizational goals should reflect actor goals (student and teacher goals) and organizations should offer opportunities for the attainment of individual goals, it is at the micro level that overarticulation of goals and means has the possibility of stifling autonomy, creativity, and individual choice. Excessively close coupling at the micro level means that the organization establishes goals for its members and provides the requisite opportunities for attainment of the goals. However, because individual organizations are capable of greater degrees of micromanagement and are better able to exercise surveillance over members than are macro-level institutions—such as state legislatures, administrative agencies, and social service bureaus—very tight coupling is likely to imply rigidity and a limitation on individual options to learn. In schools, it is likely to imply a limited number of curricula geared to the needs of the modal student and faculty member, as well as forced compliance to rules and regulations. At the macro level, where surveillance is more difficult, tight coupling suggests only that education provides access to real careers by providing the requisite skills and opportunity structures (such as economic support for programs to meet needs of teachers and students, or to stimulate innovation). Tight coupling does not mandate micromanagement from superordinate levels of authority—such as the implementation of a universal curriculum by a legislature.

Table 10.1 displays the impacts of tight coupling, loose coupling, and uncoupling on the macro and micro levels of school and societal organization with respect to the goals/means to goals scheme of strain theory. Tight coupling at the classroom and campus level is likely to correspond to a single organizational viewpoint, uniform goals, and a hierarchical structure wherein individual differences among teachers, students, the student body as a whole, and campus environments are ignored and curricula and pedagogy become rigid and stereotypical. Innovation is discouraged and communication flows only along established and legitimated routes; commands flow downward and data flow upward.

By contrast, loose coupling at the micro level of schools and classrooms ensures autonomy and adaptation to unique situations and needs. This enhances organizational commitment by students and teachers, provided that higher levels of the organization (e.g., at the district level) have a shared vision of the goals for teachers and students. A critical part of such goals includes a view that the promotion of campus-level inputs is legitimate. Micromanagement (excessive management) by officials in district offices or above is thus avoided.

Uncoupled school systems fail to have any consistent dreams or goals, nor do they assure that the attainment of goals can be facilitated. They thus permit anarchy at the micro level until legislative or public outcry initiates intervention. This is because uncoupled systems lack the clear goals and professional commitment to quality control that render loosely coupled systems, by contrast, more coherent. Uncoupled systems lack microsystems to articulate and mediate goals; hence in the face of crises they are at the mercy of autocratic administrative response. All too often this involves imposition of systems of accountability, excessive surveillance, and despotic forms of control by authorities external to the school building.

Coupling at the Macro Level

At the macrosystem level, the role of coupling is distinctly different. Here, rather than referring to the linkages of control and communication *within* an organization, the term *uncoupling* reflects the failure of the schools to keep step with changes in the society. Uncoupled systems are those in which the organizational goals of schools and the pedagogical means for attaining those goals fail to match with new or emerging demographic, economic, cultural, and structural characteristics of the society. Schooling that is uncoupled from society or, at best, very loosely coupled to it tends to "fit people for unfit fitnesses," as Merton (1968) once noted. Such schools become warehouses for children too young to work and repositories for employees (teachers and administrators) who cannot find work elsewhere. Schools train students to enter careers that no longer exist; teachers rely upon family support systems that are not present; colleges of education educate students to perform in school settings that are long gone. By contrast, tighter coupling means that education becomes relevant to a variety of student needs and that careers in education can be rewarding. It is important to note that extremely tight coupling between schools and society is an alternative we do not advocate; it is exemplified by societies in which state-centralized human resources planning dominates educational policy.

EXPLORING THE REALM OF POSSIBLE AND PROBABLE CHANGE

What we propose is a redistribution of patterns of coupling and control in school systems. We believe that schools should be more *loosely coupled* at the micro or local level as well as within and between the components internal to educational systems—at the level of the conditions of teaching and relationships between adults and children in schools—while they should be more *tightly coupled* at the macro level—or between components of the society such as the labor market, family structures, and professional training. Such an arrangement would move both the practices and consequences of schooling toward the middle range of Table 10.1, rather than at the poles, where we believe that they currently are located.

Considerable resistance exists, however, to implementing change at any level of schooling. In general, school people exhibit three classes of response to avoid implementing change in what they do. First, they focus blame for the crisis in education on factors that they actually *cannot* change, such as increasing urbanization, changes in the structure of families and the labor force that increase the number of single-parent families and families in which both parents work, and the rising tide of crime and drug abuse in society at large. Second, they blame the misfeasance and nonfeasance of outsiders for failure to change or control what school people themselves also cannot change or control. Third, they abdicate responsibility for many factors over which they *do* exercise some measure of control—such as criminal and deviant behavior of students, pathological school bureaucracies, disinterested and apathetic students, and the effects of dysfunctional families—by defining them as being *out* of their realm of control. At the micro level of school practice, educators blame their plight on issues at the macro level, while at the macro level of policymaking and finance, blame is placed upon teachers and school staff. As a remedy, micromanagement is imposed at all levels. The strain is, in fact, toward tighter coupling, but it is tighter coupling of the wrong kind.

In the following pages, we would like to accomplish the following. First, we will discuss those issues over which we feel that school people really do not have much control. Second, we want to satisfy the genuine need of school people to answer the question, What do I do in school tomorrow? in practical, rather than theoretical, language. The immediacy of life on the firing line of school practice makes this common plea no trivial request. Grand theoretical statements about how students do and should learn and how social structures do and do not operate are useless to practitioners who need concrete advice about daily pedagogy and administration. To do so we will focus on changes that are possible; we also redefine as changeable some factors often deemed out of control by school people. We accomplish this redefinition both by making our expectations for change more realistic and by changing the level at which the desired changes occur.

FACTORS SCHOOLS CANNOT CHANGE

The factors we discuss in this section are those that both profoundly affect the conduct of schooling and over which school people have no control at all. They constitute the most serious challenge to a school's ability for adaptive and creative response.

Recruitment. One factor over which schools have no control is that of supply-and-demand issues in the recruitment of teachers. For the foreseeable future, minority teachers will be in short supply, in large part because of the small numbers of minorities who (a) graduate from college and (b) choose to enter the teaching profession. Further, schools will be handicapped in their ability to tap what once was a "captive pool" of highly qualified prospective teachers (i.e., well-educated white middle-class females) for whom teaching represented the "glass ceiling" of desirable employment above which patterns of discrimination in the labor force prevented them from reaching. Schools desiring to institute innovative programs also will be unable to "wipe the slate clean" by firing disaffected and entrapped teachers already on their employment rosters or to avoid lowering of certification standards for certain specialty areas—such as math, science, and bilingual education—when no legitimately qualified candidates for the jobs are found.

Declining wages. Although the reward held out for success in school has been future success in the wage structure, the fact is, as we have indicated, the wages paid to most working people are declining. In fact, the U.S. Bureau of Labor Statistics (1990) observes that, as of fall 1990, the cost of living is 393% of what it was in 1967. Thus a teacher starting at $25,000 to $30,000 per year today is earning $6,361 to $7,633 in constant dollars—actually less than his or her counterpart earned some 20 years ago. Inflation has taken its toll, but more important is the fact that schools no longer hold out sufficient rewards for diligence, to either teachers or students. This is because the majority of new jobs students can anticipate are in traditionally low-paying sectors where school success is less relevant, and teacher work has become too arduous and lacking in intrinsic payoff to compensate for the low salaries teachers earn.

Working mothers. Schools cannot control the fact that a once-rich source of volunteer labor and school support—full-time homemakers—has dried up. As the structures of families and the exigencies of the labor market change, the percentage of mothers of young children who work full-time will continue to increase. Further, the percentage of teachers themselves who are both parents and full-time workers will increase.

Urbanization and demographic change. Schools can neither control nor avoid confronting the consequences of urbanization, which both generates and concentrates income inequality and ethnic and cultural diversity in enrollment. Schools also cannot control population shifts that bring increasing percentages of poor, ethnic and language minority, and immigrant children into classrooms.

Fiscal bases. While they can and do act as vigorous lobbies, schools cannot control the limited willingness and capability of the public to pay for public education as long as schools are dependent upon taxes and have no independent power to levy those taxes.

REDEFINING FACTORS TO INCREASE COUPLING: A MARSHALL PLAN FOR AMERICAN EDUCATION

Notwithstanding these intractable constraints, we still feel that there is much that can be done. While we are trying to hold our suggestions to those approaches that cost little in actual dollars, there truly is a need for more fiscal support for schools. Some of the ideas contained in this section would, in fact, be easier to implement were many schools not so pitifully underfunded (despite the polemic of current fiscally conservative politicians). We feel that what is needed is nothing less than a Marshall Plan for education. The Marshall Plan not only provided aid for the survival of the populations of war-torn Europe, but assumed that continued survival required rebuilding of the infrastructure of European economies. A Marshall Plan for education in the United States needs to start with the premise that conditions in many schools are below survival level—these schools lack the infrastructure essential to proper teaching and learning.

Providing the Essential Infrastructure and Supplies

It is commonplace to find schools without textbooks, pencils and paper, libraries, gymnasiums, and places to teach music and art. These are not frills. Try to teach a middle school child the geometric concepts of volume when he or she has had insufficient training in symbolic representation to understand perspective drawings. Try to get homework turned in when children cannot take textbooks home because they do not have any. The first step of an educational Marshall Plan needs to be a realistic appraisal—in every school in the country—of the extent to which minimum conditions needed for adequate pedagogy are absent. These conditions include up-to-date textbooks, paper, crayons and pencils for every child, well-supplied science laboratories and libraries, class sizes of no more than 30 children, heat and air conditioning, roofs that do not leak or fall in, buildings that are regularly cleaned and maintained, bathrooms and cafeterias that are sanitary and in good working order, and adequate transportation to school for all who need it.

The second step is to see to it that this infrastructure is available to every child in the country. Appraisals of deficit must not be done on a district-by-district basis; rather, the unit of analysis needs to be the individual school. We have learned too well from the research of the past that inter-district differences often are not as dramatic as within-district differences in the provision of educational opportunities for children.

Barring a vast increase in the dollars available for education, however, there still is much that educators can do to tighten the degree of coupling at the macro level while at the same time eliminating a good deal of the micromanagement that, by reducing teachers' sense of professional autonomy, contributes greatly to their alienation and burnout. We begin with factors that we previously defined as outside the purview of schools. We now examine aspects of these same topics to describe creative ways in which schools can adapt to the changing social circumstances around them.

Accommodate to Changes in Family Structure

While educators cannot bring back the two-parent, one-wage-earner family, they can couple more tightly with the needs of the families they do encounter: single-parent families, families in which both parents work, families in which neither mother nor father serves as guardian, and families headed by minor children. As long as school people define these as "dysfunctional" families, no progress will be made. When current family configurations are redefined as the reality of family life—and we have clearly indicated that these do constitute reality for the majority of American children—then creative adaptation can begin, and tighter coupling between the needs of families and the services and capabilities of the schools can be achieved.

Institute flexible scheduling. The first category of needs for such families is for more flexible scheduling of school activities. For children who must work to support themselves and their families, more convenient and decentralized night school programs may be a solution. Working parents of students constitute another issue. As we have indicated, a primary reason parents become alienated from school and teachers subsequently come to believe that parents do not care about the education of their children is the difficulty that working parents encounter finding the time and transportation to get to school for conferences. We suggest that evening conference hours—separate from the yearly "parents' nights" that all parents are invited to attend—be scheduled consistently. Further, we feel that the wedge between school and community that pressures to work and the increasing diversity of student enrollments create can be reduced only by more insistent and consistent school outreach. It is the responsibility of school personnel to take the initiative to reduce the fear and hostility that poor and minority families feel toward the institution, which means that teachers and principals must leave the campus and contact in their homes those parents who cannot or will not come to the school. Obstacles to such outreach include the discomfort that school personnel feel when forced to venture into strange neighborhoods, the time outside the classroom that visitations require, and the belief that the effort will be ineffective. These obstacles might be ameliorated if outreach times are scheduled during regular conference times, "field training" is provided to teachers who need desensitizing, and teachers are actually compensated in some way for their effort, for example, with extra pay or time off in which to engage in professional development.

Increase articulation with social services. A second need is for closer articulation and coordination among all the social service agencies that bear responsibility for children. Historically, the "service sector" (Bennett & LeCompte, 1990) of schools increased in proportion to demands that schools serve *in loco parentis* to students. However, there are literally hundreds of social service agencies that concern themselves with the health and welfare of students—from tutoring to medical and mental health care, food and clothing, housing, and foster care. While it is true that many of these agencies are overworked and underfunded, it also is true that the lack of coordination between these agencies and schools fragments the overall care of children, just as pullout programs fragment their learning experiences. Were school personnel to take the lead in articulating services from the community more closely with needs that school staff perceive children to have, the school systems themselves might in many cases be able to reduce their social work burden to one of diagnosing the need for services and prescribing referrals to appropriate agencies. Such coordination will require extra social services or counseling staff to augment already overcrowded counseling staff.

Provide on-site day care. A third need is for on-site day care for students who have babies. We have pointed out that students with babies do not drop out because they have babies; they drop out because they cannot find adequate day care and they cannot both work to support their children and stay in school. While day-care centers and parenting classes for teenaged parents still are few and underfunded, those that do exist report that the services they provide make a profound difference in the self-esteem of the young parents, their ability to care for their babies, and their ability to continue their education. One such facility in Kayenta, Arizona, reported that it could serve only 14 of the 34 young women who applied for services in its first year of operation.

Provide health care services. A current Department of Health and Human Services report indicates that while 15.5% of the total population is not covered by any health insurance (public or private), 30% of young adults, more than 25% of single, separated, and divorced women, and up to 30% of racial and ethnic minorities are likewise uncovered (Short, Monheit, & Beauregard, 1989). Clinics for poor and working-class people are few, and their hours correspond to the times that children are in school and parents are at work. To provide minimal health care for an increasing number of children, health care facilities for all students need to be provided on school campuses, facilities with authority to do more than screen for health problems and dispense aspirin. It may be possible, for example, to permit local health care agencies to locate clinics in school buildings, thereby relieving school districts of the financial burden of running clinics themselves.

Provide Teachers With Training

In Chapter 2 we spoke of the difficulty teachers have in keeping up with new developments in their field. Aside from the problems of finding time to engage in serious study, teachers find that their ability to learn more about their field is severely circumscribed by limited library services and their inability to leave the classroom to attend conferences. In-service training activities resemble the old "telephone" game, wherein staff development personnel—who may or may not have attended conferences themselves—teach teachers a watered-down version of what they themselves were taught, with attendant omissions, biases, and inaccuracies. As a remedy, we propose a looser form of coupling. We believe that schools need to redefine the way in-service training is handled and time is provided for professional development. Redefinition requires "restructuring"; it mandates that teachers define problems themselves, that in-service training no longer be a top-down affair, delivered with little follow-up and only by in-house individuals.

Time for learning. Teachers need to be given time to define collaboratively what problems they see in their teaching and how they, as a group and individually, might develop projects to solve those problems. Release time can be provided by hiring substitutes or letting staff development personnel or master teachers take over classrooms so that interested teachers can visit each other during the school day to brainstorm and plan. Teachers can be grouped so that several work together while one takes responsibility for all their students. Hourly pay could also be provided to compensate teachers for working after school or on weekends. The population of teachers now in schools who do not have graduate degrees should be afforded sabbaticals and stipends to complete their graduate training (or training in their substantive fields for those who have education undergraduate degrees). Similarly, opportunities for teacher aides to complete degrees and become certified should be encouraged. The salary structure of current teachers would be affected by their completion of graduate course work. It is expected that no more than a small percentage of teachers can take sabbaticals during any given academic year. Where teachers have specializations with direct analogues in industry, sabbatical years can be spent as interns in the corporate sector for academic credit. Likewise, professionals in the corporate sector can be loaned out to the schools to replace the teachers on sabbatical in industry. This would be especially possible in high school science, math, engineering, and industrial arts departments.

School-university partnerships. Looser coupling between teacher training and school districts may mean tighter linkages between school districts and universities. School-university programs of collaboration such as Partners in Education (PIE) at the University of Colorado, wherein classroom teachers are given leave from their districts to serve for a year or more as clinical faculty at the university, can broaden the scope for learning. Clinical faculty teach methods courses in teacher certification programs and attend university classes of interest to them. In return, the school districts involved receive in-service training and consultant services from university faculty, many of whom work collaboratively on research projects and curriculum development with practicing teachers. An analogue is school-business partnerships, in which teachers are given sabbaticals to work in businesses or industries relevant to their fields. Teachers also can be encouraged to take university-level workshops and courses for credit to upgrade their skills.

Link What Is Learned in School to What Is Needed on the Job

In general, we do not support increased vocational and narrowly conceived skills training as a means to make schooling "relevant" for non-college-bound students. While tighter coupling between the schools and the labor market is desirable, we believe that it can be achieved only, paradoxically, by instituting *looser coupling* in classroom instruction and the organization of the curriculum.

Eliminate tracking. We have elsewhere called for the "mainstreaming" of all children. By that we mean eliminating remedial tracks as an overall and perpetual curriculum and providing all students with rigorous training in problem solving, thinking, writing, calculating, and communication. As we have pointed out, ability grouping does more to create differences in student achievement than any other single variable, and once established, these differences are virtually immutable. We propose, then, a dramatic reorganization of the curriculum of schools. Students must be taught how to learn, not simply trained on more updated lathes or farmed out to menial tasks, because the most "relevant" curriculum for all children is, in fact, a firm grounding in basic cognitive skills so that they acquire the capacity to move from job to job as labor market needs change.

Institute better record keeping. To accomplish this, closer articulation between achievements in school and payoffs in the job sector is needed. We have indicated that non-college-bound students have little extrinsic incentive to achieve high grades, since they know that the difficulty of obtaining transcripts in a timely fashion means that employers do not consider grades in hiring decisions. Part of the problem lies in the antiquated and decentralized nature of school record keeping (see LeCompte & Goebel, 1987). However, recent advances in electronic record-keeping techniques and developments in the facility with which data can be translated from one processing system to another promise that these issues need no longer serve as disincentives. A priority for whatever funding does become available for school improvement should be the enhancement of record-keeping systems—for greater accessibility, consistency, and interchangeability. This is essential for adequate program planning, to address the needs of a mobile population, and to achieve tighter coupling between hard work in school and higher wages in the job sector.

Upgrade training equipment. A second way to tighten the links between non-college-preparatory training and the labor market is to assure that in those cases where specific skills training is provided, the equipment that students use and the techniques they learn are as up-to-date as those currently required in the industry in which students desire placement. Old-fashioned automobile mechanics, for example, is of little use in an industry where much of what goes on under the hood of a car is run by computer chips.

Teach for problem solving and intellectual flexibility. A third way to tighten the links between labor market and schools is to train for intellectual flexibility. Paradoxically, this requires loosening up the curriculum and training teachers to be more effective diagnosticians and facilitators of diverse learning styles. Here, new research on "situated" or contextualized learning is instructive. Culturally informed cognitive psychologists such as Tharp and Gallimore (1988) have rediscovered the work of Lev Vygotsky (1962), which militates against the fragmentation and decontextualization of teaching and learning that has characterized the past two decades of educational practice. It also obviates the one-size-fits-all approach to pedagogy and educational reform. This approach transforms the locus of control in classrooms, making children active participants in the learning process and turning teachers into diagnosticians and facilitators as well as vendors of information. It is reflected in new standards for assessment and curricular development published by the Commission for Standards in School Mathematics (1990) and the National Council of Teachers of English (1990), which stress a multidisciplinary and integrated approach to skills and problem solving. Literacy, for example, is not viewed simply as reading, but as encompassing all the skills associated with language—reading, writing, listening, and speaking. Mathematics no longer involves merely memorizing isolated skills, but is presented in long, complex—and often very practical—everyday word problems in which process is more important than product, and where there may actually be more than one right answer (see Calkins, 1986; Cobb, Yackel, & Wood, 1989; Graves, 1983; Lampert, 1990).

Institute alternative assessment and diagnosis. New forms of pedagogy are being thrust upon teachers at the same time as assessment programs in many states change standardized assessments and exit examinations to reflect new kinds of pedagogy. Thus "teaching to the test" will require that teachers transform the way they teach. This is another paradox: Loosening up teaching may require teaching closely to a new kind of test—one that assesses new kinds of skills. This may take some time, because it requires changes in the degree to which teachers appear to control the classroom as well as in the confidence with which teachers approach subject-matter content. It is clear that most of these approaches have not filtered down into classroom practice. For example, directions for pilot mathematics tests for a new state assessment based upon the NCTM standards urged third graders to "use a table" to help them keep track of the many steps in a particular problem. The answer sheets came back covered with strange pictures drawn—and erased—all over them. The scorers finally found two pictures still intact; the children had drawn pictures of a dining-room table and four chairs! (Roberta Flexer, personal communication, 1991).

Locate learning in the experience of the student. Even more important, these approaches require that teachers change from viewing learners as empty vessels in need of filling to active participants who actually know a great deal more than they can display on tests. It becomes the teacher's task to build bridges—or "scaffolds"—between what the child knows well and what still has not been internalized (Tharp & Gallimore, 1988). This means tighter coupling between home and school knowledge bases. Particularly for elementary students, knowledge of the child's home culture assumes new importance, because teachers are required to build on what children already know, and what they know best is what they bring from home. One end of the bridge that teachers build must be firmly rooted in that home cultural background for the information and skills presented to have any real meaning at all (Moll, 1990; Reyes, in press; Tharp, n.d.)

We have argued in favor of mainstreaming students and have contended that all students can learn necessary cognitive skills and information bases. However, not all students can learn in the same environments. Some students can achieve effectively (if not optimally) in restrictive and even academically impoverished environments, while other students cannot even survive in such settings. The still all-too-common educational factory of the 1950s (see LeCompte & Dworkin, 1988) is not suitable for all learners.

Manage Unmanageable Students

Behavior problems are a significant concern for most schools. In some instances the disruptive behavior of a few students causes teachers to ignore the education of the majority of the class in order to discipline those few. Some teachers have reported to us that their principals instruct them not to send disruptive students out of the room because doing so requires a report to the district central office. This spoils the school's record for good deportment. In some instances disruptive students are bored students who see no connection between their education and their future goals.

While a reformed and enlightened curriculum that establishes closer links among schooling, work, and life goals may ameliorate many of the problems of disruption, we are not so naive as to assume that adverse student behavior always has a curricular solution. Some students remain incorrigible, in part because other societal institutions have failed them. Often, factors beyond the control of schools are involved. For example, children born of drug-addicted and alcoholic parents now are entering school in increasing numbers. These children have difficulty controlling their emotions, are easily distracted, and may have impaired motor, cognitive, and social functions. Children with severe emotional problems exhibit many of the same behaviors. It must be recognized that in these cases mainstreaming in regular classrooms may not provide the most appropriate and "least restrictive" environment for such children. They may well need to be removed from schools as we conceptualize them today and placed in work-related apprenticeship programs. Some students may achieve significantly more in environments that conjoin apprenticeships in the workplace with academic training—but this must be real training leading to real jobs that pay a decent wage (see Dorris, 1989, for a portrayal of attempts to educate a fetal alcohol syndrome-afflicted child).

Restructure School Organization

Characteristic of numerous educational solutions that have been proposed is the tendency to select a single strategy and apply it to all settings, all schools, students, and teachers. This uniform strategy ignores individual variations in contexts, people, and problems. One such educational strategy that has gained considerable currency has been termed "restructuring." Restructuring has been called the "garbage can" of reform (Elmore et al., 1990):

> Restructuring has become a general label for new strategies of school reform that respond to disillusionment with the results of state legislation of the middle 1980s that sought to mandate stiffer standards for students and teachers. . . . [It is] a synonym for market mechanisms of choice, or teacher professionalization and empowerment, or decentralization and school site management, or involving parents more in their children's education, or national standards in curriculum with tests to match, or deregulation, or some or all of these in combination. (quoted in Tyack, 1990, pp. 170-171)

Restructuring seems to be a superb solution to the alienating bureaucratic processes cited in previous chapters, and it is seductive because it seems also to be a "no-cost" reform. In principle, it can be effective. However, problems arise when restructuring of governance at the top is the only strategy used, when it is provided without substantive input and guidance about alternative forms of governance and pedagogy, or when it is imposed uniformly on all teachers. Effective campus-based management is likely to be useful in reducing teacher burnout and student tune-out only when it leads to the empowerment of *competent and dedicated* professionals. These often are in short supply. As evidence, we submit the fact that educators often rank among the bottom quartile in achievement on standardized tests and performance in their university courses; they may remain in teaching because they can find no other line of work (Dworkin, 1987).

More important, programs to help those who are creative and energetic often are ill conceived and poorly designed to provide support to school efforts. Recently, the Texas Education Agency initiated a request for proposals under its 1990-1991 Innovative Education Grant Program. Campus administrators were invited to submit proposals for innovative programs that could raise student achievement, reduce dropout rates, increase parental involvement in the schools, and improve the learning climate on campuses. The legislation that created the program mandated that school staff were to assist in the writing of the research/evaluation component.

Dworkin met with several public school administrators to assist in drafting their proposals. Many of the projects suggested by principals and other school staff were at best inane. Typically, the principals said that they did not have any ideas, but would gladly accept the money. Several simply read off the 24 examples in the request for proposal booklet and declared that they wanted to do "some of those." Two administrators wanted to provide enrichment in the homes of at-risk children, but they had no awareness of the multitude of problems that face their students. For example, some wanted to have parents read more to their children, and proposed sending books home with the children. However, given the large Central American immigrant population of the community, and the lack of English literacy among many parents, sending books home for parents to read without first teaching them English would have had little utility.

Another principal proposed to encourage single welfare mothers to provide more help for their children with math homework; the principal assumed that the mothers were themselves competent enough at math, but just had never been asked to assist. Finally, one principal said that he could not think of anything innovative to do, but just wanted the money to buy newer tables and chairs for the teachers' lounge. One significant difficulty with the state's program was that it asked many of the same actors who have consistently failed to address the current educational crisis to come up with solutions to the problems of schooling.

Individualize restructuring. The answer is not to abandon the concept of campus-based management, but to apply it to individual situations and in a considered manner—perhaps even with a built-in component of evaluation research. Central administration, perhaps with the assistance of affiliated universities and other concerned groups, can solicit proposals from campuses for decentralization on a trial basis. Regular evaluation of the progress of the program can be mandated and sufficient funds can be provided to ensure that the programs have a modicum of a chance to succeed. However, it must be recognized that sufficient time should be allocated to ensure that the treatment effect (the particular strategy) would have a chance to operate. Since any change is likely to have an initial disruptive effect that could decrease morale, and any program that tightens standards could elevate dropout rates, evaluation cannot be limited to initial results. Likewise, programs should not be limited to campuses with minimal problems, where success is most likely. Some schools with virtually intractable problems should be given an opportunity to participate. In time, the individual campuses, the participating universities, and the central district can become a cooperative research and development shop. Master teachers can work with the university during the summer as adjunct faculty, examining what worked and why. This model is similar to that discussed by Elmore (1990) in the Michigan State model, but involves an application of the research and development shop as a component in decentralization.

In such a model, individual campuses would develop program proposals with evaluation components to be conducted by the research and development partnerships between universities and the schools. The role of the central administration would be to evaluate the proposals and to provide technical assistance in the implementation of the programs. The central administration would serve as the gatekeeper for implementation of plans.

Build in teacher participation. Effective restructuring means more than permitting the principal to run the school as his or her little fiefdom. It means decentralization of decision making within the campus, too. This means "empowerment" of teachers, as we have described earlier, giving them real power over what and how they teach in their classrooms. The PIE model at the University of Colorado, and the kinds of programs advocated by Goodlad (1983), Joyce and Clift (1984), Joyce, Hersh, and McKibbin (1983), and Sizer (1984-1985) can serve as starting points for developing this kind of teacher leadership.

Creating a Professional Teacher Work Force

What we have offered thus far are suggestions that do not require a significant change in the teaching population. However, should the opportunity arise, as demographics suggest it will in the early years of the next century, a change in the professional status of teachers would resolve numerous faculty problems. However, to accomplish this, the following suggestions ought to be implemented.

Professional status, and especially high professional status, is contingent upon three central elements: *selective recruitment*, or some gatekeeping practice to limit supply; *specialized training*, often in a setting in an institution of higher education; and the *license to independent judgment and autonomy*. Public school teaching fails on two of these criteria, and so has often been termed a semiprofession (Etzioni, 1969).

The professionalization of teachers involves a circular problem. Professional autonomy and salaries commensurate with true professional status are unlikely to accrue to teachers unless states, school districts, and the public demand greater teacher accountability. When this is defined as countless reports and paperwork, it compromises teacher autonomy. However, without greater autonomy and better salaries, it will be difficult to attract highly qualified teachers, retain the best of the current teaching population, and generate a sense of commitment in which teachers make extra efforts on behalf of their students. Strategies directed toward raising the professional status of teachers cannot focus upon recruitment of new and better candidates alone, but must enhance the skills and attitudes of the present teaching force. Additionally, repeated studies point to the significant role of the principal in creating in teachers feelings of job commitment, job satisfaction, and the ability to cope with job-related stressors. Thus the strategy for improving the professional status of teachers must be multiple and complex, addressing issues of recruitment and retention, teacher education, administrative support, and new measures of accountability.

Selective recruitment and specialized training. Teaching is in part a lower-status profession (or semiprofession) because the supply of teachers has been relatively plentiful and college-level teacher training programs are considered easy to enter and complete. When there was still talk of a teacher "glut,"

Stinnett and Henson (1982) and Gideonse (1982) proposed that teacher preparation should take six years and result in either a master's or doctoral degree. Since that time there has been growing support for the elimination of the undergraduate education major. As preservice teachers increasingly are required to attain both a baccalaureate degree in an arts and sciences college and certification in pedagogy, teacher training could become exclusively a graduate program. Teachers will, therefore, come from the ranks of undergraduates who, like their nonteaching counterparts, have met similar entrance and exit requirements for academic programs. As a consequence, it could be expected that new teachers will be selected from a more able population.

Mandating a graduate degree for new teachers will impose greater control by universities, legislatures, or accrediting agencies over access to teaching careers. This also will reduce the supply. To prevent teaching from becoming class and race segregated, financial aid should be provided by the state and the business sector for low-income and minority teacher candidates. Student loans could be canceled with the completion of two or three years of classroom teaching.

Shortfalls in the teaching population can be rectified through alternative certification programs in which individuals with undergraduate or graduate degrees enroll in graduate programs in education while teaching in school districts under the supervision of master teachers. The salary structure of public education would come to resemble that of other occupations requiring a graduate degree.[1]

Competency testing of teachers at the point of certification should be matched to college-level norms rather than to eighth-grade reading levels, as current examinations are set. Failure to pass such examinations, either by newly recruited teachers or by the extant population of teachers, should mean mandatory remedial training and training, followed by termination of those unable to pass the examinations after a third trial (for a description of the Texas experience with such testing, see Shepherd & Kreitzer, 1987).

The issue of termination for teachers who fail to pass competency examinations is a thorny one. The Texas experience revealed that almost 97% of the state's teaching population passed a minimum competency test (gauged to a junior high school achievement level), but that those who failed were predominantly black teachers, most of whom were themselves products of segregated and inferior school systems (M. Smith, 1991). While these teachers possessed classroom management skills, they did not understand some of the subject matter they were supposed to teach to their students. Others who failed the competency examinations were younger teachers educated by equally disadvantaged teachers working in central-city schools. If the competency tests had been designed to assess college-level abilities, the failure rate would have risen exponentially, thereby reducing significantly the supply of teachers, and especially the already dwindling supply of minority teachers.

To permit incompetent teachers to remain in the classroom ensures that yet another generation of children will be given a second-rate education. However, the number of such teachers is relatively small. Rather than propose the wholesale firing of older teachers who cannot pass competency examinations on repeated attempts, as was done in Texas (M. Smith, 1991), we recommend that new duties, including child-care responsibilities (perhaps in the on-site day-care facilities we recommended earlier), be found for older teachers who find themselves in this situation. Younger teachers who fail the examinations repeatedly, however, should be fitted with new skills and helped to find new jobs. Academic tenure should replace "continuing contracts" and should be granted after three to five years only to those who demonstrate competent teaching.

Specialized apprenticeships and training. Student teaching, the most significant portion of the certification process for most new teachers, constitutes a poorly supervised substitute for the highly monitored and rigorous apprenticeships served by novices in other fields. Alternatives might included a variation of the plan adopted in Michigan through Michigan State University (Elmore, 1990), in which colleges of education function somewhat like medical schools and new teachers are similar to medical residents. Currently, practice teaching serves as a poor surrogate for experience in schools in the central city.

An alternative plan would have didactic training occur during the first year of graduate-level teacher education, followed by a clerkship with a rotation through different subject matters and different kinds of schools—all prior to receipt of the teaching degree. For example, minority and inner-city public schools in a specified area would become the lab schools for the various colleges and schools of education throughout the region, making it impossible for preservice teachers to escape significant experience with culturally and economically different students. The current faculty in the allied public schools would serve as the teachers of record for the classroom, but they would be assigned a group of interns to provide more individualized instruction to students. Children in the affiliated, generally inner-city, schools would receive much more personalized attention (perhaps five-to-one student-teacher ratios, a reduction that would significantly affect student achievement; Finn & Achilles, 1990), classroom teachers would be afforded teaching assistants to reduce their paperwork, and the preservice interns would experience first-hand classroom teaching in realistic settings. This clerkship would not replace, but rather would precede, the assignment of a recent graduate of a college of education to a class of his or her own, under the supervision of a master teacher. This latter assignment would parallel residency in medical school.

The license to independent judgment and autonomy. Tenured teachers should be considered autonomous professionals who develop their own curricular plans and are free to implement them. They also should serve as mentors to junior faculty. With the possession of a graduate degree, the successful passage of examinations and evaluations, and the granting of tenure, teachers should be given considerable freedom to develop curricula and to manage their classes without interference from district or campus officials, except in cases of flagrant malfeasance. Merit pay should be tied to demonstrated productivity in terms of innovations in teaching, student achievement gains (corrected for differences among cohorts of students), and peer evaluations. It is expected that substantial merit pay will be matched with excellence in teaching.

Parent volunteers, administrative assistants, preservice teaching interns and teachers' aides could assume much of the paperwork and nonteaching duties currently burdening teachers. For example, staff members or teachers' aides could be assigned lunchroom and recess duties, thereby affording teachers free time during the day. If the proposed internship model for alliances between colleges of education and public schools is adopted, the teachers' aides would come from preservice student intern programs in colleges of education.

The school year also should be extended so as to guarantee year-round and more stable employment of teachers. Where such plans have been implemented in the past, they have been in response to logistics of overcrowding or the scholastic needs of students; we feel it imperative to include this step as a rationale resolving the needs of teachers.

Changing Principals' Administrative Style to Enhance Teacher Morale

Principal behavior has been shown to be significant in maintaining teacher morale (Dworkin, 1987; Dworkin et al., 1988, 1990). Principals should be required to have management training that addresses issues of employee morale and productivity. They should be rewarded for the extent to which they encourage planning on the part of their teachers, and should be evaluated on the extent to which they are responsible for voluntary turnover at their campuses. Excessive teacher turnover should be seen as a sign of ineffective campus management.

CONCLUSION

There is no question that educational reform is needed in American schools. However, it is the content of the reform and, in particular, the manner in which reform is implemented that will determine whether the reform exacerbates the problems of teachers or ameliorates them. The key may be in the development of campus-based management strategies that empower those who actually work with America's children. However, simply empowering teachers without ensuring that those so empowered are capable of quality instruction does little more than produce happy school employees and poorly educated students, given current levels of teaching competence (Darling-Hammond, 1984; Schlechty & Vance, 1981; Vance & Schlechty, 1982). Omnibus educational reform legislation is needed in states where academic performance is low, but state legislatures are unqualified to micromanage educational policies by specifying curricula and accountability procedures that increase the paperwork of teachers and are not factored in as influences on the experience of students. One real challenge for the future of education is the recruitment of excellent teachers, their retention, and the development of curricula that challenge students. Reliance upon minimum competency tests to determine the abilities of teachers or students ensures only that both perform no better than several years behind grade level. Such performances continue to put our "nation at risk."

Our analysis of the causes of teacher and student alienation remains one informed by the somewhat gloomy perspective of sociologists who refuse to view schools as the engine for social transformation. As we have indicated, societies run schools; schools do not run society. We have few illusions about the capacity for policymakers and the public to initiate the kinds of social structural reforms necessary to "put schools right" with their economic and social context. For this reason, many of our concrete suggestions are relatively modest. Nevertheless, our explanatory frame for the crisis in education adheres to an integrated and multilevel view of schooling. It is an analysis that, however pessimistic, eschews naive thinking about what schools can and cannot do. We hope that it will constitute a necessary first step toward remediating those most painful symptoms of educational crisis that form the focus of this volume: the propensity for teachers and students to give up on school.

NOTE

1. For example, in the Houston Independent School District, the fourth largest in the nation, starting salaries during the 1989-1990 academic year were $20,500 for a teacher with a B.A., $21,200 for a teacher with an M.A., and $22,200 for a teacher with a Ph.D., while the peak salaries for 20+ years of teaching were $29,500, $33,500, and $36,500, respectively. Especially at the doctoral level these are not competitive, even with academia, which also operates with 9-month contracts—for example, 10-month starting salaries for Ph.D.s exceed $30,000 in AAUP Category I schools (see Dworkin, 1990a).

References

Alutto, J. A., Hrebiniak, L. G., & Alonzo, R. C. (1973). On operationalizing the concept of commitment. *Social Forces, 51,* 448-454.

American Association of University Professors. (1989). Annual report on the economic status of the profession: 1988-89. *AAUP Bulletin, 75,* 10.

Anderson, B. D., & Mark, J. H. (1977). Teacher mobility and productivity in a metropolitan area: A seven year case study. *Urban Education, 12,* 15-36.

Apple, M. W. (1979). *Ideology and curriculum.* Boston: Routledge & Kegan Paul.

Apple, M. W. (1986). *Teachers and texts: A political economy of class and gender relations in education.* New York: Methuen.

Apple, M. W. (1989). American realities: Poverty, economy, and education. In L. Weis, E. Farrar, & H. G. Petrie (Eds.), *Dropouts from school: Issues, dilemmas, and solutions* (pp. 205-223). Albany: State University of New York Press.

Archer, E. L., & Dresden, J. A. (1987). A new kind of dropout: The effect of minimum competency testing on high school graduation in Texas. *Education and Urban Society, 19,* 269-280.

Aronowitz, S. S., & Giroux, H. (1985). *Education under siege.* South Hadley, MA: Bergin & Garvey.

Asin, S. (1989, October 20). Diploma forfeited: Klein won't graduate honors student attending USC. *Houston Chronicle,* p. 21A.

Asin, S. (1990, January 13). Dropout rates fall in two area ISDs in research by A&M. *Houston Chronicle,* p. 25A.

Bacharach, S., Bamberger, P., & Conley, S. (1990). Models of teacher militancy. *Industrial and Labor Relations Review, 43,* 570-586.

Bachman, J. G., Green S., & Wirtanen, I. D. (1971). *Dropping out: Problem or symptom.* Ann Arbor, MI: Institute for Social Research.

Bailin, M. (1990). Social, political and economic factors impacting upon educational reform: Comments on the Greater Houston Plan for Educational Excellence. In Greater Houston Partnership (Ed.), *A framework for educational excellence: 1990.* Houston: Greater Houston Partnership.

Bane, M. J., & Ellwood, D. T. (1989). One-fifth of the nation's children: Why are they poor? *Science, 245,* 1047-1053.

Barr, R. (1974). Instructional pace differences and their effect on reading acquisition. *Reading Research Quarterly, 9,* 526-554.

Barringer, F. (1989, October 18). 32 million lived in poverty in '88, a figure unchanged. *New York Times,* p. 1.

Barron, J. (1989, September 15). The silent majority. *New York Times* (Education Suppl.).

Bartholomew, J. (1976). Schooling teachers: The myth of the liberal college. In G. Whitty & M. Young (Eds.), *Explorations in the politics of school knowledge* (pp. 114-124). Nefferton, Driffield, England: Nefferton.

Bayes, J. (1988). Labor markets and the feminization of poverty. In H. R. Rodgers, Jr. (Ed.), *Beyond welfare: New approaches to the problem of poverty in America* (pp. 86-114). Armonk, NY: M. E. Sharpe.

Becker, G. S. (1964) *Human capital: A theoretical and empirical analysis, with special reference to education.* New York: Columbia University Press.

Becker, H. S. (1960). Notes on the concept of commitment. *American Journal of Sociology, 66,* 32-40.

Becker, H. S., & Strauss, A. (1956). Careers, personality, and adult socialization. *American Journal of Sociology, 62,* 253-263.

Bennett, E. W. (1988). *James Madison High School.* Washington, DC: U.S. Office of Education.

Bennett, K. P. (1986). *Study of reading ability grouping and its consequences for urban Appalachian first graders.* Unpublished doctoral dissertation, University of Cincinnati.

Bennett, K. P., & LeCompte, M. D. (1990). *The way schools work: A sociological analysis of education.* White Plains, NY: Longman.

Bennett, N., Desforges, C., Cockburn, A., & Wilkinson, B. (1984). *The quality of pupil learning experiences.* London: Lawrence Erlbaum.

Berger, J. (1989, June 18). New York study of welfare clients: False practices of trade schools. *New York Times,* p. A9.

Berger, J. (1990, March 21). Victory: Why one school can read. *New York Times,* p. A16.

Berkeley Planning Associates. (1977). Project management and worker burnout. In *Evaluation of Child Abuse and Neglect Demonstration Projects, 1974-1977* (Vol. 9). Springfield, VA: National Technical Information Service.

Bernstein, B. (1970). *Class, codes, and control: Vol. 1. Theoretical studies towards a sociology of language.* London: Routledge & Kegan Paul.

Bernstein, B. (1977). *Class, codes, and control: Vol. 3. Towards a theory of educational transmission.* London: Routledge & Kegan Paul.

Bidwell, C., & Kasarda, J. D. (1975). School district organization and student achievement. *American Sociological Review, 40,* 55-70.

Bishop, J. H. (1989). Why the apathy in American high schools? *Educational Researcher, 18,* 6-11.

Blakeslee, S. (1989, September 17). Crack's toll among babies: A joyless view of even toys. *New York Times,* p. 12.

Blau, Z. S. (1981). *Black children/white children: Competence, socialization, and social structure.* New York: Free Press.

Blauner, R. (1964). *Alienation and freedom.* Chicago: University of Chicago Press.

Bloom, A. (1987). *The closing of the American mind.* New York: Simon & Schuster.

Bluestone, B., & Harrison, B. (1982). *The de-industrialization of America.* New York: Basic Books.

Bluestone, B., & Harrison, B. (1987, February 1). The grim truth about the job miracle. *New York Times,* p. E3.

Blumberg, R. L. (1979). A paradigm for predicting the position of women: Policy implications and problems. In J. Lipman-Blumen & J. Bernard (Eds.), *Sex roles and social policy* (pp. 113-142). Beverly Hills, CA: Sage.

Blumer, H. (1969). *Symbolic interactionism: Perspective and method.* Englewood Cliffs, NJ: Prentice-Hall.

Blumer, H. (1978). Social unrest and collective protest. *Studies in Symbolic Interaction, 1,* 1-54.

Borko, H., & Eisenhart, M. (1986). Student's conceptions of reading and their reading experience in school. *Elementary School Journal, 86,* 589-612.

Bose, C., & Spitz, G. (Eds.). (1987). *Ingredients for women's employment policy.* Albany: State University of New York Press.

Boudon, R. (1974). *Education, opportunity, and social inequality.* New York: John Wiley.

Bourdieu, P., & Passeron, J. (1977). *Reproduction in education, society and culture.* London: Sage.

Bourgeois, P. (1989, November 12). Just another night on crack street. *New York Times Magazine,* pp. 31-79.

Bowles, S. S., & Gintis, H. M. (1976). *Schooling in capitalist America.* New York: Basic Books.

Bowles, S. S., & Levin, H. M. (1968). More on multicollinearity and the effectiveness of schools. *Journal of Human Resources, 3,* 393-400.

Braun, C. (1976). Teacher expectation: Sociopsychological dynamics. *Review of Educational Research, 46,* 185-213.

Briar, S., & Piliavin, J. (1965). Delinquency, situational inducements and commitment to conformity. *Social Problems, 13,*35-45.

Brice-Heath, S. (1982). Questioning at home and school: A comparative study. In G. F. Spindler (Ed.), *Doing the ethnography of schooling* (pp. 102-131). New York: Holt, Rinehart & Winston.

Brophy, J. E. (1983). Research on the self-fulfilling prophecy and teacher expectations. *Journal of Educational Psychology, 75,* 631-661.

Butler, J. S. (1976). Inequality in the military: An examination of promotion time for black and white enlisted men. *American Sociological Review, 41,* 807-818.

Byrnes, D. A. (1989). Attitudes of students, parents and educators toward repeating a grade. In L. A. Shepherd & M. L. Smith (Eds.), *Flunking grades: Research and policies on retention* (pp. 108-132). Philadelphia: Falmer/Taylor & Francis Group.

Calculus: Crisis looms in mathematics future. (1988). *Science, 239,* 1491-1492.

Calkins, L. (1986). *The art of teaching writing.* Portsmouth, NH: Heineman.

Camus, A. (1946). *The stranger.* New York: Knopf.

Carnegie Council on Adolescent Development. (1989). *Turning points: Preparing American youth for the 21st century.* Washington, DC: Carnegie Council of New York, Task Force on Education of Young Adolescents.

Carnegie Forum on Education and the Economy. (1986). *A nation prepared: Teachers for the 21st century*. Hyattsville, MD: Author.

Caroll, J. F. X., & White, W. L. (1982). Theory building: Integrating individual and environmental factors within an ecological framework. In W. S. Paine (Ed.), *Job stress and burnout: Research, theory, and intervention perspectives* (pp. 41-60). Beverly Hills, CA: Sage.

Catterall, J. S. (1987). On the social costs of dropping out of school. *High School Journal, 71*, 19-30.

Cedoline, A. J. (1982). *Job burnout in public education: Symptoms, causes and survival skills*. New York: Teachers College Press.

Center for National Policy Review and National Institute of Education. (1977a). *Trends in black school segregation, 1970-1974* (Vol. 1). Washington, DC: Government Printing Office.

Center for National Policy Review and National Institute of Education. (1977b). *Trends in Hispanic segregation, 1970-1974* (Vol. 2). Washington, DC: Government Printing Office.

Chafetz, J. S. (1980). Conflict resolution in marriage: Toward a theory of spousal strategies and marital dissolution rates. *Journal of Family Issues, 1*, 397-421.

Chafetz, J. S. (1984). *Sex and advantage: A comparative, macro-structural theory of sex stratification*. Totowa, NJ: Rowman & Allanheld.

Chafetz, J. S., & Dworkin, A. G. (1986). *Female revolt: Women's movements in world and historical perspective*. Totowa, NJ: Rowman & Allanheld.

Chafetz, J. S., Dworkin, R. J., & Dworkin, A. G. (1975). *New migrants to the rat race: A systems model for changes in work force allocation and role expectations, by gender, race and ethnicity*. Unpublished manuscript, University of Houston.

Charters, W. W., Jr. (1970). Some factors affecting teacher survival in school districts. *American Educational Research Journal, 7*, 1-27.

Cherniss, C. (1980). *Professional burnout in human service organizations*. New York: Praeger.

Cherniss, C. (1982). Cultural trends: Political, economic, and historical roots of the problem. In W. S. Paine (Ed.), *Job stress and burnout: Research, theory, and intervention perspectives* (pp. 83-94). Beverly Hills, CA: Sage.

Cherniss, C., Egnatios, E. S., & Wacker, S. (1976). Job stress and career development in new public professionals. *Professional Psychology, 7*, 428-436.

Children's Defense Fund. (1987). *Declining earnings of young men: Their relationship to poverty, teen pregnancy and family formation*. Boston: Author.

Chira, S. (1989, October 1). In 1990s, what price scarce labor? *New York Times* (Careers Suppl.), p. 29.

Cicourel, A., & Kitsuse, J. (1963). *The educational decision-makers*. Indianapolis: Bobbs-Merrill.

Cipollone, A. (1990). "New Futures" approach for addressing at-risk students: Address social institutions involved with all youth. In Greater Houston Partnership (Ed.), *A framework for educational excellence: 1990* (pp. C1-C6). Houston: Greater Houston Partnership.

Clark, B. R. (1960). The "cooling out" function in higher education. *American Journal of Sociology, 75*, 569-576.

Clifton, R., Perry, R., Parsonson, K., & Hryniuk, S. (1986). The effects of ethnicity and sex on teachers' expectations of junior high school students. *Sociology of Education, 59*, 58-67.

Clignet, R. P., & Foster, P. (1966). *The fortunate few: A study of secondary schools and students in the Ivory Coast.* Evanston, IL: Northwestern University Press.

Cloward, R. A. (1959). Illegitimate means, anomie, and deviant behavior. *American Sociological Review, 24,* 164-176.

Cobb, P. M., Yackel, E., & Wood, T. (1989). Young children's emotional acts while doing mathematical problem solving. In D. B. McLeod & V. M. Adams (Eds.), *Affect and mathematical problem solving: A new perspective* (pp. 117-148). New York: Springer-Verlag.

Coleman, J. S. (1961). *The adolescent society.* Glencoe, IL: Free Press.

Coleman, J. S., Campbell, E. Q., Hobson, C. J., McPartland, J., Mood, A. M., Weinfeld, F. D., & York, R. L. (1966). *The equality of educational opportunity.* Washington, DC: Government Printing Office.

Coleman, J. S., & Hoffer, T. (1987). *Public and private schools: The impact of communities.* New York: Basic Books.

Coleman, J. S., Hoffer, T., & Kilgore, S. (1982). *High school achievement: Public, Catholic and private schools compared.* New York: Basic Books.

Collins, R. (1971). Functional and conflict theories of educational stratification. *American Sociological Review, 36,* 1002-1019.

Collins, R. (1974). Where are educational requirements for employment highest? *Sociology of Education, 47,* 419-442.

Collins, R. (1979). *The credential society.* New York: Academic Press.

Commission for Standards in School Mathematics. (1990). *Curriculum and evaluation standards for school mathematics.* Reston, VA: Author.

Compton, D. (1983). *H. P. Carter Career Center progress report, 1982-1983.* Houston: Houston Independent School District, Department of Planning, Research and Evaluation.

Conley, S. C. (1989). Who's on first? School reform, teacher participation and the decision-making process. *Education and Urban Society, 21,* 366-380.

Cook, J. (1989, October 16). Will Wall Street fade? *Forbes,* pp. 38-139.

Cooper, H. M. (1979). Pygmalion grows up: A model for teacher expectation communication and performance influence. *Review of Educational Research, 49,* 389-410.

Corcoran, T. B., Walker, L. J., & White, J. L. (1988). *Working in urban schools.* Washington, DC: Institute for Educational Leadership.

Corwin, R. G. (1973). *Reform and organizational survival: The Teacher Corps as an instrument of educational change.* New York: John Wiley.

Crano, W. D., & Mellon, D. M. (1978). Causal influence of teachers' expectations on children's academic performance: A cross lagged panel analysis. *Journal of Educational Psychology, 70,* 39-49.

Cricklow, W. (1986). *Responses of Afro-American students to processes of education in urban high schools.* Paper presented at the annual meeting of the American Educational Research Association, San Francisco.

Croke, K. (1989, October 1). Women moonlighting to make ends meet. *Houston Chronicle,* p. 6H.

Cummins, N. L., & Miramontes, O. B. (1989). Perceived and actual linguistic competence: A descriptive study of four low-achieving Hispanic bilingual students. *American Educational Research Journal, 26,* 443-473.

Daniels, L. A. (1989, October 18). Cavazos presses parental choice in public schools. *New York Times*, p. 19.

Danziger, S. (1988). The economy, public policy and the poor. In H. R. Rodgers, Jr. (Ed.), *Beyond welfare: New approaches to the problem of poverty in America* (pp. 3-14). Armonk, NY: M. E. Sharpe.

Darling-Hammond, L. (1984). *Beyond the commission reports: The coming crisis in teaching*. Santa Monica, CA: RAND Corporation.

Dean, D. G. (1961). Alienation: Its meaning and measurement. *American Sociological Review, 26*, 753-758.

Delpit, L. (1988). The silenced dialogue: Power and pedagogy in educating other people's children. *Harvard Educational Review, 58*, 280-298.

Deyhle, D. (1989). Pushouts and pullouts: Navajo and Ute school leavers. *Journal of Navajo Education, 6*, 36-51.

Deyhle, D. (1992, Winter). Empowerment and cultural conflict: Navajo parents and the schooling of their children. *International Journal of Qualitative Studies in Education*.

Djerassi, C. (1989). The bitter pill. *Science, 245*, 356-361.

Donnenworth, G., & Cox, H. G. (1978). Attitudinal militancy among teachers. *Sociological Quarterly, 19*, 459-468.

Dorris, M. (1989). *The broken cord*. New York: Harper & Row.

Duke, D. L. (1984). *Teaching: The imperiled profession*. Albany: State University of New York Press.

Durkheim, E. (1933). *The division of labor in society*. New York: Macmillan.

Durkheim, E. (1958). *Professional ethics and civic morals*. Glencoe, IL: Free Press.

Dusek, J. B. (1975). Do teachers bias children's learning? *Review of Educational Research, 45*, 661-684.

Dusek, J. B. (Ed.). (1985). *Teacher expectancies*. Hillsdale, NJ: Lawrence Erlbaum.

Dworkin, A. G. (1968). No siesta mañana: The Mexican American in Los Angeles. In R. W. Mack (Ed.), *Our children's burden: Studies of desegregation in nine American communities* (pp. 387-439). New York: Random House.

Dworkin, A. G. (1980). The changing demography of public school teachers: Some implications for faculty turnover in urban areas. *Sociology of Education, 53*, 65-73.

Dworkin, A. G. (1982). *Work commitment and quitting behavior: A study of urban public school employees*. Paper presented at the annual meeting of the Southwestern Sociological Association, San Antonio, TX.

Dworkin, A. G. (1984). *Teacher burnout in the public schools: Final report to the Hogg Foundation for Mental Health*. Unpublished manuscript.

Dworkin, A. G. (1985). *When teachers give up: Teacher burnout, teacher turnover, and their impact on children*. Austin, TX: Hogg Foundation for Mental Health and Texas Press.

Dworkin, A. G. (1987). *Teacher burnout in the public schools: Structural causes and consequences for children*. Albany: State University of New York Press.

Dworkin, A. G. (1990a). The salary structure of sociology departments. *American Sociologist, 21*, 48-59.

Dworkin, A. G. (1990b). *Teacher morale in the public schools: Final report to the Hogg Foundation for Mental Health*. Unpublished manuscript.

Dworkin, A. G., & Caram, D. F. (1987). *Evaluation of the "Career and Education Day" program: 1987.* Unpublished manuscript, Houston Hispanic Forum.

Dworkin, A. G., & Chafetz, J. S. (1983). *Work commitment among male and female urban public school employees: An application of Kanter's approach to a semi-profession.* Unpublished manuscript.

Dworkin, A. G., Chafetz, J. S., & Dworkin, R. J. (1986). The effects of tokenism on work alienation among urban public school teachers. *Work and Occupations, 13,* 399-420.

Dworkin, A. G., & Dworkin, R. J. (1982). *The minority report: Introduction to race, ethnic, and gender relations* (2nd ed.). New York: Holt, Rinehart & Winston.

Dworkin, A. G., Haney, C. A., Dworkin, R. J., & Telschow, R. L. (1990). Stress and illness behavior among urban public school teachers. *Educational Administration Quarterly, 26,* 59-71.

Dworkin, A. G., Haney, C. A., & Telschow, R. L. (1988). Fear, victimization, and stress among urban public school teachers. *Journal of Organizational Behavior, 9,* 159-171.

Dworkin, A. G., Joiner, V. W., & Bruno, P. (1980). *Locus of control and intention to remain in unpleasant situations: The case of the public school teacher.* Paper presented at the annual meeting of the Southwestern Sociological Association, Houston.

Dworkin, A. G., Lorence, J., & LeCompte, M. D. (1989). *Organizational context as determinant of teacher morale.* Paper presented at the annual meeting of the Southwestern Sociological Association, Little Rock, AK.

Dworkin, A. G., Sanders, J., Black, F., McNamara, J., & Webster, W. (1978). *The Singleton ratio: The impact of faculty desegregation upon faculty alienation and student achievement in an urban public school system.* Paper presented at the annual meeting of the Southwestern Sociological Association, Houston.

Easterlin, R. A. (1987). *Birth and fortune: The impact of numbers on personal welfare.* Chicago: University of Chicago Press.

Eder, D., & Parker, S. (1987). The cultural production of reproduction of gender: The effect of extra-curricular activities on peer-group culture. *Sociology of Education, 60,* 200-213.

Eisenhart, M. A., & Graue, E. (1990). Socially constructed readiness for school. *Qualitative Studies in Education, 3,* 253-269.

Ekstrom, R. B., Goertz, M. E., Pollack, J. M., & Rock, D. A. (1986). Who drops out of school and why? Findings from a national study. *Teachers College Record, 87,* 356-373.

Elam, S. M., & Gallup, A. M. (1989). The 21st annual Gallup Poll of the public's attitudes toward the public schools. *Phi Delta Kappan, 71,* 42-54.

Elam, S. M., & Gough, P. B. (1980). Comparing lay and professional opinion on Gallup Poll questions. *Phi Delta Kappan, 62,* 47-48.

Elmore, R. F. (1990). School organization, governance, teacher preparation. In Greater Houston Partnership (Ed.), *A framework for educational excellence: 1990* (pp. F1-F6). Houston: Greater Houston Partnership.

Elmore, R. F., & Associates. (1990). *Restructuring schools: The next generation of educational reform.* San Francisco: Jossey-Bass.

England, P. (1984). Wage appreciation and depreciation: A test of neoclassical economic explanations of occupational sex segregation. *Social Forces, 62,* 726-749.

England, P., Chassie, M., & McCormack, L. (1982). Skill demands and earnings in male and female occupations. *Sociology and Social Research, 66,* 147-168.

England, P., & Dunn, D. (1988). Evaluating work and comparable worth. *Annual Review of Sociology, 14,* 227-248.

Erickson, F. (1984). School literacy, reasoning and civility: An anthropologist's perspective. *Review of Educational Research, 54,* 525-546.

Essen, J., & Wedge, P. (1982). *Continuities in childhood disadvantage.* London: Heineman.

Etzioni, A. (Ed.). (1969). *The semi-professions and their organization: Teachers, nurses and social workers.* New York: Free Press.

Experts alarmed by rise in AIDS among teenagers. (1989, October 8). *New York Times,* pp. 1, 15.

Falk, W. W., Grimes, M. D., & Lord, G. H., III. (1982). Professionalism and conflict in a bureaucratic setting: The case of a teachers' strike. *Social Problems, 29,* 551-560.

Falk, W. W., & Lyson, T. (1987). *High tech, low tech, no tech.* Albany: State University of New York Press.

Farber, B. (1982). *Stress and burnout in human service professions.* New York: Pergamon.

Farnworth, M., & Leiber, M. J. (1989). Strain theory revisited: Economic goals, educational means, and delinquency. *American Sociological Review, 54,* 263-274.

Feagin, J. R., & Eckberg, D. L. (1980). Discrimination: Motivation, action, effects, and context. *Annual Review of Sociology, 6,* 1-20.

Feitelson, D. (1988). *Facts and fads in beginning reading: A cross language perspective.* Norwood, NJ: Ablex.

Ferrell, B., & Compton, D. (1986). The use of ethnographic techniques for evaluation in a large school district: The Vanguard case. In D. Fetterman & M. A. Pitman (Eds.), *Educational evaluation: Ethnography in theory, practice, and politics* (pp. 171-192). Beverly Hills, CA: Sage.

Festinger, L. (1964). *Conflict, decision, and dissonance.* Stanford, CA: Stanford University Press.

Fine, M. (1986). Why urban adolescents drop into and out of public high school. *Teachers College Record, 87,* 403-410.

Fine, M. (1987). Silencing in public schools. *Language Arts, 64,* 157-174.

Fine, M., & Zane, N. (1989). Bein' wrapped too tight: Why low-income women drop out of high school. In L. Weis, E. Farrar, & H. G. Petrie (Eds.), *Dropouts from school: Issues, dilemmas, and solutions* (pp. 23-55). Albany: State University of New York Press.

Finn, J. D., & Achilles, C. M. (1990). Answers and questions about class size: A statewide experiment. *American Educational Research Journal, 27,* 557-577.

Firestone, W. A., & Rosenblum, S. (1988). Building commitment in urban high schools. *Educational Evaluation and Policy Analysis, 10,* 285-299.

Fiske, E. (1989, April 12). Lessons. *New York Times,* p. 16.

Fitzgerald, F. (1987). *Cities on a hill.* New York: Simon & Schuster.

Foltz, K. (1989, November 2). Ad drive seeks to stem drug abuse by blacks. *New York Times,* p. A15.

Fordham, S., & Ogbu, J. U. (1986). Black students' school success: Coping with the "burden" of "acting white." *Urban Review, 18,* 176-206.

Foster, P. (1965). *Education and social change in Ghana.* Chicago: University of Chicago Press.

Fox, W. S., & Wince, M. H. (1976). Structure and determinants of occupational militancy among public school teachers. *Industrial and Labor Relations Review, 30,* 47-58.

Francis, R. G. (1963). The anti-model as a theoretical concept. *Sociological Quarterly, 4,* 197-205.

Freudenberger, H. J. (1974). Staff burn-out. *Journal of Social Issues, 30,* 159-165.

Friedenberg, E. Z. (1970). Curriculum as educational process: The middle class against itself. In N. V. Overly (Ed.), *The unstudied curriculum: Its impact on children.* Washington, DC: National Education Association, ASCD Elementary Education Council.

Fromm, E. (1955). *The sane society.* New York: Rinehart.

Frymier, J. (1987). Bureaucracy and the neutering of teachers. *Phi Delta Kappan, 69,* 9-14.

Fuhrman, S., Clune, W. H., & Elmore, R. R. (1988). Research on educational reform: Lessons on the implementation of policy. *Teachers College Record, 90,* 237-259.

Furlong, M. (1980). Black girls in a London comprehensive. In R. Deem (Ed.), *Schooling for women's work.* London: Routledge & Kegan Paul.

Gallup, G. H. (1982). The 14th annual Gallup Poll of the public's attitudes toward the public schools. *Phi Delta Kappan, 64,* 37-50.

Gibson, M. A. (1988). *Accommodation with assimilation: Punjabi Sikh immigrants in an American high school.* Ithaca, NY: Cornell University Press.

Gideonse, H. D. (1982). The necessary revolution in teacher education. *Phi Delta Kappan, 64,* 15-18.

Ginsburg, M. B. (1988). *Contradictions in teacher education and society: A critical analysis.* London: Falmer.

Ginsburg, M. B., & Newman, K. K. (1985). Social inequalities, schooling and teacher education. *Journal of Teacher Education, 36,* 49-54.

Giroux, H. A. (1983). *Theory and resistance in education: A pedagogy for the opposition.* South Hadley, MA: Bergin & Garvey.

Giroux, H. A. (1988a). *Schooling and the struggle for the public: Critical pedagogy in the modern age.* Minneapolis: University of Minnesota Press.

Giroux, H. A. (1988b). *Teachers as intellectuals: Toward a critical pedagogy of learning.* South Hadley, MA: Bergin & Garvey.

Gitlin, A., & Smyth, J. (1989). *Teacher evaluation: Educative alternatives.* New York: Falmer.

Glaser, D. (1978). *Crime in our changing society.* New York: Holt, Rinehart & Winston.

Gleick, J. (1987). *Chaos: The making of a new science.* New York: Penguin.

Goldenberg, C. N. (1989). Parents' effects on academic grouping for reading: Three case studies. *American Educational Research Journal, 26,* 329-353.

Goodlad, J. I. (1983). *A place called school.* New York: McGraw-Hill.

Gore, P., & Rotter, J. B. (1963). A personality correlate of social action. *Journal of Personality, 31,* 58-64.

Gottlieb, D. (1964). Teaching and students: The views of Negro and white teachers. *Sociology of Education, 37,* 345-353.

Gouldner, A. (1979). *The future of intellectuals and the rise of the new class.* New York: Seabury.

Grant, G. (1989). *The world we created at Hamilton High.* Cambridge, MA: Harvard University Press.

Grant, W. T. (1988). *The forgotten half: Pathways to success for America's youth and young families.* Washington, DC: Commission on Work, Family and Citizenship.

Graves, D. (1983). *Writing: Teachers and children at work.* Portsmouth, NH: Heineman.

Gray, H., & Freeman, A. (1987). *Teaching without stress.* London: Paul Chapman.

Greater Houston Partnership, Chamber of Commerce Division. (Ed.). (1990). *A framework for educational excellence: 1990.* Houston: Author.

Greenberger, E., & Steinberg, L. (1986). *When teenagers work: The psychological and social costs of adolescent employment.* New York: Basic Books.

Grossberg, R. (1989). Pedagogy and the present: Politics, post-modernity and the popular. In H. A. Giroux & R. I. Simon (Eds.), *Popular culture: Schooling and everyday life* (pp. 91-118). Westport, CT: Bergin & Garvey.

Growing inventory of lenders yields farm land redistribution. (1987, March 29). *Washington Post,* pp. A10-A11.

Gurin, P., & Epps, E. (1975). *Black consciousness, identity, and achievement.* New York: John Wiley.

Gurin, P., Gurin, G., & Morrison, B. M. (1978). Personal and ideological aspects of internal and external control. *Social Psychology, 41,* 275-296.

Haberman, M. (1987). *Recruiting and selecting teachers for urban schools* (ERIC/CUE Urban Diversity Series 95). New York: ERIC Clearing House on Urban Education.

Haberman, M. (1989). More minority teachers. *Phi Delta Kappan, 71,* 771-776.

Hahn, A., & Danzberger, J. (1987). *Dropouts in America: Enough is known for action.* Washington, DC: Institute for Educational Leadership.

Halberstam, D. (1986). *The reckoning.* New York: Avon.

Haller, E. J., & Davis, S. A. (1981). Teacher perceptions, parental social status and group for reading instruction. *Sociology of Education, 54,* 162-173.

Hammack, F. M. (1986). Large school systems; dropout reports: Analysis of definitions, procedures and findings. *Teachers College Record, 87,* 324-342.

Hargroves, J. S. (1987). The Boston Compact: Facing the challenge of school dropouts. *Education and Urban Society, 19,* 303-311.

Louis Harris & Associates. (1985). *The Metropolitan Life survey of former teachers in America.* New York: Author.

Peter D. Hart Research Associates. (n.d.). *Democracy's next generation: a survey of youth values in America.*

Hawking, S. W. (1988). *A brief history of time: From the big bang to black holes.* Toronto: Bantam.

Hayes, C. D. (Ed.). (1987). *Risking the future.* Washington, DC: National Academy Press.

Heath, D. (1981). *Faculty burnout, morale, and vocational adaptation.* Boston: National Association of Independent Schools.

Herbers, J. (1986, December 14). U.S. suburbs absorbing more of immigrants, mostly affluent and educated. *New York Times,* p. 22.

Herriott, R., & Firestone, W. A. (1984). Two images of schools as organizations: A refinement and elaboration. *Educational Administration Quarterly, 21*, 41-57.

Hess, G. A. (1986). Educational "triage" in an urban school setting. *Metropolitan Education, 2*, 39-52.

Hess, G. A. (1991). *School restructuring: Chicago style.* Newbury Park, CA: Corwin.

Hess, G. A., & Addington, H. (1990). *Chicago school reform: What it is and how it came to be.* Chicago: Chicago Panel on School Policy and Finance.

Hess, G. A., & Green, D. O. (1988). *Invisibly pregnant: A study of teenaged mothers and urban schools* (Chicago Panel on Public School Policy and Finance). Paper presented at the annual meeting of the American Anthropological Association, Phoenix, AZ.

Hess, G. A., Wells, E., Prindle, C., Liffman, P., & Kaplan, B. (1987). Where's room 185? How schools can reduce their dropout problem. *Education and Urban Society, 19*, 320-330.

Heyns, B. (1990). The changing contours of the teaching profession. In M. T. Hallinan, D. M. Klein, & J. Glass (Eds.), *Change in societal institutions* (pp. 123-141). New York: Plenum.

Hilts, P. J. (1990, February 15). US is decades behind Europe in contraceptives, experts report. *New York Times*, p. 1.

Hirsch, E. D. (1988). *Cultural literacy: What every American should know.* New York: Vintage.

Hirschi, T. (1969). *The causes of delinquency.* Berkeley: University of California Press.

Hodgkinson, H. L. (1985). *All one system: Demographics of education, kindergarten through graduate school.* Washington, DC: Institute for Educational Leadership.

Hodgkinson, H. L. (1989). *The same client: The demographics of education and service delivery systems.* Washington, DC: Institute for Educational Leadership.

Hoffman, L. (1974). The effects of maternal employment on the child: A review of the research. *Developmental Psychology, 10*, 204-228.

Holley, F. M., & Doss, D. A. (1983). *Mother got tired of takin' care of my baby* (Publication No. 82.44). Austin, TX: Austin Independent School District, Office of Research and Evaluation.

Holmes, C. T. (1989). Grade level retention effects: A meta-analysis of research studies. In L. A. Shepherd & M. L. Smith (Eds.), *Flunking grades: Research and policies on retention* (pp. 16-33). Philadelphia: Falmer/Taylor & Francis Group.

Holmes Group. (1986). *Tomorrow's teachers.* East Lansing, MI: Author.

Horswell, C., & Markley, M. (1989, October 21). High school students stage mass walkout. *Houston Chronicle*, p. 1.

House, J. S., & Wells, J. A. (1978). Occupational stress, social support and health. In A. McLean, G. Black, & M. Colligan (Eds.), *Reproducing occupational stress: Proceedings of a conference* (HEW [NIOSH] Publication No. 78-140; pp. 8-29). Washington, DC: Government Printing Office.

Houston Independent School District, Department of Research and Evaluation. (1989). *HISD dropout report for 1987-1988.* Houston: Author.

Houston Independent School District Task Force on Restructuring. (1990, June 18). *A declaration of beliefs and visions for the Houston Independent School District.* Unpublished manuscript.

Hungry children increase in survey. (1989, December 21). *New York Times,* p. 20.

Hyman, H. H. (1942). The psychology of status. *Archives of Psychology, 269* (whole issue).

Iwanicki, E. F., & Schwab, R. L. (1981). A cross validation study of the Maslach burnout inventory. *Educational and Psychological Measurement, 41,* 1167-1174.

Jackson, P. (1968). *Life in classrooms.* Chicago: University of Chicago Press.

Jackson, S. E., Schwab, R. L., & Schuler, R. S. (1986). Toward an understanding of the burnout phenomenon. *Journal of Applied Psychology, 71,* 630-640.

Jacob, E. (1987). Qualitative research traditions: A review. *Review of Educational Research, 57,* 1-51.

Janis, I. L., & Mann, L. (1977). *Decision-making: A psychological analysis of conflict, choice, and commitment.* New York: Free Press.

Jessor, R., Graves, T. D., Hanson, R. C., & Jessor, S. (1968). *Society, personality, and deviant behavior.* New York: Holt, Rinehart & Winston.

Johnson, S. M. (1984). Merit pay for teachers: A poor prescription for reform. *Harvard Educational Review, 54,* 175-185.

Johnston, L. D., O'Malley, P. M., & Bachman, J. G. (1989). *Illicit drug use, smoking, and drinking by America's high school students, college students, and young adults: 1957-1987* (DHHS Publication No. [ADM] 89-1602). Washington, DC: Government Printing Office.

Jordan, M. (1987a, March 29). Lack of housing changes the course of people's lives. *Washington Post,* p. A16.

Jordan, M. (1987b, March 29). Renovations come and residents go: Poor left with few options. *Washington Post,* pp. A1, A16.

Joyce, B., & Clift, R. (1984). The Phoenix agenda: Essential reform in teacher education. *Educational Researcher, 13,* 5-18.

Joyce, B., Hersh, R., & McKibbin, M. (1983). *The structure of school improvement.* New York: Longman.

Kahn, R. L., Wolfe, D. M., Quinn, R. P., Snoek, J. D., & Rosenthal, R. A. (1964). *Organizational stress: Studies in role conflict and ambiguity.* New York: John Wiley.

Kanter, R. M. (1968). Commitment and social organization: A study of commitment mechanisms in utopian communities. *American Sociological Review, 33,* 499-517.

Kanter, R. M. (1977). *Men and women of the corporation.* New York: Basic Books.

Kaplan, H. B. (1983). Psychological distress in sociological context: Toward a general theory of psychosocial distress. In H. B. Kaplan (Ed.), *Psychosocial stress: Trends in theory and research* (pp. 195-264). New York: Academic Press.

Kelley, H. H. (1952). Two functions of reference groups. In G. E. Swanson, T. M. Newcomb, & E. L. Hartley (Eds.), *Readings in social psychology* (pp. 410-414). New York: Holt, Rinehart & Winston.

Kilborn, P. T. (1990, February 16). For many women, one job just isn't enough. *New York Times,* p. 1.

Kirby, S. N., Darling-Hammond, L., & Hudson, L. (1989). Non-traditional recruits to mathematics and science teaching. *Educational Evaluation and Policy Analysis, 11,* 301-324.

Kohl, H. (1967). *36 Children.* New York: World.

Kolata, G. (1986, November 26). Despite its promise of riches, the crack trade seldom pays. *New York Times,* pp. 1, 18.

Kolata, G. (1989, July 19). A new toll of alcohol abuse: The Indians' next generation. *New York Times,* p. 1.

Kozol, J. (1967). *Death at an early age.* Boston: Houghton Mifflin.

Kreitzer, A. E., Madaus, G. F., & Haney, W. (1989). Competency testing and dropouts. In L. Weis, E. Farrar, & H. G. Petrie (Eds.), *Dropouts from school: Issues, dilemmas, and solutions* (pp. 129-152). Albany: State University of New York Press.

Labaree, D. F. (1984). Setting the standard: Alternative policies for student promotion. *Harvard Educational Review, 54,* 67-87.

Labaton, S. (1989, December 5). The cost of drug abuse: $60 million a year. *New York Times,* pp. 27, 30.

Lampert, M. (1990). When the problem is not the question and the solution is not the answer: Mathematical knowing and teaching. *American Educational Research Journal, 27,* 29-63.

LaPointe, A. E., Mead, N. A., & Phillips, G. W. (1989). *A world of differences: An international assessment of mathematics and science.* Princeton, NJ: Educational Testing Service.

LaRocco, J. M., House, J. S., & French, J. R. P., Jr. (1980). Social support, occupational stress, and health. *Journal of Health and Social Behavior, 21,* 202-218.

Learning conditions in the U.S. get C+ on "report card." (1989, September 12). *New York Times,* p. 20.

LeCompte, M. D. (1978). Culture shock: It happens to teachers, too. In B. D. Felder, J. Weinstein, L. Carmichal, L. Faseler, G. Goodman, W. R. Houston, & H. B. W. Poindexter (Eds.), *Focus on the future: Implications for education* (pp. 102-113). Houston: University of Houston, College of Education.

LeCompte, M. D. (1985a). Defining the differences: Cultural subgroups among mainstream children. *Urban Review, 17,* 111-128.

LeCompte, M. D. (1985b). *HISD dropout study #1: Issues in defining and enumerating dropouts.* Houston: Houston Independent School District, Department of Planning, Research and Evaluation.

LeCompte, M. D. (1987, February). *The cultural context of dropping out: Why good dropout programs don't work.* Paper presented at the annual meeting of the American Association for the Advancement of Sciences.

LeCompte, M. D., & Dworkin, A. G. (1988). Educational programs: Indirect linkages and unfulfilled expectations. In H. R. Rodgers, Jr. (Ed.), *Beyond welfare: New approaches to the problem of poverty in America* (pp. 135-168). Armonk, NY: M. E. Sharpe.

LeCompte, M. D., & Ginsburg, M. B. (1987). How students learn to become teachers: An exploration of alternative responses to a teacher training program. In G. W. Noblitt & W. T. Pink (Eds.), *Schooling in social context: Qualitative studies* (pp. 3-22). Norwood, NJ: Ablex.

LeCompte, M. D., & Goebel, S. (1987). Can bad data produce good program planning? An analysis of record keeping on school dropouts. *Education and Urban Society, 19,* 250-269.

LeCompte, M. D., & Preissle, J. (1992). Toward an ethnology of student life in schools and classrooms: Synthesizing the qualitative tradition. In M. D. LeCompte, W. L. Millroy, & J. Preissle (Eds.), *The handbook of qualitative research in education.* San Diego, CA: Academic Press.

Lee, F. R. (1989a, October 28). Impact of testimony worries district. *New York Times,* p. 10.

Lee, F. R. (1989b, November 14). Violence outside New York schools. *New York Times,* p. 16.

Lee, V., & Bryk, A. S. (1988). Curriculum tracing as mediating the social distribution of high school achievement. *Sociology of Education, 61,* 78-94.

Lefcourt, H. M. (1976). *Locus of control: Current trends in theory and research.* Hillsdale, NJ: Lawrence Erlbaum.

Levin, H. M. (1972). *The costs to the nation of inadequate education* (Study prepared for the U.S. Senate Select Committee on Equal Educational Opportunity). Washington, DC: Government Printing Office.

Lewin-Smith, N. (1981). *Youth employment during high school.* Chicago: National Opinion Research Center.

Lieberman, M. (1989). *Privatization and educational choice.* New York: St. Martin's.

Lindquist, K. M., & Mauriel, J. J. (1989). School-based management: Doomed to failure? *Education and Urban Society, 21,* 393-403.

Liska, A. A. (1981). *Perspectives on deviance.* Englewood Cliffs, NJ: Prentice-Hall.

Litt, M. D., & Turk, D. C. (1985). Sources of stress and dissatisfaction in experienced high school teachers. *Journal of Educational Research, 78,* 178-185.

Littwin, S. (1987). *The postponed generation: Why America's grown-up kids are growing up later.* New York: Morrow.

Lortie, D. C. (1969). The balance of control and autonomy in elementary school teaching. In A. Etzioni (Ed.), *The semi-professions and their organization: Teachers, nurses and social workers* (pp. 1-53). New York: Free Press.

Lortie, D. (1975). *Schoolteacher.* Chicago: University of Chicago Press.

Lutz, F. W., & Hutton, J. B. (1989). Alternative teacher certification: Its policy implications for classroom and personnel practice. *Educational Evaluation and Policy Analysis, 11,* 237-255.

Malcolm, A. H. (1987, February 4). What five families did after losing the farm. *New York Times,* pp. 1, 9.

Malen, B., & Hart, A. W. (1987). Career ladder reform: A multi-level analysis of initial efforts. *Educational Evaluation and Policy Analysis, 9,* 9-23.

Mann, D. (1987). Can we help dropouts? Thinking about the undoable. In G. Natriello (Ed.), *School dropouts: Patterns and policies* (pp. 3-19). New York: Teachers College Press.

Mark, J. H., & Anderson, B. D. (1978). Teacher survival rates: A current look. *American Educational Research Journal, 15,* 379-383.

Mark, J. H., & Anderson, B. D. (1985). Teacher survival rates in St. Louis, 1969-1982. *American Educational Research Journal, 22,* 413-421.

Markely, M. (1989, November 7). Teacher to fight transfer over student petition. *Houston Chronicle*, p. 12A.

Marotto, R. A. (1986). Posin' to be chosen: An ethnographic study of in-school truancy. In D. Fetterman & M. A. Pitman (Eds.), *Educational evaluation: Ethnography in theory, practice, and politics* (pp. 193-215). Beverly Hills, CA: Sage.

Marrett, C. B. (1990). The changing composition of schools: Implications for school organization. In M. T. Hallinan, D. M. Klein, & J. Glass (Eds.), *Change in societal institutions* (pp. 71-90). New York: Plenum.

Martin, D. (1988, April 26). A blend of student voices on drugs. *New York Times*, p. 14.

Marx, K. (1959). *Basic writings on politics and philosophy* (L. S. Feuer, Ed.). Garden City, NY: Anchor.

Maslach, C. (1976). Burned-out. *Human Behavior, 5*, 16-22.

Maslach, C. (1978a). The client role in staff burn-out. *Journal of Social Issues, 34*, 111-124.

Maslach, C. (1978b). Job burnout: How people cope. *Public Welfare, 36*, 56-58.

Maslach, C. (1982). Understanding burnout: Definitional issues in analyzing a complex phenomenon. In W. S. Paine (Ed.), *Job stress and burnout: Research, theory, and intervention perspectives* (pp. 29-40). Beverly Hills, CA: Sage.

Maslach, C., & Jackson, S. E. (1979). Burned-out cops and their families. *Psychology Today, 12*, 59-62.

Maslach, C., & Jackson, S. (1981). The measurement of experienced burnout. *Journal of Occupational Behavior, 2*, 99-113.

Maslach, C., & Jackson, S. (1982). After-effects of job-related stress: Families as victims. *Journal of Occupational Behaviour, 3*, 63-77.

Maslach, C., & Pines, A. (1979). Burnout: The loss of human caring. In A. Pines & C. Maslach (Eds.), *Experiencing social psychology*. New York: Knopf.

Mason, W. S. (1961). *The beginning teacher: Status and career orientations* (DHEW Publication). Washington, DC: Government Printing Office.

Mattingly, M. A. (1977). Sources of stress and burnout in professional child care work. *Child Care Quarterly, 6*, 127-137.

Matza, D. (1964). *Delinquency and drift*. New York: John Wiley.

McDermott, R. (1987). Achieving school failure: An anthropological approach to illiteracy and social stratification. In G. Spindler (Ed.), *Education and cultural process: Anthropological approaches* (pp. 173-204). Prospect Heights, IL: Waveland.

McDill, E. L., Natriello, G., & Pallas, A. M. (1985). Raising standards and retaining students: The impact of the reform recommendations on potential dropouts. *Review of Educational Research, 55*, 415-433.

McLaren, P. (1980). *Cries from the corridor: The new suburban ghettos*. Toronto: Methuen.

McLeod, J. (1987). *Ain't no makin' it: Levelled aspirations in a low-income neighborhood*. Boulder, CO: Westview.

McNeil, L. M. (1984). *Lowering expectations: The impact of student employment in classroom knowledge*. Madison, WI: Center for Educational Research.

McNeil, L. M. (1986). *Contradictions of control: School structure and school knowledge*. London: Routledge & Kegan Paul.

McNeil, L. M. (1988a). Contradictions of control, part I: Administrators and teachers. *Phi Delta Kappan, 69*, 333-339.

McNeil, L. M. (1988b). Contradictions of control, part II: Teachers, students and curriculum. *Phi Delta Kappan, 69,* 432-438.

McNeil, L. M. (1988c). Contradictions of control, part III: Contradictions of reform. *Phi Delta Kappan, 69,* 478-485.

Merton, R. K. (1964a). Social structure and anomie. In R. K. Merton (Ed.), *Social theory and social structure* (pp. 131-160). New York: Free Press.

Merton, R. K. (1964b). Continuities in the theory of social structure and anomie. In R. K. Merton (Ed.), *Social theory and social structure* (pp. 161-194). New York: Free Press.

Merton, R. K. (Ed.). (1968). *Social theory and social structure* (rev. ed.). New York: Free Press.

Merton, R. K., & Kitt (Rossi), A. S. (1950). Contributions to the theory of reference group behavior. In R. K. Merton & P. F. Lazarsfeld (Eds.), *Continuities in social research: Studies in the scope and method of "The American soldier"* (pp. 40-105). Glencoe, IL: Free Press.

Meyer, J., & Rowan, B. (1978). The structure of educational organizations. In M. Meyer & Associates (Eds.), *Environments and organizations: Theoretical and empirical perspectives* (pp. 78-109). San Francisco: Jossey-Bass.

Mickelson, R. A. (1990). The attitude-achievement paradox among black adolescents. *Sociology of Education, 63,* 44-61.

Modest gains seen in improving schools. (1989, November 8). *New York Times,* p. 24.

Moll, L. C. (Ed.). (1990). *Vygotsky and education: Instructional implications and applications of sociohistorical psychology.* New York: Cambridge University Press.

Morales, E. (1989). *Cocaine: White gold rush in Peru.* Tucson: University of Arizona Press.

Moreno, A., & Dworkin, A. G. (1988). *Evaluation of the "Career and Education Day" program: 1988* (Report to the Houston Hispanic Forum). Unpublished manuscript.

Moreno, A., & Dworkin, A. G. (1989). *Evaluation of the "Career and Education Day" program: 1989* (Report to the Houston Hispanic Forum). Unpublished manuscript.

Morrow, G. (1986). Standardizing practice in analysis of school dropouts. *Teachers College Record, 87,* 342-356.

Mottaz, C. J. (1981). Some determinants of work alienation. *Sociological Quarterly, 22,* 515-530.

Murnane, R. J. (1975). *The impact of school resources on the learning of inner city children.* Cambridge, MA: Ballinger.

Murnane, R. J., & Phillips, B. (1981). Learning by doing, vintage, and selection: Three pieces of the puzzle relating teaching experience and teaching performance. *Economics of Education Review 1,* 453-466.

Nadelmann, E. A. (1989). Drug prohibition in the United States: Costs, consequences, and alternatives. *Science, 245,* 939-946.

National Center for Educational Statistics. (1982). *The High School and Beyond study.* Washington, DC: U.S. Department of Education.

National Center for Educational Statistics. (1984). *The condition of education.* Washington, DC: U.S. Department of Education.

National Center for Educational Statistics. (1985). *The condition of education.* Washington, DC: U.S. Department of Education.

National Commission on Excellence in Education. (1983). *A nation at risk.* Washington, DC: U.S. Department of Education.

National Council of Teachers of English. (1990). *Standards for assessment and curriculum development.* Reston, VA: Author.

National Education Association. (1967). *School dropouts: Research summary 1967-S1.* Washington, DC: Author.

National Education Association. (1983). *Teacher supply and demand in public school, 1981-82.* Washington, DC: Author.

National Education Association. (1987a). *Status of the American public school teacher, 1985-86.* Washington, DC: Author.

National Education Association. (1987b). *Teacher supply and demand guidebook.* Washington, DC: Author.

National Endowment for the Humanities. (1989). *Fifty hours: A core curriculum for college students.* Washington, DC: Author.

National Institute of Education. (1976). *The desegregation literature: A critical approach.* Washington, DC: Government Printing Office.

National Institute of Education. (1978). *Violent schools—safe schools: The Safe School Study report to Congress* (Vol. 1). Washington, DC: Government Printing Office.

National Science Foundation. (1984). *Program announcement: Grants for research on the teaching and learning of science and mathematics* (84-74, OMB 3145-0058). Washington, DC: Author.

Nettler, G. (1957). A measure of alienation. *American Sociological Review, 22,* 670-677.

Newmann, F. M. (1981). Reducing student alienation in high schools: Implications of theory. *Harvard Educational Review, 51,* 546-564.

Newmann, F. M., Rutter, R. A., & Smith, M. S. (1989). Organizational factors that affect school sense of efficacy, community, and expectations. *Sociology of Education, 62,* 221-238.

Oakes, J. (1985). *Keeping track: How schools structure inequality.* New Haven, CT: Yale University Press.

Ogbu, J. U. (1974). *The next generation.* New York: Academic Press.

Ogbu, J. U. (1978). *Minority education and caste: The American system in cross-cultural perspective.* New York: Academic Press.

Ogbu, J. U. (1983). Minority status and schooling in plural societies. *Comparative Education Review, 27*(2), 168-190.

Ogbu, J. U., & Matute-Bianchi, M. (1986). Understanding socio-cultural factors: Knowledge, identity and school adjustment. In California State Department of Education, Bilingual Education Office (Ed.), *Beyond language: Social and cultural factors in schooling language minority children* (pp. 73-142). Los Angeles: California State University, Evaluation, Dissemination and Assessment Center.

Ogintz, E. (1989). Cries in the dark. *Northwestern Perspective, 2,* 2-5.

Olson, P. (Ed.). (1963). *America as a mass society.* New York: Free Press.

On welfare and truants. (1990, March 20). *New York Times,* p. A8.

O'Neill, D. M., & Sepielli, P. (1985). *Education in the United States: 1940-1983* (CDS-85-1). Washington, DC: U.S. Department of Commerce, Bureau of the Census.

Orfield, G. (1975). Examining the desegregation process. *Integrated Education, 13*, 127-130.

Ornstein, A. C. (1980). Teacher salaries: Past, present, future. *Phi Delta Kappan, 61*, 677-679.

Ornstein, A. C., & Levine, D. U. (1981). *An introduction to the foundations of education* (2nd ed.). Boston: Houghton Mifflin.

Orum, L. S. (1984). *Hispanic dropouts: Community responses.* Washington, DC: National Council of La Raza, Office of Research, Advocacy, and Legislation.

PACE. (1989). *Conditions of children in California.* Berkeley: University of California, School of Education.

Page, R. (1989). The lower track curriculum at a "heavenly" high school: "Cycles of prejudice." *Journal of Curriculum Studies, 21*, 197-221.

Paine, W. S. (1982). Overview: Burnout stress syndrome and the 1980s. In W. S. Paine (Ed.), *Job stress and burnout: Research, theory, and intervention perspectives* (pp. 11-28). Beverly Hills, CA: Sage.

Patchen, M. (1982). *Black-white contact in schools: Its social and academic effects.* West Lafayette, IN: Purdue University Press.

Pavalko, R. (1965). Aspirants to teaching: Some differences between high school girls and boys. *Sociology and Social Research, 50*, 47-62.

Pavalko, R. (1970). Recruitment to teaching: Patterns of selection and retention. *Sociology of Education, 43*, 340-353.

Peng, S. (1983). *High school dropouts: Descriptive information from high school and beyond.* Washington, DC: National Center for Educational Statistics.

Persell, C. H. (1977). *Education and inequality: The roots and results of stratification in America's schools.* New York: Free Press.

Peters, T., & Waterman, R. (1982). *In search of excellence: Lessons from America's best run companies.* New York: Warner.

Philips, S. U. (1972). Participant structures and communicative competence: Warm Springs children in community and classroom. In C. Cazden, V. P. John, & D. Hymes (Eds.), *Functions of language in the classroom* (pp. 370-394). New York: Teachers College Press.

Porter, L. R., Steers, R., Mowday, R., & Boulian, P. (1974). Organizational commitment, job satisfaction, and turnover among psychiatric technicians. *Journal of Applied Psychology, 59*, 603-609.

Powell, A. G., Farrar, E., & Cohen, D. K. (1985). *The shopping mall high school: Winners and losers in the educational marketplace.* Boston: Houghton Mifflin.

Price, J. L. (1977). *The study of turnover.* Ames: Iowa State University Press.

Puckett, J. L. (1989). *Foxfire reconsidered: A twenty year experiment in progressive education.* Urbana: University of Illinois Press.

Puga, A., & DeSoto, B. (1989, November 5). AIDS on the street: The lost children of Mexico. *Houston Chronicle* (Special Suppl.).

Putnam J. F., & Tankard, G. G., Jr. (1964). *Pupil accounting for local and state school systems* (State Educational Records and Reports Series, Handbook 5, DHEW Bulletin No. 39). Washington, DC: Government Printing Office.

Ranbom, M., & Lewis, J. (1986). *School dropouts: Everybody's problem.* Washington, DC: Institute for Educational Leadership.

Reinhold, R. (1990, June 12). California tally: Apathy on the rise. *New York Times*, p. A10.

Resnick, D. P., & Resnick, L. B. (1985). Standards, curriculum and performance: A historical and comparative perspective. *Educational Researcher, 14,* 5-20.

Reyes, M. de la L. (1990). *A process approach to literacy using dialogue journals and literature logs: How effective is it for second language learners?* Unpublished manuscript, University of Colorado.

Reyes, M. de la L. (in press). Challenging venerable assumptions: A multicultural language arts alternative. *Language Arts.*

Richardson, V., Casanova, U., Placier, P., & Guilfoyle, K. (1989). *School children at-risk.* Philadelphia: Falmer/Taylor & Francis Group.

Riger, S. (1977). Locus of control, belief, and female activism. *Psychological Reports, 41,* 1043-1046.

Riggar, T. F. (1985). *Stress burnout.* Carbondale: Southern Illinois University Press.

Rist, R. C. (1970). Social class and teacher expectations: The self-fulfilling prophecy in ghetto education. *Harvard Educational Review, 40,* 411-451.

Rist, R. C. (1973). *The urban school: Factory for failure.* Cambridge: MIT Press.

Ritzer, G., & Trice, H. (1969). An empirical study of Howard Becker's side-bet theory. *Social Forces, 47,* 475-478.

Rodgers, H. R., Jr. (1988). Reducing poverty through family support. In H. R. Rodgers, Jr. (Ed.), *Beyond welfare: New approaches to the problem of poverty in America* (pp. 39-66). Armonk, NY: M. E. Sharpe.

Roman, L. G. (1989). *Double exposure: The politics of feminist materialist ethnography.* Paper presented at the annual meeting of the American Educational Research Association, San Francisco.

Rosenfeld, R. A. (1980). Race and sex differences in career dynamics. *American Sociological Review, 45,* 583-69.

Rosenholtz, S. J. (1989). *Teachers' workplace: The social organization of schools.* New York: Longman.

Rosenholtz, S. J., & Simpson, C. (1990). Workplace conditions and the rise and fall of teachers' commitment. *Sociology of Education, 63,* 241-257.

Rosenthal, R., & Jacobson, L. (1968). *Pygmalion in the classroom.* New York: Holt, Rinehart & Winston.

Rotter, J. B. (1966). Generalized expectancies for internal versus external control of reinforcements. *Psychological Monographs, 80,* 1-28.

Rumberger, R. W. (1983). Dropping out of school: The influence of race, sex, and family background. *American Educational Research Journal, 20,* 199-220.

Rumberger, R. W. (1987). High school dropouts: A review of issues and evidence. *Review of Educational Research, 57,* 101-121.

Sarason, S. B. (1971). *The culture of the school and the problem of change.* Boston: Allyn & Bacon.

Sarason, S. B. (1977). *Work, aging, and social change.* New York: Free Press.

Sarason, S. B. (1978-1979). Again, the preparation of teachers: Competency and job satisfaction. *Interchange, 10,* 1-11.

Sarason, S. B., Davidson, K. S., & Blatt, B. (1962). *The preparation of teachers: An unstudied problem in education.* New York: John Wiley.

Schell, J. (1982). *The fate of the earth.* New York: Avon.

Schelling, T. C. (1956). An essay on bargaining. *American Economic Review 46,* 281-306.

Schelling, T. C. (1960). *The strategy of conflict.* Cambridge, MA: Harvard University Press.

Schlechty, P. C., & Vance, V. S. (1981). Do academically able teachers leave education? The North Carolina case. *Phi Delta Kappan, 63,* 106-112.

Schwab, R. L., & Iwanicki, E. F. (1982). Received role conflict, role ambiguity, and teacher burnout. *Educational Administration Quarterly, 18,* 60-74.

Seeman, M. (1959). On the meaning of alienation. *American Sociological Review, 24,* 783-791.

Seeman, M. (1967). On the personal consequences of alienation in work. *American Sociological Review, 32,* 273-285.

Seeman, M. (1975). Alienation studies. *Annual Review of Sociology, 1,* 91-123.

Selznick, P. (1951). Institutional vulnerability in mass society. *American Journal of Sociology, 56,* 320-331.

Sewell, W. H., Haller, A. O., & Ohlendorf, G. W. (1970). The educational and early occupational attainment process: Replication and revision. *American Sociological Review, 35,* 1014-1027.

Sewell, W. H., Haller, A. O., & Portes, A. (1969). The educational and early occupational attainment process. *American Sociological Review, 34,* 82-92.

Sewell, W. H., & Hauser, R. M. (1975). *Education, occupation and earnings.* New York: Academic Press.

Shaw, M. E., & Constanzo, P. R. (1970). *Theories of social psychology.* New York: McGraw-Hill.

Shaw, S. F., Bensky, J. M., & Dixon, B. (1981). *Stress and burnout: A primer for special education and special services personnel.* Reston, VA: Council for Exceptional Children.

Shearer, L. (1990, January 14). Intelligence report. *Parade Magazine,* p. 8.

Shepherd, L. A., & Kreitzer, A. (1987). The Texas teacher test. *Educational Researcher, 16,* 22-31.

Shepherd, L. A., & Smith, M. L. (Eds.). (1989a). *Flunking grades: Research and policies on retention.* Philadelphia: Falmer/Taylor & Francis Group.

Shepherd, L. A., & Smith, M. L. (1989b). Introduction and overview. In L. A. Shepherd & M. L. Smith (Eds.), *Flunking grades: Research and policies on retention* (pp. 1-16). Philadelphia: Falmer/Taylor & Francis Group.

Shibutani, T. (1955). Reference groups as perspectives. *American Journal of Sociology, 60,* 562-569.

Shils, E. (1963). The theory of mass society. In P. Olson (Ed.), *America as a mass society* (pp. 30-47). New York: Free Press.

Shinn, M. (1982). Methodological issues: Evaluating and using information. In W. S. Paine (Ed.), *Job stress and burnout: Research, theory, and intervention perspectives* (pp. 61-82). Beverly Hills, CA: Sage.

Shoemaker, D. J., Snizek, W. E., & Bryant, C. D. (1977). Toward a further clarification of Becker's side-bet hypothesis applied to organizational and occupational commitment. *Social Forces, 56,* 598-603.

Short, J. F., Jr., & Strodtbeck, F. L. (1959). *Group process and gang delinquency.* Chicago: University of Chicago Press.

Short, P., Monheit, A., & Beauregard, K. (1989). *A profile of uninsured Americans* (National Medical Expenditure Survey Research Findings 1, DHHS Publication No. PHS 89-3443). Rockville, MD: U.S. Department of Health and Human Services.

Shultz, J., & Erickson, F. (1982). *The counselor as gatekeeper.* New York: Academic Press.

Sizer, T. R. (1984-1985). *Horace's compromise: The dilemma of the American high school.* Boston: Houghton Mifflin.

Sleeter, C. S., & Grant, C. A. (1987). *Race, class, and gender and abandoned dreams.* Paper presented at the annual meeting of the American Educational Research Association, Washington, DC.

Smeeding, T. M., & Torrey, B. B. (1988). Poor children in rich countries. *Science, 242,* 873-878.

Smith, M. (1991, February 24). Teachers' test leaves pain in its wake. *Houston Chronicle,* pp. 1D, 3D.

Smith, M. L. (1989). Teachers' beliefs about retention. In L. A. Shepherd & M. L. Smith (Eds.), *Flunking grades: Research and policies on retention* (pp. 132-151). Philadelphia: Falmer/Taylor & Francis Group.

Smith, M. L., & Shepherd, L. A. (1989). Flunking grades: A recapitulation. In L. A. Shepherd & M. L. Smith (Eds.), *Flunking grades: Research and policies on retention* (pp. 214-237). Philadelphia: Falmer/Taylor & Francis Group.

Sorotnik, K. A. (1983). What you see is what you get: Consistency, persistency and mediocrity in classrooms. *Harvard Educational Review, 53,* 16-32.

Sowers, L. (1989, October 15). The adoption option. *Houston Chronicle,* p. 1C.

Sparks, D., & Hammond, J. (1981). *Managing teacher stress and burnout.* Washington, DC: ERIC Clearinghouse on Teacher Education.

Stern, S. P. (1987). *Black parents: Dropouts or pushouts from school participation.* Paper presented at the annual meetings of the American Anthropological Association, Chicago.

Stevens, J. H., Beyer, J. M., & Trice, H. M. (1978). Assessing personal, role, and organizational predictors of managerial commitment. *Academy of Management Journal, 21,* 380-396.

Stinchcombe, A. L. (1964). *Rebellion in a high school.* Chicago: Quadrangle.

Stinnett, T. M., & Henson, K. H. (1982). *America's public schools in transition: Future trends and issues.* New York: Teachers College Press.

Stinson, J. F., Jr. (1986). Moonlighting by women jumped to record highs. *Monthly Labor Review, 109,* 22-25.

Stouffer, S. A., Suchman, E. A., Devinney, L. C., Star, S. A., & Williams, R. M., Jr. (1949). *The American soldier: Vol. 1. Adjustment during army life.* Princeton, NJ: Princeton University Press.

Student debt level raises worry. (1987, January 29). *New York Times,* pp. 1, 7.

Swick, K. J. (1989). *Stress and teaching.* Washington, DC: National Education Association.

Swick, K. J., & Hanley, P. E. (1983). *Teacher renewal: Revitalization of classroom teachers.* Washington, DC: National Education Association.

Sykes, G., & Matza, D. (1957). Techniques of neutralization: A theory of delinquency. *American Sociological Review, 22,* 664-670.

Teachers' report cards. (1990, May 15). *Houston Chronicle,* sec. 3, p. 2.

Tharp, R. G. (n.d.). *Psychocultural variables and constants: Effects on teaching and learning in schools.* Unpublished manuscript, University of Hawaii, Center for Studies of Multicultural Higher Education.

Tharp, R. G., & Gallimore, R. (1988). *Rousing minds to life: Teaching, learning and schooling in social context.* Cambridge: Cambridge University Press.

Tizard, B., Blatchford, P., Burke, J., Farquhar, C., & Plewis, I. (1989). *Young children at school in the inner city.* London: Lawrence Erlbaum.

Toffler, A. (1970). *Future shock.* New York: Random House.

Toffler, A. (1981). *The third wave.* New York: Bantam.

Touraine, A. (1971). *The post-industrial society.* New York: Random House.

Tubesing, N. L., & Tubesing, D. A. (1982). The treatment of choice: Selecting stress skills to suit the individual and the situation. In W. S. Paine (Ed.), *Job stress and burnout: Research, theory, and intervention perspectives* (pp. 155-171). Beverly Hills, CA: Sage.

Turner, R., Camilli, G., Kroc, R., & Hoover, J. (1986). Policy strategies, teacher salary incentive and student achievement: An explanatory model. *Educational Researcher, 15,* 5-11.

Tyack, D. (1990). "Restructuring" in historical perspective: Thinking toward Utopia. *Teachers College Record, 92,* 170-191.

Tyack, D., & Hansot, E. (1984). Hard times, then and now: Public schools in the 1930s and the 1980s. *Harvard Educational Review, 54,* 33-67.

U.S. Bureau of the Census. (1963). *Statistical abstract of the United States: 1964* (84th ed.). Washington, DC: Government Printing Office.

U.S. Bureau of the Census. (1964). *Statistical abstract of the United States: 1965* (85th ed.). Washington, DC: Government Printing Office.

U.S. Bureau of the Census. (1966). *Statistical abstract of the United States: 1967* (87th ed.). Washington, DC: Government Printing Office.

U.S. Bureau of the Census. (1971). *Statistical abstract of the United States: 1972* (92nd ed.). Washington, DC: Government Printing Office.

U.S. Bureau of the Census. (1979). *Statistical abstract of the United States: 1980* (100th ed.). Washington, DC: Government Printing Office.

U.S. Bureau of the Census. (1981). *Statistical abstract of the United States: 1982* (102nd ed.). Washington, DC: Government Printing Office.

U.S. Bureau of the Census. (1985). *Statistical abstract of the United States: 1986* (106th ed.). Washington, DC: Government Printing Office.

U.S. Bureau of the Census. (1986). *Statistical abstract of the United States: 1987* (107th ed.). Washington, DC: Government Printing Office.

U.S. Bureau of the Census. (1988). *Statistical abstract of the United States: 1989* (109th ed.). Washington, DC: Government Printing Office.

U.S. Bureau of the Census. (1989). *Statistical abstract of the United States: 1990* (110th ed.). Washington, DC: Government Printing Office.

U.S. Bureau of Labor Statistics. (1990, December). *Consumer price index for all urban consumers* (CPI-U). Washington, DC: U.S. Department of Labor.

Valverde, S. (1986). *A comparative study of Hispanic LEP and non-LEP dropouts and Hispanic LEP and non-LEP high school graduates in an urban public school system in the southwestern United States.* Unpublished doctoral dissertation, University of Houston, College of Education, Department of Educational Leadership and Cultural Studies.

Valverde, S. (1987). A comparative study of Hispanic high school dropouts and graduates. *Education and Urban Society, 19,* 320-330.

Vance, V. S., & Schlechty, P. C. (1982). The distribution of academic ability in the teaching force: Policy implications. *Phi Delta Kappan, 64,* 22-27.

Vogt, L. A., Jordan, C., & Tharp, R. G. (1987). Explaining school failure, producing school success: Two cases. *Anthropology and Education Quarterly, 18,* 277-286.

Vygotsky, L. S. (1962). *Thought and language* (E. Hanfmann & G. Vakar, Trans.). Cambridge: MIT Press.

Walberg, H. J. (1989). District size and student learning. *Education and Urban Society, 21,* 154-164.

Warren, S. (1990, March 4). Parents face fines, jail for children's truancy. *Houston Chronicle,* pp. 1A, 22A.

Wax, R. H., & Thomas, R. K. (1961). American Indians and white people. *Phylon, 22,* 305-317.

Weatherley, R. A. (1988). Teenage parenthood and poverty. In H. R. Rodgers, Jr. (Ed.), *Beyond welfare: New approaches to the problem of poverty in America* (pp. 114-134). Armonk, NY: M. E. Sharpe.

Weaver, W. T. (1978). Educators in supply and demand: Effects on quality. *School Review, 86,* 552-593.

Weber, M. (1947). *The theory of social and economic organization.* New York: Oxford University Press.

Weick, K. (1976). Educational organizations a loosely coupled system. *Administrative Science Quarterly, 21,* 1-19.

Weintraub, B. (1989, September 13). Bush urges youngsters to help friends on drugs. *New York Times,* p. 10.

Weis, L. (1988). High school girls in a de-industrializing society. In L. Weis (Ed.), *Class, race and gender in American education* (pp. 183-209). Albany: State University of New York Press.

Weis, L. (1990). *Working class without work: High school students in a de-industrializing economy.* New York: Routledge.

Weitzman, L. (1985). *The divorce revolution.* New York: Free Press.

Whelage, G. A. (1983). *Effective programs for the marginal high school student.* Bloomington, IN: Phi Delta Kappa Foundation.

Whelage, G. A. (1989). Dropping out: Can schools be expected to prevent it? In L. Weis, E. Farrar, & H. G. Petrie (Eds.), *Dropouts from school: Issues, dilemmas, and solutions* (pp. 1-23). Albany: State University of New York Press.

White, T. F. (1986). *A study of high school seniors, 1986.* Bloomington, IN: Phi Delta Kappa.

Whitford, L. (1986). [Chapter]. In G. W. Noblitt & W. T. Pink (Eds.), *Schooling in social context: Qualitative studies.* Norwood, NJ: Ablex.

Wigginton, E. (1985). *Sometimes a shining moment: The Foxfire experience.* Garden City, NY: Doubleday.

Wilkerson, I. (1989a, October 16). Chicago picks new school chief to guide major changes in system. *New York Times,* p. 6.

Wilkerson, I. (1989b, October 22). Chicago schools try radical new cure. *New York Times,* p. 3.

Williams, S. (1987). A comparative study of black dropouts and black high school graduates in an urban public school system. *Education and Urban Society, 19,* 311-330.

Willis, P. (1977). *Learning to labor: How working class kids get working class jobs.* Lexington, MA: D. C. Heath.

Wills, C. (1989). *The wisdom of the genes: New pathways in evolution.* New York: Basic Books.

Wilson, B. L., & Corbett, H. D. (1983). Organization and change: The effects of school linkages on the quality of implementation. *Educational Administration Quarterly, 19,* 85-104.

Wilson, W. J. (1987). *The truly disadvantaged: The inner city, the underclass, and public policy.* Chicago: University of Chicago Press.

Wittig, M. A., & Lowe, R. H. (1989). Comparable worth: Theory and policy. *Journal of Social Issues, 45*(4), 1-22.

Zelnik, M., & Kantner, J. F. (1980). Sexual activity, contraceptive use and pregnancy among metropolitan-area teenagers. *Family Planning Perspectives, 13*(5), 205-217.

Zuboff, S. (1988). *In the age of the smart machine: The future of work and power.* New York: Basic Books.

Zukav, G. (1979). *The dancing Wu-Li masters: An overview of the new physics.* New York: William Morrow.

Author Index

Subject Index